POLITICS   STUDY   ROOM

PLEASE   DO   NOT

REMOVE

IN SEARCH OF AUTHORITY
Twentieth-Century Political Thought

HISTORY OF WESTERN POLITICAL THOUGHT

GENERAL EDITOR: Andrew Hacker, *Cornell University*

HISTORY OF GREEK POLITICAL THOUGHT
By Donald Kagan, *Cornell University*

HISTORY OF MEDIEVAL POLITICAL THOUGHT
By Ewart Lewis

HISTORY OF CONTINENTAL POLITICAL THOUGHT
By Michael Walzer, *Princeton University*

HISTORY OF BRITISH POLITICAL THOUGHT
By Wilfrid Harrison, *University of Liverpool*

HISTORY OF TWENTIETH-CENTURY POLITICAL THOUGHT
By Henry S. Kariel, *Bennington College*

HISTORY OF AMERICAN POLITICAL DOCTRINES
By Thomas P. Jenkin, *University of California, Riverside*

IN SEARCH
OF AUTHORITY

Twentieth-Century Political Thought

By Henry S. Kariel
Bennington College

THE FREE PRESS OF GLENCOE

Collier-Macmillan Canada, Ltd., Toronto, Ontario

Library of Congress Catalog Card Number: 64–21205

EDITOR'S FOREWORD

The history of political theory is a compendium of books and authors, of writings and writers who have attempted to describe the political order and its proper constitution. Yet of the countless scribes who have set pen to paper in each generation only a few are reread and remembered. It is often argued that the exceptional books, the books that last, survive because they have adumbrated principles which are applicable in every political epoch. There is, however, another way of explaining why it is that some writings live on while others are forgotten.

At any moment in history there will be a dozen would-be philosophers convinced that they can sense the direction in which events are moving. Drawing on their powers of prediction or prescience they believe they can detect amid the swirl of the present those incipient trends that will give shape to the future. Inevitably most such forecasts are wrong. The reason is simple enough: any society will contain not one but a vast multitude of potential "trends"; and most of these will fail to develop, for they represent patterns of events whose days are numbered. Writers who venture to predict—and any theory is at heart such a prediction—almost invariably misplace their emphases. Thus the history of political theory ends up being the chronicle of those few writers who happen to have placed their bets on the winning side.

A theory achieves "greatness," then, if events bear out its major propositions. It is added to the shelf of works presumed to be timeless and is memorialized in textbooks and monographs. The remainder of our theoretical literature is consigned to the back stacks of antiquarian archives, perhaps to be perused by zealous graduate students in search of neglected authors. Hence the suspicion arises that it is history which elevates theories to eminence, that their ascent has little to do with their literary purity or even profundity. If the writings of Karl Marx are renowned in our time it is because China and the Soviet Union have chosen to adopt him for their patron saint. Marx is remembered because powerful men invoke him to justify their deeds of state. Had the politicians of these systems chosen another writer—or indeed no writer at all—then dialectical materialism might intrigue scholars but would hardly concern those outside the academic coterie.

These observations may serve as a preface to any consideration of recent political theory. Which of the writers of recent generations will be counted among the ranks of the winners? To answer such a question we, too, would have to have advance knowledge of the political forms and forces that will characterize the century opening before us. If the world continues to be marked by violence, bloodshed, and irrationality then Friedrich Nietzsche and Georges Sorel may be raised to the circle now occupied by writers like Aristotle, Hobbes, and Marx. But if societies succeed in organizing themselves with sophisticated patterns of institutional controls, then it will be writers like Max Weber and Elton Mayo who will be candidates for immortality. Or if the stresses and tensions of modern life continue to take an increasing emotional toll then Sigmund Freud and Erich Fromm will be remembered as foreseeing the conditions that were later to engulf man and society. These are by no means the only alternatives to come to mind, and the writers discussed on the pages which follow present an array of approaches, moods, and outlooks. At least one of them will surely be considered as required reading by our children's grandchildren. But which one? That decision is for them to make, not for us.

What also emerges in Henry Kariel's study is that theory can spring from a variety of sources. Men in or close to the centers of political affairs have written as perceptively as have scholars cloistered in academies. Thus in the chapters to come we will encounter politicians as well as professors, propagandists no less than philosophers. The hands of a Lenin, for example, are stained with blood no less than with ink. But he remains, for all that, a theorist of no small stature. Suppose it is protested that Lenin is not a serious thinker, that he is merely a pamphleteer who sought to provide a grim rationalization for his party's rise to power. Well and good. And yet: Is there no measure of ideology to be found in the theories of Michael Oakeshott, Elton Mayo, or John Dewey? Surely these writers, all holders of august professorships at respected universities, were not immune from political commitment. They, no less than Lenin, are concerned to perceive the *status quo* through a moral lens, to attack or defend prevailing arrangements in their pursuit of political truth.

Only the man with an engaged mind can see a pattern to politics. The writer who seeks after objectivity, who begins every second paragraph with the phrase "on the other hand," who adduces long lists of reservations and qualifications to anticipate the objections of any and all critics—such a man may have an open mind, but it can be a sadly empty mind as well. Ideological preconceptions undoubtedly distort a perception of social reality. Yet the mind of a theorist, eschewing common sense and stressing one factor to the exclusion of others, can often see what the rest of us cannot. Out of the hyperbole of a Nietzsche, a Freud, a Sorel, a Camus can come an understanding of the political life that never emerges from writers who through their fear of failure try to satisfy everyone and thus enlighten no one.

Are we witnessing the passing of politics? In our age it is statecraft that will decide whether or not whole populations will survive; and surely this in itself should make political power a central concern of man and societies. Yet theories and theorists have never been comfortable generalizing about the politics of the international arena, and today the subject is more complex and unpredictable than ever before. But on the domestic scene, in the Western world at least, there seems to be little interest in defining the goals of public life. We are in an age of psychology and sociology rather than a time of politics and power. Yet public problems can hardly be said to have been solved. There is still injustice, both economic and social, even if the sufferers are minorities rather than the vast mass of the population. And justice is a political matter, in definition and distribution, even if the means used to achieve this goal are often outside normal political channels. Economists may speak of an affluent society, but the problem for political theory is of an indifferent society. Henry Kariel's analysis demonstrates that the problems of politics are being neglected at our peril. If the goals of public life are left undefined there is no guarantee that the dilemmas we choose to ignore will resolve themselves. The task of the theorist is to raise to the surface those uncomfortable facts and values that most of society would prefer to see submerged. However there is reason for hope: that at least one reader is interested in the subject of these pages is evidence that there exists an audience for the enterprise of political theory.

ANDREW HACKER

CONTENTS

Fables can instruct grown men;
but one must tell the truth to children.
—JEAN-JACQUES ROUSSEAU

ACKNOWLEDGMENTS

Six Bennington College seniors—Ellen Bernstein, JoAnn Bromberg, Ellen Jacobowitz, Sheilah Marlowe, Sheila White, and Sally Wolter—helped temper my various interpretations of contemporary political thought in a series of weekly class meetings. To them, primarily, I am indebted. By relentlessly taking issue, they provided a forum, sparked a dialogue, and kept me aware of my audience.

I am only slightly less indebted to my colleagues on the Bennington College faculty for their uninhibited criticism of portions of my manuscript: Richard Blake, Louis Carini, Stanley Edgar Hyman, Anne Schlabach, and Rush Welter.

Parts of the manuscript which formed the basis for this book have also been read, attacked, and ultimately chastened by Professors Michael Curtis, Robert V. Daniels, Hans Gerth, Andrew Hacker, Stanley Hoffmann, George Kateb, Walter Kaufmann, Max Salvadori, Judith N. Shklar, and Neal Wood. To all of these critics I am most grateful—doubly so because they responded with so much vigor, pertinence, and wit that their correspondence would make a worthy companion volume.

Miss Isabel B. Sherwood's precision and patience in converting successive drafts into clean typescripts freed me for other work. A grant from the Huber Foundation, I am pleased to acknowledge, gave financial backbone (and a measure of psychological support) to my enterprise. Stanford University Press permitted me to borrow from my *The Decline of American Pluralism* (1961). And finally, the editors of *The Massachusetts Review* and *The Journal of Politics* gave me permission to draw on articles of mine that first appeared in their publications.

In fact, I have leaned so much on the research of others and received such generous backing that I am suddenly most reluctant to follow convention, as I must, and assume sole responsibility for all that follows.

HENRY S. KARIEL

Bennington, Vermont
June, 1963

IN SEARCH OF AUTHORITY
Twentieth-Century Political Thought

Introduction

This study intends primarily to illuminate the present state of political philosophy. It does not seek to provide, as textbooks properly do, a pleasing synthesis of available interpretations. It embodies a point of view which, I would hope, is focused, consistent, and comprehensive enough to allow the reader to take issue.

There are various ways of encouraging him to become critical. He might feel moved to disagree with me after being exposed to one of my academic colleagues who, teaching a course surveying modern political thought, offers a different perspective. He might also feel invited to take issue by considering such secondary works (listed in the end-of-chapter bibliographies) as proceed from premises differing from mine. Or he might feel invited by his independent review of the primary sources (similarly listed).

This study, in any case, proposes to proceed in the light of a general proposition. As it considers a succession of leading writers who have systematically reflected on political issues, it will be guided by the belief that political philosophy seeking to elucidate our ultimate common purposes, seeking to define the good life and the just state, has become increasingly inapplicable to our public realm. In fact, the very possibility of political philosophy having such aims has been put in jeopardy.

Our first concern will be to inquire what, on the level of theory, has produced this critical state of affairs. That is, what philosophical approach has challenged the possibility of engaging in discourse about the wisdom of public goals? And our second concern will be to probe, one by one, the variety of contemporary responses to the crisis in theory.

To say that a group of thinkers has created a crisis by subverting traditional political philosophy would be to give too much credit to their labors. But although these men have not produced the major revolutions of our time, they have both foreshadowed and reflected them. By casting experience in a rational mold, political thinkers have given it systematic and coherent form. In effect, their work rationally expresses the collapse of traditional political philosophy, if not the end of ideology. This collapse was fully anticipated by the achievement of Hegel, and it was he who furnished a point of departure for both Marx and Nietzsche. Their radical break with the past, their deflation of the enterprise of philosophy, had at least two consequences: it opened the way to the mindless politics which culminated in Naziism, and it prepared the ground for the widely held belief that "organizational theory" and "constitutional theory" provide the only kinds of generalizations relevant to our common public affairs.

What distinguishes the contemporary situation is the conviction that the "realistic" political theorist is concerned with "neutral" and "objective" information about the condition of politics, that value-neutral "practical" theory alone has integrity and merits our respect. The result has been to deprecate and exhaust discussion of the goals of political action. The abandonment of substantive political values has not, of course, put an end to political philosophy. Much of it, however, has become dangerously personal, immoderate, exotic, and shrill. At the same time it has become increasingly directed toward private realms: the small community and the easily managed enterprise. Ultimately the student himself will have to determine what gains and losses inhere in this development.[1]

This approach to contemporary political thought indicates what may properly be omitted here. No consideration

1. He can best do so by turning to the primary works, a task made easier by the volume of readings designed to accompany this interpretive study, *Sources in Twentieth-Century Political Thought* (1964).

will be given the discussion which continues today within the contours of Marxism. The reason, quite simply, is that Chinese, Russian, Hungarian, and even Polish political thought remains so constricted and so idiomatically burdened by the framework of Marxism that it fails to provide fresh insights, not to mention prescriptions. Second, no explicit consideration will be given to British logical and linguistic empiricism. This omission can be justified only by observing that while British empiricism has assuredly chastened speculative activity, it has not so far been brought to bear comprehensively on the political order. Third, no consideration will be given to present-day Far Eastern or Middle Eastern philosophy, because analyzing it requires understanding the historical setting giving it its distinctive point. To proceed without such understanding would be parochial; but to attempt to provide it for the Western student in the available space would merely add presumptuousness to parochialism. Finally, no consideration will be given ideological conflicts between Left and Right, liberalism and conservatism, laissez-faire and welfare state. The structure of this study should make these traditional categories irrelevant, or at least show them to be no longer illuminating. Not unintentionally, my approach may thus contribute to a situation it seems merely to describe.

HENRY S. KARIEL

I. THE ECLIPSE OF POLITICAL PHILOSOPHY

Three figures—Friedrich Nietzsche (1844–1900), Sigmund Freud (1856–1939), and Karl Mannheim (1893–1947)—compellingly introduce us to the predicaments of twentieth-century political thought. The momentum of the logic they set in motion has not diminished. In reviewing their work we are in fact reviewing, at its most articulate, the unsorted political notions we carry in our own minds. They help make explicit and open to criticism beliefs which for us remain simply axiomatic and unquestioned.

The logic of their work has the effect of removing a good deal of traditional political philosophy from the public scene. Their work has the effect of disclosing that it is impossible, in principle, to establish with certainty what is just and good for man in common. It attempts to represent our ideas of justice and goodness as no more than the expression of our drive for power (Nietzsche), of our complex psychic mechanisms (Freud), or of our historical situation (Mannheim). At the same time it summons man to establish himself. It summons him to form and re-form the infinite potentialities which are truly his. Insofar as the public order cannot validly be filled with any timeless, substantive Truth, the individual person is expected to make his own truth, thereby satisfying his own diverse needs. In accordance with this political approach, it becomes necessary to uphold the distinction between the morally indifferent state and a highly diversified society, between the public order and the private order.

Yet it has always proved to be difficult in practice to found a political regime which does justice to this approach.

Nietzsche, who accepted and elaborated it, did nothing whatever to implement it. Freud's psychoanalytic technique for
implementing it turned out to imply a new elitism; this was
to repress the mass of men so effectively that half of the
formula—the half insisting that men must create their own
private truth—was all but sacrificed. And insofar as Mannheim's way of implementing his view happened in the end to
uphold both parts of the formula, this was a merely lucky
circumstance; not his theory but his political interests, his
slowly maturing respect for the tradition of English constitutional procedures, were responsible.

We are less concerned, however, with testing the machinery Nietzsche, Freud, and Mannheim favored to preserve the
tension between the public and the private realm than with
expounding the way they defined these two realms. In their
definitions they in effect reformulated the perennial problem
of political philosophy, the problem of the proper relation
between the individual and the state.

We shall have to become fully alert to their distinction
between a public order of means and a private order of ends,
for this should help us grasp the various contemporary
reactions to it. Recognizing that each has made such distinction, we may understand the efforts (1) to obliterate the
distinction, as in the activism of fascism, (2) to ignore it, as
in the conservative acquiescence in the supposed dictates
of history, (3) to transcend it, as in in the acceptance of
"science" as arbiter of alternative social strategies, and (4)
to reinforce it, as in the theories which, while they burden
the private arena with moral imperatives, keep the public
arena free from ultimate objectives.

The Demands of Life:
Friedrich Nietzsche

Do you know what "the universe" is to my mind? Shall I show it to you in my mirror? This universe is a monster of energy, without beginning or end; a fixed and brazen quantity of energy which grows neither bigger nor smaller, which does not consume itself, but only alters its face. . . . It is . . . energy everywhere, the play of forces and force-waves, at the same time one and many, agglomerating here and diminishing there, a sea of forces storming and raging in itself, forever changing, forever rolling back over incalculable ages to recurrence . . . producing the most complicated things out of the most simple structures . . . a becoming which knows not satiety, or disgust, or weariness: this, my Dionysian world of eternal self-creation, of eternal self-destruction, this mysterious world of twofold voluptuousness; this, my "Beyond Good and Evil," without aim, unless there is an aim in the bliss of the circle. . . . Would you have a name for my world? A *solution* of all your riddles? Do you also want a light, you most concealed, strongest, and most undaunted men of the blackest midnight? This world is the *Will to Power*—and nothing else! And even you yourselves are this will to power—and nothing besides!

Nietzsche's specific idiom, the explosiveness and stridency of his aphorisms, are easily confused with his basic position. It is tempting to conclude, moreover, that his work has little significance independent of the historical conditions which precipitated it. Although these conditions may explain his distinctive style, they do not in the end account for what he

7

said. His experiments in language generated a tension between the conflicting demands of private and public life
with which we ourselves must come to terms. Refusing to
resolve this tension, he elaborated and intensified it. His
predicament remains ours even after the fall of the specific
institutions he besieged.

Nietzsche's work has helped, on the level of theory, to
clear the way for the dual state composed of (1) a public
order whose policies merit support to the extent that they
serve the infinitely varied interests of men—not to the
extent that they serve some timeless, transcendental purpose—and (2) a private order in which men are expected
to realize themselves, to fulfill their infinite promises. Moreover, it has helped provide us with a definition of leadership
accepted in democratic practice but still unaccommodated
by democratic theory.

Like Rousseau before him, Nietzsche assaulted the official
formulas of his day in behalf of a richer, more ample existence for man. So unconscious and secure did he believe to be
the current consensus, that he pushed on to challenge not
only the values which in fact prevailed but the very belief
in the possibility of publicly testifying about a realm of
truth and justice. He thereby transcended his times and
posed questions of durable pertinence.

Nevertheless, the controlled fury of Nietzsche's writing
is scarcely comprehensible without an understanding of the
society of his day. The prevailing moral agreement, the
existing political, cultural, and religious establishment, as
well as the academic philosophies which lent respectability
to the suffocating conventions of the late nineteenth century
—all these gave his work its specific edge. To explain the
sharpness of Nietzsche's attack it is necessary to recall his
image of the softness and stuffiness of the burgeoning
empire of the Hohenzollerns. He looked on Bismarck's paternalistic socialism as parochial and nationalistic; he saw
organized religion as shallow and hypocritical; and he experienced the great showpieces of nineteenth-century culture

—including Wagner's *Parsifal*—as vulgar and ugly monuments catering to the rising masses.

Above all, Nietzsche perceived philosophy as a discipline which did no more than to rationalize the status quo. Both English empiricism and Continental positivism, as Nietzsche viewed them, uncritically buttressed the existing institutions. He beheld a society which took pride in material achievements, and which consequently supported scholarship dedicated to providing objective descriptions of the facts. The facts, it seemed, needed only to be compiled. Without being prompted, they would then tell their own story. The statistical method would at last emerge as the appropriate one for understanding man's social and natural universe. It was a method designed to flatten out the unique event, the dramatic incident, or the eccentric genius, encouraging everything truly individual to become absorbed by the "historical process." The historical process, as Hegel had conceived it, could be counted on to vindicate itself. It was Reason marching ever onward and upward. Thus the mere accretion of historical monographs and scientific experiments would automatically reveal that the movement of events was inevitably progressive. Whatever hindered progress would be eliminated by an advancing technology, by philanthropy, and by public education. All this would take place under the auspices of a beneficent state equitably protecting established rights and removing the more annoying of economic inequalities.

If Nietzsche indecorously mocked this vision, this was because of the decorum, the refinement, and the smugness of his contemporaries. Where he stressed the motive power of evil, his contempories were certain of the triumph of goodness. He emphasized irrationalism where the utilitarians celebrated rationalism; he negated what a positivistic natural science affirmed. In the face of a growing bureaucratization and standardization of public life, his prose bore witness to the impulsive and the personal. In the face of pleas for clarity and objectivity, he counseled mystery, darkness, and subjectivity. He opposed finally the great political settlement of the nineteenth century—the belief in moderation and the faith that good sense was so widely distributed that it would always tell the individual citizen which of his notions and actions were in bad taste. It was the innocent, uncritical optimism of his age, its pompous insipidness and its self-indulgent philistinism, which gave Nietzsche's writing its drive and overlaid it with his sense of exasperation.

He raised his voice to affirm the great promise of man's existence. Elucidating the unperceived or corrupted potentials of life, he attempted to humanize them, to make them rational. He sought to capture them for the conscious mind. One of the notes that was to make up *The Will to Power* (1880–1890) consisted of his unambiguous declaration: "A book for thinking, *nothing else:* it belongs to those for whom thinking is a *delight,* nothing else." He proposed to vindicate man not by doing anything, certainly not by leading a revolutionary movement, but by remaining reflective and illuminating.

Given these intentions, he was confounded at the very outset by a dilemma which was to agonize him throughout his career. Somehow he had to move his readers—his students, his disciples, ultimately his public—to a rational conception of the irrational roots of their existence. Somehow he had to lead them to such understanding. Yet what tactics of leadership could he possibly employ? Would his reliance on rationality not deny the very point he wanted to make? To shine a bright light on the dark sources of man's power was to make it impossible to perceive their true nature. "A spirit who is sure of himself," he wrote, "speaks softly; he seeks secrecy, he lets himself be awaited. A philosopher is recognized by the fact that he shuns three brilliant and noisy things—fame, princes, and women: which is not to say that they do not come to him. He shuns every glaring light: therefore he shuns his time and its 'daylight.'" In committing himself to this view, Nietzsche blocked the road of political activism for himself. Instead of giving force to his ideas by organizing, bargaining, and compromising, he did no more than to expose his dilemma, to give it the fullest possible expression.

His logical starting point was his conviction that whatever may be our impressions of events, these impressions are tied together and made into coherent generalizations or moral propositions exclusively by virtue of our determination to give them such unity. We ourselves—not God, not Natural Law, not History, not Reason—give authenticity to judgments. We may, for example, call a sequence of action "honorable," using that adjective to link fragments of human behavior. But there is nothing honorable (or dishonorable) in behavior as such; no behavior is naturally honorable (or dishonorable). It is whatever we choose to designate it. Its quality depends on our determination, our will. And our will, in turn, expresses our interests as living beings, as beings concerned with getting on in the world, and surviving. Such propositions as "He conducted himself honorably" are therefore but expressions of the imperious forces of life.

But if our intellect is governed by our instinctual desires, Nietzsche asked, how can we claim that our moral propositions are valid? What is the relation between man's private will and public judgments? This was and is Nietzsche's central question, and he never dropped it. Thus he was concerned not with this or that moral judgment, but with the very possibility of making and communicating moral judgments. All the specific ones that had been piling up since the first moralist propounded his doctrine, so Nietzsche claimed, merely deflected attention from the more basic issue. Conventional intellectual moralizing was merely a kind of avoidance, a narcotic. What seemed essential was to recognize the deadly effect of our reliance on the intellect. It was time to appreciate the demands of life. The demands of the intellect, Nietzsche intoned, had been heeded to excess.

Seeing the forces of life buried in the unconscious, he delineated their infinite promptings, tones, and subtleties, resolving to redeem for the private man what was being repressed by the public man, always in the hallowed name of reason. What was public was shared; it was necessarily partial and incomplete, at best a precondition for the fullness of life. This was as true of public institutions as it was of public philosophies. Using life in all of its amplitude as the measure of those philosophers who claimed rational knowledge, Nietzsche characterized them as mere partisans. They broke life into segments; and, happy with the segments, they never troubled to see it whole and true. Their pursuit of truth could express but part of their being. To regain wholeness they would have to give a full hearing to the calls of their sensibilities and instinctive powers.

In an unprecedented fashion, then, Nietzsche aspired to give recognition to the depth and intensity of the irrational in man. His problem was how to retain a commitment both to life in all of its *personal* idiosyncrasies and to moral truth as a *social* construction, how to keep both in a state of suspense—and to do so while thoroughly aware of their respective demands.

Later thinkers, less probing in their skepticism, often found it easier to maintain the balance and to mediate between subjective volition and objective reason; so had earlier ones. Francis Bacon had challenged prevailing "idols" to enable him to move closer to a genuine understanding of the natural world. Machiavelli, doubting that those who lived in palaces speak the truth to outsiders, had sought to unmask beliefs about the political order. Helvetius, Condillac, and other thinkers of the French Enlightenment had wanted to rid us of our social and religious prejudices. Marx had been determined to show how the language of the bourgeoisie was but a cover for exploitation. Schopenhauer had maintained that by our logic and language we were led to an immoral, sinister world, and that our feelings of compassion demanded its negation. It was Nietzsche who laid waste to the public domain of moral truth still guarded by each of these endeavors. He radically jeopardized an axiom his predecessors had left untouched: the ultimate authority of a shared human rationality. He cast into doubt what Aristotle had called the rational principle within us. He systematically questioned man's capacity to grasp abstract moral truth by the use of his rational intellect, by the use of his common language. The island of moral truth protected by his precursors, the very island on which they took their stand against *false* idols, prejudices, and ideologies, Nietzsche exposed to erosion. What had saved his skeptical predecessors was their faith that whatever stand they took, they took it as human beings able to make rational distinctions, able to use a common language to value some things over others. And they had believed that their distinctions were not merely a function of their instincts, not merely an expression of their feelings of pain and pleasures—after all, even animals could express these—but rather, in Aristotle's terms, their "perceptions of good and evil, of the just and the unjust." With Nietzsche it was the rational principle within man that came under attack, for he could not convince himself that rational discourse has some ultimate point. Like Machiavelli, Hobbes, Hume, and Rousseau, he thereby subverted the classical conception of the city, the public square, the political forum, the parliamentary assembly. Like the framers of the American Constitution, he did not think these institutions of politics were suitable instruments for establishing the ends of life and instituting virtue. It follows that he radically criticized the kind of righteous public action based on the premise that our convictions and our language are derived from an objective realm of moral truth. Having assailed language, Nietzsche challenged the classical conception of public man as philosopher in quest of the ideal community.

In 1869, at the age of twenty-five, having studied art history, archaeology, and philology, Nietzsche accepted a professorship at the University of Basel. His inaugural lecture turned out to be a sharply concentrated preview of his later exercises in measured irony. As the newly appointed professor of classical philology, he proceeded quite properly to defend his discipline against its enemies. But as he restated the case of the enemies of philology, they seemed to have the best of the argument. Nietzsche spoke as if he deplored their attack: he noted that they were sniping from all directions, deriding philological scholarship as dull and useless. They considered philologists a breed of dust-swallowing moles who "for the eleventh time were pushing up some clod of dirt which had been pushed up ten times before." Or worse, they objected to the elevated idealism of the philologists. But in fact, Nietzsche said apologetically, philology was a marvelous make-believe empire incorporating history, science, aesthetics, and pedagogy. Did it not teach what was of durable value? Without destroying by dissecting, did it not lead the student to a renewed appreciation of the classical ideal?

Nietzsche extended his ambiguous observations on philology in a striking section of his *Thoughts out of Season* (1874)—"The Use and Abuse of History." There he turned toward historical scholarship more generally, questioning the real utility of the accounts of the past that human language makes available. After all, what goes into the countless volumes of history seems to be utterly useless; it hardly quickens our sensibilities. On the contrary, historical knowledge makes us self-conscious, reflective, and inactive. For Nietzsche this did not mean that we can dispense with history but rather that we must discriminate in favor of the kind of history which sustains life and action. We must discriminate against those historians whom Nietzsche called the "jaded idlers in the garden of knowledge," for they failed to perceive the life-destructive character of their work.

How did Nietzsche come to see one kind of history as essentially destructive of life? We are distinguished, he reasoned, by our capacity to remember the past, to recollect our past action. We are distinctively historical beings, as animals are not. Our experience—more accurately, our consciousness of our experience—distinguishes us. And it rests upon us like a burden. Our consciousness of our past, our conscious knowledge, is our curse. Fully to take the past into account—indeed, fully to take the future into account—confounds all action. Full knowledge of the past, full knowledge of the future (including our inescapable death), produces either delirium or paralysis. Thus history, experience, consciousness, intellectual awareness, rational knowledge—all these are the enemies of life. If we favor life, we have no choice but to repress these. Life requires repression, forgetfulness, deception. And from this it follows that those of us who are self-deceived or who have been deceived by others will lead the least inhibited lives. To be oriented by something less than full knowledge, to make one's way in the light of myth and illusion, is to make one's life bearable. On the other hand, the undeceived person, the one aware of past and future possibilities, is hindered in his movements. His very rationality mutilates his capacity to define himself in action.

It becomes evident, therefore, that the kind of history which will enhance man's capacity for action cannot be the kind provided by the customary academic discipline of history. The traditional discipline has been addressing itself to the past in the light of the most common of prevailing opinions. This is what "objectivity" in the teaching of history has actually amounted to. There would seem but one way of overcoming what is most common and shallow in the age of the historian—and this is to write and teach "subjective" history. Historians truly concerned with enlarging man's life and enhancing his capacity for action must not adjust to existing modes of thought but impose their vision of a higher standard. They must transcend what is common in the present and work in reference to what is most elevated and noble in it. By no means is the discipline of history to be deserted: it must be turned against itself. If the old history negates life, let a new history negate life-negating history.

Thus history can and must be used as a life-affirming discipline. This, indeed, is the historian's moral imperative.

The moment, however, that it became apparent to Nietzsche that he had arrived at a moral imperative, he realized he was confronted again by his central dilemma: man's highest vocation is dedication to moral truth, and yet moral truth denies life. Thus man is fated to be destroyed by his very dedication. Nietzsche's basic question—how can man arrive at moral truth and yet resist the life-destructive nature of history, consciousness, rational knowledge—remained unsolved.

The fact that Nietzsche saw no way of transcending his question did not mean that he ceased to pose it. On the contrary, he persisted in reformulating his predicament until his language became increasingly loaded, playful in its puns, light at its most serious points, self-confident in its irony, and rich in its allusions. Each of his works had the effect of complicating his problem, and this without loss in dramatic suspense. None of them offered the solution he could accept as final. In his *Beyond Good and Evil* (1886), however, an untempered skepticism began to gain the upper hand. Pursuing ideas he had set forth previously, Nietzsche now observed that philosophers sought to speculate about moral truths not because they loved truth as such but because they loved their *own* truth. The source of their quest, the very genesis of moral discourse, was to be found in the drives of those who engaged in it. Noting this, Nietzsche systematically unmasked the entire enterprise of traditional philosophy. He pointed to the meaninglessness of its claim that it can lead man to a realm of objective values. Like history, aesthetics, and linguistics, which he dealt with in turn, it struck him as deceptive in its very nature. Philosophers did not strive for truth; instead, they sought such understanding of the world which enables men to live happily. They searched precisely for what all art searches: the symbols that give depth and meaning to human life and action. They work, Nietzsche pointed out, in order to console themselves, in order to reconcile themselves to the absurdity of their existence. They thus furnished not Truth but conceptual systems, systems they themselves conceived. These systems, indistinguishable in their function from other artistic fabrications, gave cohesion to an incoherent world. Their utility, if they had any, lay in their capacity to make life bearable, their capacity to conceal its tensions and trials, to *place* those terrible facts of human existence for which, in all honesty, we cannot find a place in our minds.

It would seem that philosophers were unwittingly performing acts of mercy. They helped man repress. In fact Nietzsche did not expect philosophers to behave otherwise. "When a slave in prison dreams that he is free and relieved of his chains," Nietzsche asked, "who would be so callous as to waken him and tell him that he is merely dreaming?" Philosophy, then, was but a dream—one which was justified by its success in concealing man's unbearably tragic condition. To be sure, it rested on deceit. But this precisely gave it its credentials. Like the great works of art and theology, it filled a need. It satisfied our instinctual drives. But to truth as such it could have no relation whatever. Since our thought is but a biological function, an unconscious tool of life, it would be meaningless to inquire whether the ends it served were good or evil. All morality which still accepts this distinction, Nietzsche argued in his *Genealogy of Morals* (1887), must therefore be overcome.

The traditional rejection of evil thoughts and deeds Nietzsche now deemed not merely sentimental but downright dangerous—dangerous to civilization. To maintain a genuine civilization it was essential to rely on men whose style and manner are commonly considered "evil." These men were the true nobility, and the tasks of civilization could not be carried out without them. Civilization required such an aristocracy; it was necessarily based on human inequality. But inequality creates envy among the mass of men. When the majority encounters the potent, the noble, and the gifted, it becomes resentful and proceeds to call them evil. This, said Nietzsche, had always been the way of the weak: their guilt-ridden hostility to excellence dates back to the times of biblical antiquity. A biblical priesthood, as Nietzsche reconstructed history, had deeply resented the ancient warlords and succeeded in attaching the label "evil" to their qualities. The priesthood, with estimable forcefulness, had thundered in opposition: it provided a decalogue of Thou Shalt Nots. But while it said "No" to the forces of life—to the source of man's most noble qualities—it did so with magnificent determination. Nietzsche's respect for the energy of the priesthood was so great that, although he rejected the priesthood's code of humility and meekness, he accepted the spirit with which it was promulgated. Thus he found himself arguing that the "No" be converted into a "Yes," that the energetic impulse of biblical morality be harnessed to a life-affirming code, to a pagan morality. This pagan morality, however, he saw as a code like no other. It contains no prohibitions. Instead of repressing man, instead of forcing him to feel obliged to conform, it emancipates. It releases the impulses of life. And it does so by ignoring what passes for "good" and "evil," by ignoring all conventional "morality."

In taking this stand, in opposing conventional morality, Nietzsche still did not say that there was no such thing as morality. He merely affirmed that the perception of moral truth, that public discourse informed by the belief in the existence of a realm of final truth, was destructive of man's most distinctively human qualities. Action premised on this belief subverted humanity. For humanity, far from requiring objective truth, needed illusion, myth, and deception. These, after all, were the preconditions of life. The imperative, therefore, was to make men renounce their common quest for moral truth and yet not to deprive them of illusion. Their renunciation was to provide the basis for the full life, the life beyond good and evil, but not the life beyond illusion. Myths there would have to be, but these would be truly living constructions—made by men, expressing their own needs, projecting their own potentialities.

To be converted to this position, Nietzsche realized, is to transcend the conventions of ordinary men. It is to detach oneself from the holy causes which galvanize the masses. It is to increase the distance between rulers and subjects, to move on a superior plane with heightened awareness and enhanced power. It is to join the new priesthood of "spiritualized Caesars."

Transcending all conventional morality, the new individual will be liberated from its imperatives. He will no longer be distracted by a quest for knowledge of absolute ends. Uninhibited by values, he will be truly free to display his virtuosity, to perform, play, and create as he sees fit, incorporating the ends of life in the very process of living it.

Yet in working his way toward these conclusions in *Beyond Good and Evil,* Nietzsche did not make the final jump. He still did not free himself from the belief in a realm of moral truth. While he repudiated the very concept of truth, he did not dispense with it. Thus he did not hesitate to think more highly of those points of view which reveal the deceptive character of others. While all perspectives are illusory, some he believed to be clearly better than others. What makes some of them better is their capacity for enabling us to see through a greater variety of moral propositions, to detect and eradicate the human appetites and rationalizations retained by lesser, narrower perspectives.

If, then, some perspectives are better than others insofar as they unmask others, skepticism itself becomes a valuable tool. It enables us to move closer to truth. Yet the truth toward which it enables us to move is not any positive system of verities. It is, instead, a negative, illusion-destroying truth. It affirms nothing—but does so with vigor, force, and persuasive power.

To see this is to have at least one key to the nature of Nietzsche's work. May his work not be seen as a fully reasoned affirmation of the negative? Does it not embody the

denial of all positivism? In fact, it establishes nothing whatever. It gives sanction to no social order—to no human
community, no social class, no political regime. It bankrupts
every establishment, clearing it away, making room for the
individual. It leaves nothing as final, neither ideas nor institutions. Still it does give absolute sanctity to the individual
person, approaching him as incommensurable. It thereby
gives authority to such political arrangements, and only to
such, as are apt to preserve man's integrity.

Interestingly enough, these propositions are the heart of
the theory of democratic constitutionalism. For this theory
holds that the test of all public institutions and all public
laws is the likelihood of their enhancing the rights of individuals, that the only common goal for political action is to
keep the ends of life unplanned and personal.

Once the political philosopher has concluded that there
is no final validation for a public philosophy, and that all
attempts to provide one are presumptuous, how can he per-
suade others to see as he does? How can he persuade them
that in public life there can be no fulfillment, no final
rationality? How can he lead ordinary men to *know* that
knowledge is denied them? This ultimate insight, according
to Nietzsche, they can gain, if at all, only by direct personal
experience:

> The condition of those who have been wracked long
> and horribly by sickness . . . is not without value for gain-
> ing knowledge. . . . The victim of extreme suffering looks
> *upon* all things with a terrible coldness: for him all that
> deceptive magic in which things customarily float for the
> healthy person has disappeared. In fact, he confronts his
> very self stripped.

Just as Marx's proletarian had to be truly miserable in order
to be freed from ideology and *know* his true place, so Nietzsche's autonomous individual had to be in a state of pain to
understand the world as it really is. He had to be aware of
his self, his history, his condition. His fate had to weigh on

him. When truly down and out, he would see everything in a new light. Falsehood would disappear. Only what truly matters would stand up. And the one thing that would then matter beyond all doubt would be life itself. As illusion after illusion dropped off, true understanding would become possible.

Whoever has gained such understanding, gained it in suffering, is entitled to act autonomously in public. He is the genuine statesman. Accepting the absurdity of all so-called truth, he recognizes the truths of other men as their private achievement. He knows that making any one of these into public policy would bedevil the community: it would impose an artificial regime of Truth and deprive men of their individuality. Having won his way to the insight that the public order, while it is an order, remains inherently meaningless, he cannot feel tempted to lead a crusade in behalf of a great cause.

It should be obvious that Nietzsche was aware of the threat to individuality posed by rulers who, having failed to gain self-mastery, were hankering for a public crusade in behalf of some cause. He saw such uncontrolled rulers as able to induce the rest of the community to accept their moral truth—a myth of their own making, a product of their own weakness. But he never contemplated the possibility of depending on political machinery to frustrate the will of psychologically crippled elites. He consequently appeared to be indiscriminate in his acceptance of elitism. Impressed as he was by the immensity of the burden the mass of men would have to bear if they only knew that their public life had no final significance, he assaulted all forms of egalitarianism. After all, the ordinary man will not voluntarily expose himself to pain, fully consider his existence, and then go on despite its absurdity. To work when no public code finally makes sense demands extraordinary qualities, above all, a detached, ironic, joyous spirit. It requires the virtues of the picaresque hero—a light touch, irony, and humor. It requires a particular kind of new elite which gaily recognizes the pointlessness of our common existence and is determined to have us live our private lives to the utmost. Since this elite will accept no political cause as "given"—whether by Nature, Fate, History, Science, or Providence—it is left to its own devices, compelled to be inventive. And so as not to be unnerved by its task to keep forever on the move, it has to remain jaunty and buoyant, facing up to every crisis in a mood of insouciance.

Such a leadership would justify itself by its capacity to preserve public life as an inconclusive, interminable process. Its paramount task is to guarantee that the public order comes to no terminus, moves in an eternal cycle, forever destroying and creating itself. Whereas traditional morality had closed our horizon and given public life a goal, the new morality demands that we look for the goal of humanity not at the end but in mankind's noblest examples, in its most eminent types.

It is perfectly clear, of course, that Nietzsche was not concerned with making his prophecy concrete. No practical considerations were to temper and moderate it. While the British utilitarians or the drafters of the American Constitution were preoccupied by the instrument of government, he ignored the possible ways of implementing his views. Failing to consider what form of government would do justice to them, he left an ominous gap.[1] Had he coupled his plea for a superior leadership with recommendations for specific governmental arrangements, it might have been less easy to misinterpret him by charging him with supporting government by any elite whatever. Thus while reflection makes clear that the only kind of political machinery appropriate

1. One way of filling this gap was Freud's. To liberate man Freud sought to rely not on the institutions of constitutional politics but (1) on the procedures of empirical science and (2) on a loyal, crusading Psychoanalytic Movement whose members were "practitioners." Converting the "findings" of a positive natural science of man into public policy does, however, entail a form of generally undiscussed discrimination; such a science does not account for unexpressed, immaterial, and ultimately impractical interests. Whenever it is the exclusive basis for action, it delimits human ends—and hence is incompatible with Nietzsche's position.

to Nietzsche's basic outlook is that associated with liberal constitutionalism, it was to become possible to believe that his philosophy could justify government by elites who were victims, not masters, of their passions, who were possessed by their vision of good and evil, and unable to move beyond it.

It was surely fateful that Nietzsche refrained from asking what kind of educational system would teach the governing elite not to take politics too seriously. He might have reflected on a curriculum for making potential leaders detached, cool but respectful toward one another, and only lightly committed to public goals. Moreover, he might have considered how a two-party system keeps elected officers from becoming attached to public office, how it forces them to remain in circulation, to be forever replaceable, to stay limber and equivocal. He might thus have been impelled toward a theory of government accommodating the irrational in man, a theory making the most of man's drive for power by demanding not that men be virtuous but that their ambitions be always held in check by counterambition. A system based on such a theory will make those in power insecure and uneasy. It will make their public life hard and troublesome. In the final analysis, it will thereby turn out to be an institutional substitute for the sustained suffering Nietzsche believed to be the sole qualification for leadership.

Ignoring this substitute, Nietzsche found himself embracing an unqualified principle of human inequality. Statesmen accepting the politics of constitutionalism have long accepted this principle, recognizing that all government is inescapably minority government. But, more significantly, they have traditionally proceeded to ask *how* men who are unequal by nature might yet gain equality in public life. They consequently worked on a system which might provide aristocracy in the midst of democracy, which might consistently turn private ambition, as they put it, into public benefit. Nietzsche, however, dealt exclusively with private ambition, with the complex, irreducible, unequal individual. Brilliantly elaborating on man's manifold potentials, stressing his inalienable uniqueness, he put on trial the manners, postures, and rationalizations which debase him. In the tradition of Machiavelli, Hobbes, Hume, and Rousseau, Nietzsche's philosophy thereby cleared the way for a secular, inconclusive, godless public order. Within it meaningful debate would have to deal with means, not ends. Whatever ends men sought to preserve as holy and absolute, they would have to do so in privacy. As their public life lacked in "seriousness" and exhilaration, their private life would be venturesome, creative, and self-fulfilling.

The Triumph of Utility: Sigmund Freud

By revealing the relation between our ideals and the drives within us, by seeing all religious creeds, metaphysical systems, and political ideologies as our own repressive contrivances, Nietzsche had discredited the belief that it was meaningful to engage in philosophical discourse about ultimate public purposes. To subscribe to his skepticism was to deprive political and social philosophy of its architechtonic scope. Admittedly, men might continue to quest for ideals, discuss those they beheld, and shape their communities to accord with them. This they would do by nature, as political animals who define ends, and who, by so doing, limit opportunities. But should they wish to realize the manifold potentials within them, should they wish to be free, they could support only a regime ruled by leaders wholly indifferent to moral absolutes.

Should moral absolutes somehow still seem to have validity, this impression was merely due to the force given them by historical circumstance and individual interest. They could have no claim to permanence or universality. Behind the flux of appearance there was no finality, no absolute, no morality. Nietzsche, in any case, hoped to keep absolutes from becoming permanent or universal fixtures by entrusting the task of public leadership to a detached elite, one that would be free from the common need to submit to the tyranny of false gods. This elite would not have to discipline either itself or its subjects on grounds unrelated to human self-fulfillment.

While holding these views, Nietzsche considered no insti-

tutions that might have implemented them. He associated
them with no structure of government or process of politics.
He sought no disciples, founded no cult, nurtured no organization, and provided no technique for keeping his ideals
untarnished.

Where Nietzsche stopped, Freud was to push on. What
makes Freud a noteworthy figure for the student of modern
political thought was his sustained concern for giving force
to his insight. Like Hobbes, he wished his work to "fall into
the hands of a Soveraign, who will . . . convert this Truth
of Speculation into the Utility of Practice." Freud resolutely
attempted to gain acceptance of his view of man and society,
and toward that end he engaged in politics. What, specifically, distinguished his view? And how did he seek to convert
it into a sovereign force in society?

When, as a young man, Freud turned to the investigation
of psychological phenomena, he clearly did not do so in
order to induce action or to see his truth prevail. He quietly
began his inquiries so as to bring order to disorderly experience. He simply hoped to understand behavior that
appeared odd or extreme. He sought to make it less puzzling
by shedding light on it. It was his express aim systematically
to account for a greater variety of human experiences than
conventional natural and medical science could accommodate. As Ernest Jones, his most level-headed disciple, has
written, he desired "to furnish a *theoretical* basis for the new
discoveries he was making in psychopathology and, with the
help of that, to found a *theory* of the mind that would take
into due account the peculiar features of the unconscious;
the outcome of his endeavors is called psychoanalysis."

Proceeding empirically, Freud necessarily rejected all
teleological explanations of behavior. He was determined to
inquire exclusively how a particular mental phenomenon
functioned, how it behaved in relation to other mental
phenomena, and how the entire set of phenomena constituted an integral whole. The integral whole, as Freud saw
it, was man trying to get on, trying to augment his resources,

make the most of his life, or simply survive. All the postulated parts of the human mechanism functioned—or malfunctioned—in relation to the paramount value of human life. By consistently referring to the value of life, it became possible for Freud to perceive contradictions in our psychic machinery, to locate breakdowns, to make diagnoses. It became possible for him to construct a pathology and specify when things were not running smoothly. In the well-operating human mechanism nothing was wasted, everything was economically employed toward its maintenance. And, so Freud assumed, to maintain it meant simply to keep it in motion—not for any end or purpose but for its own sake.

To provide himself with a model for our mental processes, Freud postulated a conflict between our unconscious, instinctual urgings and that mental agency which orders them, between id and ego. The id Freud believed to be autonomous: it activates itself, presses for recognition, demands gratification. Its gratification is our deepest happiness. But the ego denies us this happiness by judiciously regulating the promptings of the unconscious. Recognizing that in the natural as well as the social world the gratification of our instinctual demands must lead to the destruction of life, it disciplines them. It prudently chooses between alternative levels and amounts of gratification, permitting some direct expression, totally repressing others, and guiding still others into socially useful channels. In performing this function, the ego is led by those norms of society which the individual has accepted, by those internalized standards that Freud, continuing in his metaphorical creation, called the super-ego.[1] Thus the ego is our rational mediator. Warned and criticized by the super-ego, pressured by the id, it maintains

1. The following from Freud's *The Problem of Anxiety* (1936) should warn us how simplified the above account is: "The separation of the ego from the id seems justified, indeed is forced upon us, by certain findings. Yet on the other hand the ego is identical with the id, is only a specially differentiated portion of it. . . . The same with the relationship of the ego to the super-ego; as regards many situations they are one and the same. . . . We have been taking abstractions too rigidly."

our balance. It keeps us, if not happy, at least alive and working. It keeps us from destroying ourselves and from being destroyed by others. It preserves our sanity, and obviously does so in the face of conflicting pressures.

Freud's respect for these pressures, his actual perception of a new dimension of the conflict between individual and society, had a dual effect. It stressed, first of all, the primacy, intensity, and obstinacy of human passions. And, second, it placed a countervailing stress on the massiveness of society's restraints. Under such conditions the results of the harassment of the ego were bound to be unnerving. Given the imperiousness of our instinctual needs, what requires explaining is the incredible fact that we manage to have a community at all. Conflicts between the individual and society, in Freud's view, were not occasioned by this or that governmental system; they inhered in any civilized society whatever. Every society being precariously constituted, the obstacles to maintaining it would seem to be overwhelming.

Since Freud realized that social controls would always have to remain proportionate to the antisocial pressures that call for their exercise, it is not surprising that he was to take an authoritarian position. He had certainly observed these pressures at their strongest. They were fully manifest in the society of his day, in his patients, and, most tellingly, in himself. Provoked by his understanding of our baser instincts, his call turned out to be for public order. Encountering individuals as patients in the extremities of crisis situations— indeed, perceiving his whole world as crashing under the impact of the newly enfranchised masses, the class struggle, industrial dislocations, and national wars—he was steadily alert to the need for authority, for a firmly civilizing leadership that would unify a disintegrating society.

In a letter to his fiancée written a half century before he published *Civilization and Its Discontents* (1930) he had already distinguished between the civilizing role of the aristocracy, with which he identified himself, and the irra-

tionality of the masses. On the one hand, he wrote, there is
the aristocracy:

> We economize with our health, our capacity for enjoy-
> ment, our forces: we save up for something, not knowing
> ourselves for what. And this habit of constant suppression
> of natural instincts gives us the character of refinement.

Acting prudently, the aristocracy remains sober, chaste, and
solitary. On the other hand, there is "the mob giving vent
to its impulses":

> The poor are too powerless, too exposed, to do as we
> do. . . . The common people judge, believe, hope, and work
> quite otherwise than we do. There is a psychology of the
> common man which is somewhat different from us.

Civilized living, then, enjoins us to control our antisocial
nature, to renounce our instinctual needs, and to pay for this
sacrifice in the form of our neuroses. This price can be paid
only by those exemplary individuals who, having faced up
to the cruel facts of life, have freed themselves from their
demands. Their leadership becomes legitimate to the extent
that they have gained independence from all base impulses,
whether these impulses reside in themselves or in society
outside. They are a heroically self-denying, self-controlled,
and ultimately self-authenticating elite. And they must be
summoned to serve because conditions objectively demand
it. As Freud put it in *The Future of an Illusion* (1928):

> It is just as impossible to do without government of the
> masses by a minority as it is to dispense with coercion in
> the work of civilization, for the masses are lazy and un-
> intelligent, they have no love for instinctual renunciation,
> they are not to be convinced of its inevitability by argu-
> ment, and the individuals support each other in giving full
> play to their unruliness. It is only by the influence of indi-
> viduals who can set an example, whom the masses recognize
> as their leaders, that they can be induced to submit to the
> labors and renunciations on which the existence of culture
> depends. All is well if these leaders are people of superior

insight into what constitute the necessities of life, people who have attained the height of mastering their own instinctual wishes.

The function of the leadership is to preserve organized life by demanding and enforcing instinctual renunciations. Its task is to reconcile man to necessity, to keep him oriented to "reality."

That Freud happened to identify necessity with the specific institutions and ideas of *fin de siècle* Vienna has been frequently noted. But the politically far more significant point, which has been elaborated in one of the essays in David Riesman's *Individualism Reconsidered* (1954), is that Freud identified reality with an economy of scarcity. His model of the "real" world was one in which goods are limited, men are fully employed, and nothing is wasted. Everything has a function and duly performs it. It is a world of no idleness, no nonsense, no *im*practical jokes. Every joke, every dream, every slip of the tongue or the pen has its place. What pleasures there are, are merely prologues to a life that is hard and earnest. Laughter helps us get relief from tension and thus supports what really matters: our work. Our very dreams conserve our energy; they keep us asleep and thus refresh us for the next day's labor.

The mature individual will accept the life of work and effort, not that of idleness and spontaneity. He will have overcome the illusions of play or art, illusions which shield him from the brutal reality of life, just as religion shields him from the brutal reality of death. For Freud there was to be no deception about the tragic nature of man's existence. He sought to be consistently clear-minded and sober, honestly facing reality. As Jones pointedly says: "Water was drunk at meals." Suffering from cancer of the jaw, Freud took aspirin tablets.

There was to be no compromise. Play, art, ethics, religion, and ultimately science itself—these were all to be unmasked. In the stunning language of Freud they are escape routes, substitute formations, and wish fulfillments; they are sublimations, projections, and rationalizations. They become intelligible in relation to the real world, the world of our drives. Our drives create them so that we can keep going in a permanently hostile and oppressive environment. By means of these formidable inventions, we get our bearings in the world. They enable us to keep living. Thus our religious codes spring from our obsessive need for the protective father in a world of insecurity. Our artistic endeavors—even though "almost always harmless and beneficent"—furnish "a temporary refuge for us from the hardships of life"; they give us "substitute gratifications," "provide the feelings of identification," and "subserve a narcissistic gratification." Nor was the activity of science exempt: "One may finally regard curiosity, the impulse to investigate," so Freud wrote a friend, "as a complete sublimation of the aggressive or destructive instinct." In 1932 he rhetorically asked Einstein whether every science does not "come in the end to a kind of mythology."

Because these varied forms of behavior have value insofar as they can be shown to contribute to our ability to survive, it becomes possible to appreciate and grade their respective merits. They do not function equally well in making life bearable, in enabling us to master the world. Understandably it was the enterprise of science which emerged in a superior position for Freud.

> It is inadmissible to declare that science is one field of human intellectual activity, and that religion and philosophy are others, at least as valuable, and that science has no business to interfere with the other two, that they all have an equal claim to truth, and that everyone is free to choose whence he shall draw his convictions and in what he shall place his belief. Such an attitude is considered particularly respectable, tolerant, broadminded, and free from narrow prejudices. Unfortunately, it is not tenable. . . .

In *The Future of an Illusion* Freud wrote that an attempt was often made to discredit science on the ground that it is so bound to our mental processes that it can only yield subjective results. But for a number of reasons, he said, this is a misunderstanding of scientific work:

> Firstly, our organization, i.e., our mental apparatus, has been developed actually in the attempt to explore the outer world, and therefore it must have realized in its structure a certain measure of appropriateness; secondly, it itself is a constituent part of that world which we are to investigate, and which readily admits of such investigation; thirdly, the task of science is fully circumscribed if we confine it to showing how the world must appear to us in consequence of the particular character of our organization; fourthly, the ultimate findings of science, just because of the way in which they are attained, are conditioned not only by our organization but also by that which has affected this or-ganization; and, finally, the problem of the nature of the world irrespective of our perceptive apparatus is an empty abstraction without practical interest.
>
> No, science is no illusion. But it would be an illusion to suppose that we could get anywhere else what it cannot give us.

The very structure of the human mind, as Freud viewed it, was formed and re-formed so as to come to terms with the physical universe. It therefore becomes possible to rely on the work of an empirical science both for gaining under-standing of the world and for fashioning the programs to overcome the threats it poses to human life. As science puts us into touch with the real world, it enables us to control it. Thus an applied science, converting Freud's ana-lytical constructs into policy directives, can facilitate our survival while it simultaneously reveals what is fruitful or fruitless in our policies. Its practitioners, aware of the waste of all ideological conflict, gain the knowledge necessary to assess alternative policies and discriminate in favor of those conducive to social health. They can thus ameliorate con-flict and provide the conditions for meaningful productivity. By defining the limits of tolerance, their authority can create social order and peace. If the body politic is to remain healthy, if it is not to be torn apart by man's natural savagery, policy scientists would have to legislate. Unless they exercise a governmental function, civilization is not likely to survive.

To maintain the basis for community, the practitioners of such a science must be reluctant to reveal what they know about the nature of man and society. Were they to speak openly, they would set forces in motion which ultimately destroy society: they would give rise to politics. Without myth, as Freud had seen, men cannot live together, or even with themselves. Given man's natural aggressiveness, mythologies are indispensable for social cohesion. The mass of men are kept in line by their shared rituals and ceremonials, their irrational commitments to dogmas and causes. When laboring under illusory beliefs, they willingly cooperate; but when they must make individual calculations about what is rationally to their mutual advantage, they are brutally competitive. Thus were one to expose and publicize the coercive foundation of civilized life by making men aware of the illusory character of their beliefs, men would be thrown into a barbaric state of nature. Such disclosure would loosen the bonds of community and destroy civilization. To deprive man of his beliefs, to liberate him from the restraints of dogma, is to atomize his society. It is to give rise to intolerable conflicts, to the assertion of individual rights against society. In short, it is to introduce politics.

If, then, the community is to be protected from politics, if civilization is to be preserved, it becomes incumbent upon its governors to keep their rational knowledge of man and society from reaching the masses. Thus rationality might be preserved—but it would have to be confined to the few. The elite might act with reasonable prudence; the masses cannot. Lest the masses revert to barbarism, they would have to be guarded against the new knowledge of mass psychology.

But under modern conditions of mass education and

mass communication, this could hardly be easy. Freud's conclusions were bound to be disseminated, and in the process they inexorably turned into the mythology of Freudianism. In consumption-oriented societies Freudian beliefs found acceptance only insofar as their unpleasant aspects were ignored. Freud had stressed the need for self-restraint and self-mastery because, as he saw it, "reality" demanded it. But where this was found to be unprofitable, "reality" was simply redefined so as to demand self-indulgence. Whereas Freud's vision led him to counsel self-control, those who saw reality in a different light advertised more abundant consumption. Indeed, ultimately even Freud's grim view of man, his unrelieved pessimism about social reform, and his dependence on authoritarian controls could be accommodated—but without becoming decisive in the actual affairs of men. "Psychology" could become still another marketable commodity to be consumed, a point of view to be entertained and hence to be merchandized with profit. It could be "placed" in college courses, in anthologies, and in the compartments of one's mind—all this without becoming the operative basis of personal conduct.

It would have been altogether reasonable for Freud to protect his knowledge, to keep it from being converted into the mythology of a self-indulgent society. But he evidently did not believe that access to his insights could be limited to a specially qualified elite. Still, he did take measures that had the effect of making it difficult first to be introduced to his ideas and then to deviate from them. His fundamental view of the world was to be transmitted to the uninitiated as part of an interminable therapeutic process. His pessimistic assessment of human life, his unshakable skepticism about the possibility of progress, his view that the mature person endures with resignation, his belief in society as repressive, his hope for a self-denying governing elite—this complex morality was to be embraced by the patient. Yet the problem was how to make the patient—and the patient was, in principle, every member of society—accept himself and the world when his very instincts made him rebellious. After all, the human mind is fundamentally so constituted as to resist Freud's doctrines. It would, if left unguided, transform them into something more pleasurable. It therefore became essential to protect their integrity. Since Freud's truth—the truth of skepticism—was such that it could not make its way into the minds of men by virtue of its own merit, it had to be actively defended.

It becomes intelligible, then, why Freud was to live up to the image of the religious crusader, the prophet armed. He was indeed concerned with gaining converts and retaining disciples. Toward that end he conscientiously worked on his organization, vigorously engaging in politics. Psychological congresses were to resemble political conventions. Freud's biographer has sketched at least one impressive picture of Freud as politician, bargaining, negotiating, and compromising at an international congress in 1910. In a hotel room he passionately appealed to his Viennese colleagues to broaden the base of the movement by accepting the nomination of Jung for president. In a different mood nine years later, but just as astutely the politician, he was to write Jones that the plan "to purge the London Society of the Jungian members is excellent." Even as Freud gained recognition he remained acutely aware of the loyalty of his supporters. When Jones informed Freud that a number of psychologists who had been analyzed by Freud personally might form an Old Guard, as he put it, to preserve the purity of psychoanalysis, Freud replied:

> What took hold of my imagination immediately is your idea of a secret council composed of the best and most trustworthy among our men to take care of the further development of psychoanalysis and defend the cause against personalities and accidents when I am no more. . . . I daresay it would make living and dying easier for me if I know of such an association existing to watch over my own

creation. First of all, this committee would have to be *strictly secret* in its existence and in its actions. . . .

Thus Freud took care to implement his view that if civilization was to be preserved against the onslaught of the masses, a self-critical and self-controlled elite must govern. While adjusting the rest of the community to its tragic condition, the members of the ruling class would somehow keep themselves in check: they would initiate their successors, analyze one another, refine their theory, and improve their technique. The institutional gap that had been left open by Nietzsche, Freud now closed. He implemented his desire to free men not by relying on the mechanisms of constitutional politics but instead by relying on an empirical science whose "findings" would be made the basis for public policy by a crusading movement of loyal practitioners.

Insofar as a natural science is necessarily deterministic, Freud's reliance on it had the logical consequences of transmitting his specific form of determinism to those whom psychoanalysis could reach. And he disarmed them by incorporating their very opposition in his deterministic system: if they claimed their religion was not merely an illusion, their art not merely an evasion of reality, their politics not merely a device for group catharsis, their play not merely "acting out," their dreams not merely tension-relieving, their joking not merely utilitarian, or their work not merely a form of renunciation but a positive pleasure— if they entered any of these claims to keep from "functioning," he could characterize them as "resisting" and proceed to practice therapy. Thus there could be no rational appeal to a tribunal outside the realm of an empirical science of man. The values authenticated by science were simply public values. The vacuum left by Nietzsche, Freud's commitment to empiricism—and to an organization to put its results into practice—was effectively filled.

The procedures employed by Freud to implement his values set illiberal forces in motion. But an element of pathos remains in this, for he had discredited man's suffocating public myths no less than Nietzsche. He had emphatically set out to liberate man. By incorporating our socially intractable self in his theory, accounting for it and dignifying it, he no less than Nietzsche sought to redeem the private man—redeem him in all his obstinate perversity, with all his primary drives intact, irreducible to society, culture, or civilization. It is thus clear that even though he did not consider reason to be the inalienable attribute of man, Freud's basic impulse was profoundly liberal. Indeed, it is hardly necessary to note that he added a dimension to our understanding of man which an equalitarian liberal theory must continuously take into account in order to remain viable. After Freud it becomes impossible to reject the proposition that, at least potentially, all of us are patients.

The Imperative of History:
Karl Mannheim

Nietzsche and Freud moved man into the center of politics: they made him, and him alone, the author of the state. They saw the state as wholly expressive of man's will, not of some timeless moral absolute or some demiurge immanent in history. The logic of their work had the effect of reducing political philosophy to psychology and sociology. It did this by making the sole test of our social institutions their conformity to our conflicting drives. They inquired to what extent our social arrangements conformed to our two mutually hostile needs: (1) the need to dominate, to defy the community in obedience to our aggressive drives, and (2) the need to submit, to satisfy our craving for union and community. It thus became irrelevant to inquire whether our institutions conformed to those needs which philosophers, discussing the moral ends of the state, had attributed to a realm of ideals, to Providence, or to History. Nietzsche as well as Freud looked upon philosophical discourse itself as but symptomatic of the needs of philosophers.

This approach replaced theoretical questions about the state, questions properly elucidated by political philosophers, with practical ones properly answered by an empirical science of man. The exclusively relevant questions became those of means: How much individual freedom can a social system tolerate without becoming unstable? How much freedom is compatible with the survival of society? By what tactics is man most effectively controlled? What degree of repression is necessary under specific conditions? In each

38

instance the given end—that is, the answer we get when we ask, "Necessary or effective for what?"—is the healthy social system. Accepting the natural need for social cohesion, the question is about the instrumentalities conducive to it. And the answer is supplied by the new science of psychology and sociology, by the ascending theorists of social organization. To such a science, the writings of Karl Mannheim are a superb introduction. Moreover they are comprehensive enough to provide an additional insight: a science preoccupied by means and the deliberately interminable politics of constitutional regimes both assume man's limited capacity to grasp the public good.

Obeying the same rational impulse that had driven Freud, Mannheim sought to impose order on the unprecedented disorder of his times. He was born in Budapest in 1893. From 1929 until the rise of Hitler he taught sociology at the University of Frankfurt. He then emigrated to England, continuing his academic career until his untimely death in 1947. Throughout his life, he searched for coherence where he beheld conflict. He saw society in a pathological condition of crisis and disorganization. It offered a spectacle of conflicting opinions and no common philosophy from which to deduce the principles for the just state. As he worked for a genuine science of society that might become the legitimate basis for public policy, he was impressed by the apparent futility of his task. In the face of the innumerable opinions each alleged to embody true knowledge, how could one possibly be certain? Considering the tremendous range and variety of beliefs—considering the absence of any shared, public philosophy—the prospects for a scientific politics would seem hopeless. One need only observe the clash of ideas in modern society: groups maintain an arsenal of ideas, develop fighting creeds, use words as ammunition, and engage in psychological warfare. Their militant language is not a means for negotiation, not a device for mediating between antagonistic views by revealing what they share. It

is not used to *disclose* the natural coherence of the social
world but rather to *establish* its coherence. It is used as an
instrument to enlist and move men, not to reveal part of the
truth to them. It is truly a weapon in our struggle for power.

In his *Ideology and Utopia* (1929) Mannheim set himself the task of inquiring how men had come to be skeptical
about the truth-revealing content of their language. Tracing
man's distrust of ideas from the thinkers of the Renaissance
to Marx, he brilliantly illustrated how a limited skepticism
became gradually transformed into an all-inclusive one. What
began as a suspicion that part of our thinking was biased
ended with the certainty that none of it was objective. Mannheim pointed to Napoleon as being but the first statesman to
recognize the unrealistic character of ideas by contemp-
tuously dismissing intellectuals as "ideologists." Theirs was a
world of illusion, while Napoleon's was the hard world of
power politics; theirs was a world of reflection, while his was
the no-nonsense world of action.[1] What had become increasingly clear ever since Machiavelli's compatriots had recognized that "the thought of the palace is one thing, that of the
public square is another," Mannheim now attempted to make
thoroughly explicit and systematic. While Marx had still protected some kinds of moral knowledge from the charge of
being biased—after all, Marx himself was morally certain
that a system that made it necessary for nine-year-old children to labor in coal mines was truly unjust—Mannheim now
proceeded to reduce all ideas to ideologies. He concluded
that our thoughts, the very style and structure of our thinking, are ineradicably biased because they find their source
in specific historical situations—situations in which groups
battle for power. His reductionism was thoroughgoing: it is
not that one set of ideas is true and another is false. None
are true or false; they are all points of view, or "perspectives."

1. In this invidious distinction between illusion and reality we encounter
again the hostility to imaginative speculation which permeated the life and
work of Freud.

This is not, Mannheim said, because we as individuals are misguided or perverse. We simply cannot help ourselves. Our various intellectual constructions—our legal norms, ethical systems, political philosophies, scientific methodologies (although Mannheim excepted formal logic and mathematics)—are incurably fragmentary. Whatever goes on in our minds is but a reflex of the process of history. And insofar as our history is but a secular record of groups in conflict, thought is merely a function of groups acting and reacting in society. The basis for all of our thinking, its genesis, lies in the active warfare of groups. In short, it lies in society. Truly to understand our thought, we must therefore uncover its social origins. This Mannheim saw as the central task of a "sociology of knowledge." Such a sociology could reveal how our language, our ideas, our very rationality, are but functions of our group membership.

Just as there can be no case studies of untroubled individuals, so there can be no histories of untroubled societies. History is a record of difficulties. Men are said to make history when they respond to challenges, whether these are the challenges of nature or of their neighbors. In a hostile environment men associate and engage in action. Assuming all groups to be action-groups competing for scarce resources, Mannheim believed that a group's rationality is tested in emergencies. It becomes sharper under increasing pressures. That is, up to a point, the tougher life is for a group— whether in the offensive or the defensive—the more stripped, rigorous, and efficient would be its rhetoric. Because pressure compels us to adjust to our real needs, we dismiss all idle thoughts and proceed to think clearly. The price of failure is decline and death. Survival is the true measure of the economy and clarity of our thought. And we gain clarity not when detached but when involved. We learn by doing. Our thought is at its most meaningful when it corresponds not to some abstract Reason but to the tested and vindicated rationality of our group. Ideas most relevant to our true interests come to us when critical circumstances compel us to act. Crisis gives us lucidity.[2]

If crisis conditions compel groups to sharpen their intellectual tools, the present epoch, Mannheim noted, provided the sociologist of knowledge with unprecedented opportunities. Certainly contemporary history was rife with conflict. Facing the Europe of his day—its cultural and social conflicts, its class antagonisms, its civil wars, its violence and disasters—Mannheim could actually take an optimistic view. At least men now *knew* what they wanted, and they were under pressure to say it clearly. Admittedly their beliefs were partisan and incomplete. But this made it possible to piece them together and behold the needs of the times in their entirety. Thus, although a climax of social disorganization had been reached, despair was uncalled for. On the contrary, the very sickness of society made it possible to understand its condition and then to practice social therapy on the basis of such understanding. The rationality which none of the social groups could claim for itself resided in the total pattern. If it could be perceived, Mannheim believed, politics could at last be made scientific. Action could be oriented by the unified pattern embedded in the historical period; it would thus be rational.

Policy prescriptions would no longer be derived from an ideal model of the just state. Nor would they be based on an abstract, formalistic sociology: any such effort would disregard uniquely human qualities. Instead, public policy would have to be extracted from the current historical situation. For Mannheim this meant that the practitioners of a

2. This is a notion much celebrated in Romantic literature. In "Under Ben Bulben," William Butler Yeats proclaimed, "Know that when all words are said/ And a man is fighting mad,/ Something drops from eyes long blind,/ He completes his partial mind. . . ." This irrational activism has always given support to those who wish to make matters worse so that men, having been enraged and purged, might be regenerated. It is echoed in the various programs for instituting crises, putting things to the test, or creating conditions of tension. Empirical science, Marxist revolutionary theory, contemporary educational practice, psychoanalysis, and a good deal of medical advice find their source in it.

sociology of knowledge, intellectuals interested in making politics truly scientific, would themselves have to partake in group action. They would have to identify themselves with social groups, participate in ideological warfare, and, as members of the intelligentsia, express the prevailing fighting creeds in the clearest, most rational idiom. Once they had exposed all the significant causes (significant, it should be noted, because groups acted in their behalf), the objectively true pattern of thought could be discerned. The merely ideological would be transcended. True knowledge of society, a genuine behavioral science anchored in actuality, would become possible. The dream of a scientific politics based on the hard realities of power would be realized.

But what would enable sociologists engaged in the analysis of thought to be so free from group bias themselves that they could be trusted to come up with the true pattern of social needs? Mannheim's answer was that one group in society, the intelligentsia, may quite properly be the bearer of the new rationality. Being a "relatively classless stratum which is not too firmly situated in the social order," it has no specific attachments. It was tied neither to society's top nor bottom. To be sure, insofar as it is a group, it is bound to have a social interest. But this is its interest in objectivity, in truth. Admirably situated, it would now have to become conscious of its mission to find the pattern of history and convert this pattern into a program for action. Its task would be to raise the historical process to consciousness, to make it coherent and rational.

Mannheim held that all beliefs may be understood in reference to the historical process, that is, to the struggle of groups for power. Accordingly, he associated conflicts between irreconcilable belief systems with historical conflicts for power in society. However much men might insist that their ideals caused them to disagree, Mannheim deemed their disagreements to be "really" determined by their drive to dominate. He saw not power in the service of ideals but ideals in the service of those groups who, historically, have or want power over others. And if the age did have a pattern of ideals, if the sociology of knowledge was to articulate a rational synthesis, it had to be the pattern embedded in the historical process. Manheim thus had to accept whatever the historical process might yield. He had to be resigned to the prevailing forces in society.

His intellectual position implies a fundamental fatalism. It suggests, but it does not prove, his faith in the ultimate goodness of history, his conviction that beneath all conflict, history surely was all right. There would be no point for him to do anything about history in reference to transhistorical ideals. All that could be required was to understand it sympathetically by taking part in it, by getting in step with the march of history and then going wherever it might take one.

But upon Hitler's ascension to power, Mannheim broke his engagement with history. The new order which history had generated proved to be intolerable. Having first produced the group anarchy of the Weimar Republic and later the barbarism of the Nazi regime, the historical process became untrustworthy. If history was blind to injustice, men did not need to be; if history failed to deliver justice, men must deliver it. They had to make a supreme effort to give meaning and purpose to events. Mannheim consequently argued for the positive reconstruction of society, and this, he said, would have to begin with the psychological reconstruction of man. Directly reacting to the threat of a totalitarian dictatorship, he noted the apparent efficacy of its tactics. He insisted that industrial society could not be moved into rational channels unless a new basis for agreement had been created. In *Diagnosis of Our Time* (1943), a treatise written under wartime pressure, he made a fervent case for a rejuvenated "militant democracy" with "the courage to agree on some basic values." The new state must aggressively inculcate the basic civil virtues traditionally associated with constitutional regimes: public-spiritedness and respect for others. While giving no further content to these virtues,

Mannheim urged conformity to them, coerced conformity if need be. He stressed especially that the educational machinery of the new state would have to create the proper conditions for freedom and finally that religion and myth had to be utilized to uphold a consensus without which modern society could not survive. Only reliance on the irrational, he wrote, could galvanize individuals and keep them dedicated to their indispensable joint enterprise. To reconstruct society, elites would have to establish the proper balance between individual freedom and public power. Elite rule was unavoidable.

But in his posthumous *Freedom, Power, and Democratic Planning* (1950) Mannheim introduced qualifications. He turned to the consideration of machinery for implementing his desire to maintain a balance, to guard against the always present danger of its being tipped in favor of the elite in power. To make the necessary elite a responsible one, he was now convinced that institutional devices had to restrain it. To keep it from becoming overbearing, it was essential, Mannheim concluded, to adhere to Anglo-American techniques of democratic constitutionalism.

Mannheim thus ended in the camp of the active state interventionists—but his interventionism was directed not toward establishing an ideal society but, more modestly, toward maintaining an equilibrium of public forces. While he had certainly echoed the totalitarian prescription for consensus, he was to remain loyal to his prior conviction that there could be no indubitable truths in the public arena. Since there was no abstract Truth to guide action, he was to settle, as he put it, for "health," for "peace," and for "rationality." These criteria, the very criteria of constitutional politics, were to orient public action. Public policy, he implied, was to concern itself with survival—and this meant fostering (1) a spirit of forbearance and non-violence toward one's opponents, (2) a determination to act rationally, to use only such means as are appropriate to the end sought, and (3) a consensus on procedures which ensure that no resolution of conflict will ever be final. And although Mannheim was to counsel wholesale planning, he did leave all specifics open, providing no blueprint for utopia. He remained preoccupied by form, not content. He merely wanted his policy makers to plan a sanctuary which would sustain the private man—and this in the face of massive industrial and social forces threatening to standardize and regiment him. Mannheim clearly hoped that the ultimate ends of life would remain unplanned, for he wanted man to plan them on his own. He thereby made his way back to that faith in natural progress which, under great pressure in the 1930's, he had momentarily lost.

In this voyage he was unique among the three thinkers we have considered so far. But no less than Nietzsche and Freud, he introduces us to the proposition that in the public realm all political philosophy concerned with ends must be seen as nothing but the expression of private views and private visions, as nothing but ideologies. Being mere ideologies, they could not be protected against public review and public revision. The ideal citizen would indeed acknowledge as much. Whatever the strain, he would remain loyal both to his private vision of justice and to the public institutions which might put it into jeopardy. The quest of that classical political philosophy preoccupied by the best regime could retain only historical interest for him, an interest to be pursued in privacy.

Recommended Reading

NIETZSCHE: ORIGINAL WORKS

The Portable Nietzsche (New York, 1954).
Beyond Good and Evil (Chicago, 1955).
Genealogy of Morals (New York, 1956).
The Use and Abuse of History (New York, 1957).
Joyful Wisdom (New York, 1960).

NIETZSCHE: SECONDARY WORKS

Heller, Erich, *The Disinherited Mind* (New York, 1957).
Kaufmann, Walter, *Nietzsche: Philosopher, Psychologist, Antichrist* (New York, 1956).
Kohn, Hans, *The Mind of Germany* (New York, 1960), Chap. 9.
Lilge, Frederic, *The Abuse of Learning* (New York, 1948), Chap. 4.
Mann, Thomas, *Doctor Faustus* (New York, 1948).

FREUD: ORIGINAL WORKS

Future of an Illusion (New York, 1957).
Civilization and Its Discontents (New York, 1958).
Group Psychology and the Analysis of the Ego (New York, 1960).

FREUD: SECONDARY WORKS

Fromm, Erich, *Sigmund Freud's Mission* (New York, 1959).
Nelson, Benjamin, ed., *Freud and the 20th Century* (New York, 1957).
Rieff, Philip, *Freud: The Mind of the Moralist* (New York, 1959).
Riesman, David, "Freud and Psychoanalysis," in *Individualism Reconsidered* (Glencoe, Ill., 1954).

MANNHEIM: ORIGINAL WORKS

* *Ideology and Utopia* (New York, 1936).
Diagnosis of Our Time (New York, 1944).
Freedom, Power, and Democratic Planning (New York, 1950).

MANNHEIM: SECONDARY WORKS

Paul Kecskemeti, "Introduction" to Karl Mannheim, *Essays on the Sociology of Knowledge* (London, 1952).

GENERAL SECONDARY WORKS

Frankel, Charles, *The Case for Modern Man* (New York, 1955).
Hughes, H. Stuart, *Consciousness and Society: The Reorientation of European Social Thought, 1890–1930* (New York, 1958).
Levi, Albert William, *Philosophy and the Modern World* (Bloomington, Ind., 1959).
Passmore, John, *A Hundred Years of Philosophy* (London, 1957).
Pennock, J. Roland, *Liberal Democracy: Its Merits and Prospects* (New York, 1950).
Shklar, Judith N., *After Utopia: The Decline of Political Faith* (Princeton, 1957).
Wolin, Sheldon S., *Politics and Vision: Continuity and Innovation in Western Political Thought* (Boston, 1960).

* Excerpts in *Sources in Twentieth-Century Political Thought* (New York, 1964).

II. THE DOCTRINE OF ACTIVISM

If only by implication, the work of Nietzsche, Freud, and Mannheim revealed anew that to honor man's conflicting claims it is essential to promote a loyalty both to one's private truth and to the public order. Twentieth-century European history provides ample evidence that this dual loyalty does not come about by itself. Were it the automatic result of the free play of natural forces, we would have been spared the totalitarian ideologies of the first half of the century. We would never have heard the ominous summons to abandon our private quest for moral truth, to establish goodness and eradicate evil in common. This plea for unity would never have been transformed into the totalitarian policies of entire nations. However enthusiastically advanced, the case for a purposeful public order would have remained one among many, confined to the sphere of the private.

The constitutional state, in short, is not the result of spontaneity. It is the product of deliberation, education, and law. And it tends to persist only when reinforced by a well-founded tradition of civility and forbearance, by a succession of only partial victories in increasingly difficult skirmishes. When such a tradition is weak or when economic or technological upheaval threatens its very foundation, the distinction between the domain of the public and the private fades, and men find themselves driven to make their personal vision of justice into a common, public creed. Infuriated by their environment, they then proceed to activate their beliefs, converting them into practice. Repudiating Nietzsche's prophecy about the end of public philosophy, they are then determined to continue the speculative quest for the ideal by giving some substantive purpose to public life. But insofar as they continue this quest in the realm of practice, they pervert its character. They put an end to its speculative nature by making it concrete. The work of Georges Sorel (1847–1922) and the more sharply focused rhetoric of fascism may provide us with a clear view of this dynamism.

The Exaltation of Violence:
Georges Sorel

Georges Sorel was born at Cherbourg in 1847, a year before the *Communist Manifesto* was published. From his
twenties until the age of forty-five he was an inconspicuous
but successful civil engineer. Not until 1892 did he decide to
devote himself fully to talking and writing about public
affairs. He helped found two political reviews, contributed
to countless others, and wrote some seventeen books, only
one of which, *Reflections on Violence* (1906), has been trans-
lated into English. Restlessly searching for a social instrument that might give energy to his moral vision, he hailed
and abandoned orthodox Marxism, democratic socialism,
revolutionary syndicalism, Maurras's monarchist nationalism,
Lenin's Bolshevik revolution, and a nascent fascism. Always
disillusioned and never finally committed, he died in 1922,
the year of Mussolini's March on Rome.

Just as Sorel's life was distinguished by his unwillingness
to betray the purity of his principles by practical considerations, so was his work distinguished by his uncompromising
distaste for anything profane, wasteful, and unchaste. ("He
did not admit that ambition should make a man change his
doctrine," Jean Variot wrote of him.) This does not mean
that his writing was either detached or clear, but rather that
a fastidious moralism consistently colored it. Since his work
acted as a kind of crude, partially clouded prism, gathering
and refracting the ideas of Vico, Nietzsche, Marx, and Berg-
son, it often revealed previously obscure relationships. Joining the diverse views of Nietzsche and Marx, it enables us

to perceive the irrational drive behind a presumably rational indictment of the capitalist economy; it enables us to perceive the link between a rational effort to add to our scientific knowledge of society and the irrational foundation on which the effort rests. Furthermore, Sorel's work gives coherent expression to the incoherent dynamism of the political mass movements of the twentieth century, and thus makes it understandable that both the Russian and the Italian governments should have offered in the early 1930's to erect a monument in his honor at his graveside. Finally, it clarifies how the drive to enlist *all* our resources so as to give the individual a sense of destiny and fulfillment generates an ungovernable activism. It thereby reveals the politically explosive character of an undiluted private moralism.

This radical nature of Sorel's stand is best explained by his view of the existing social order as totally decadent, as beyond redemption by ordinary piecemeal efforts. His demand for unmitigated violence was but an integral part of his catastrophic perspective. In what way did he believe modern society to be sick? What therapy did he prescribe? And what assumptions guided his diagnosis and prescription?

The perspective of Marx had made Sorel forcefully aware of the incongruities of a capitalist economy, of French society, and of the politics of the Third Republic. Focusing on the economy, Sorel was enraged by its manifest waste of human energy. He was appalled by a system of production, distribution, and consumption that he considered inefficient in its very foundations. By every engineering criterion the system was a patent failure. It was perpetually off balance. Its internal friction made it unproductive. Worst of all, it produced nothing that anyone could truly value. On the face of it, industry was so organized as to separate workers from meaningful work. It gave them nothing to do worth doing. What they did during the best hours of their day could not possibly satisfy them as human beings. The *use* of the work force, already extensively described and deplored by Marx, was so blatantly incongruous because it was really possible, after all, to produce wealth. Clearly, productive resources and machinery were being wasted. In the midst of poverty, so it could be said with a freshness of idiom now difficult to recapture, there was plenty.

But material abundance itself, and this was Sorel's new point, served no purpose whatever. It satisfied no human need, not even that of the wealthy. Workers, in short, were not the only class dehumanized by the system. Those whom the system assigned the position of exploiters, members of the bourgeoisie, were in fact no better off. Had the bourgeoisie victimized the proletariat with any sense of exhilaration—that is, had it at least experienced a sense of psychological satisfaction from its exploitative practices—the system would have served at least one function. But not even the members of the bourgeoisie worked with a sense of purpose. On the contrary: they seemed slack, dilettantish, apologetic, and understandably bewildered. They behaved not like autonomous men but like victims of the system. They lived off its economic surplus, slowly decaying and dissipating. The divorce rate, Sorel pointed out, was highest in capitalist nations. The ruling class was increasingly soft and flabby. Even in warfare it remained essentially pacific. Thinking of war as a sport, it remained faithful to the rules of fair play. In 1900, so Sorel observed, English officers went into the Boer War like gentlemen to a football game. To them the conflict did not *matter*, did not seem to be about anything vital. The class in power, it was clear, lacked all heroic virtues. Its members were not dedicated to anything productive, inspiring, or moving. They had no purpose in life other than improving their material comfort. As their life was flat and stale, so their existence had no point.

Sorel's sweeping indictment was based on his presumed knowledge of both economic and psychological health. It was easy for him to conclude that the industrial system and man within it were diseased as long as productive energies remained pathologically dormant. How might man's energy be freed?

Certainly liberal democracy presented no alternatives. Like Marx, Sorel saw its politics as but a façade for maintaining economic inequalities; its public enactments merely reflected election victories purchased by money. In the face of economic inequality, political equality was a sham. If a remedy was to be found, it was therefore necessary to act outside such traditional institutions of liberalism as popular elections, representative assemblies, political debate, and legislative compromise. This machinery for controlling violence, Sorel recognized, rested on the dubious assumption that the conciliation and reconciliation of conflicting interests was possible.

While he disdained the mechanism of politics, Sorel did not believe that the groups active in society were in fact irreconcilable. Indeed, he believed that they might well be seduced by the promises of liberalism. He therefore insisted that under existing economic conditions there *should* be irreconcilable groups; there *should* be no common ground on which the bourgeoisie might pacify the proletariat by introducing it to politics. For Sorel, there should be no meeting ground, no political forum beyond class loyalty, beyond the domain of the private. Bourgeois ideology to the contrary, rationality was not the common property of all social groups. Every group in society, each in obedience to its distinct passions, had its own rationality—or, more properly, its own ideological rationalization. There was no shared truth, no rational principle to which all men, whatever their private loyalty, might appeal in public.

If justice was to be done despite the absence of a common rationality, it was necessary to turn to force. In order to revitalize the system, in order to escape the interminable talk of politicians, it was necessary to enlist those social forces which the industrial system kept inherently uncorrupted and virile. And those forces, Sorel believed, were embodied in the proletariat.

Only the proletariat could be trusted not to collapse under pressure. Obviously it was impossible to build on the bourgeoisie. Not only had Marx's theory of history marked it for inevitable extinction. Nietzsche's morality condemned it no less: it had gone soft. It lacked the courage of its convictions. The proletariat, however, could not conceivably collapse under pressure. It could not retreat, for it had nowhere to go. Having no other possessions, it inevitably possessed the rawest of animal drives; of necessity it was stubborn, courageous, and unyielding. In noting this Sorel did not romanticize the worker. Unlike D. H. Lawrence, he did not feel that workers had any special virtues. They merely knew what truly mattered. Pressure cleared their vision. Life for them was not a game played by previously determined rules. Their rules were improvised in action. If they believed in themselves, it was not some abstract self they believed in but their real, pulsating, living selves. It was no wonder that they were made of heroic stuff. The system under which they labored drove them inexorably to a state of rage, lucidity, and action. Utterly oppressed, compelled to fall back on themselves, they alone carried the seed of freedom. Within them, all energy was concentrated. And this had been demonstrated again and again in the worker's resolve to take direct action. The worker, Sorel pointed out, was prepared to stake all, his very life if need be, on the outcome of a strike. Experience showed that when all was said and done he could be counted on.

But aside from these practical considerations, there was a telling moral reason for relying on the working class. Workers, after all, were the only authentic producers in society, and productivity, for Sorel, was an indubitable good. In affirming this, Sorel gave full support to the syndicalist movement in France. While he did keep aloof from all of its organizational manifestations, as he carefully kept himself unaffiliated throughout his life, his work articulated the revolutionary zeal and the class antagonisms of French trade unionism. At the same time, however, Sorel expressed no direct interest in improving the well-being of workers, in making them personally more satisfied consumers. His concern was with the process and quality of their production. What they were compelled to do day in and day out, so he believed, was just not worthy of them. It was not so much that they were deprived of the fruits of their labor but rather that their labor did not result in objects which a man could be proud to have produced. In fact, they could not claim to be the producers of anything. The system was the producer of things and they were but parts of the system. If work was to become dignified, mass production would have to be reorganized. Workers themselves would have to become masters of the system of industrial production. Sorel did not go on to speculate why, under such changed conditions, workers would in fact produce only those goods which were "useful" and which would therefore give them pride in their work. Nor did he ask why the new masters would not acquire the outlook and habits of the old. His sole concern was with the building of a society in which no one would be superfluous by virtue of his nonproductivity, his inactivity. And he elevated activity—anticipating the theme of later existentialists—because he associated it with human freedom.

It is not hard to see why Sorel should have done so. He believed, as both Hobbes and Vico had, that men can never finally know the things they have not made themselves. The objects of nature they can at best grasp hypothetically, but never with finality. It is otherwise, however, with the products of their own making. Insofar as they create their own environment, insofar as they make their own history, men have knowledge of their world—a world of man-made goods. Knowledge is gained in the doing, in the making of things. As men are active and industrious, they gradually enlarge the range of knowledge. Not detached contemplation or abstract speculation, but work, industrial practice, extends their grasp. By leaving the realm of nature behind, they in fact leave that over which they have no control. And they enter the realm which, in principle, they can control, for they themselves can make it. They can create their own environment, thus overcoming the realm of necessity. And insofar as they triumph over necessity and act on their own, they become free. It is therefore incumbent upon them, if they seek freedom, to be fully engaged in productivity, to construct an artificial mileu, as Sorel called it. They will then become authentic creators and masters of their fate. They will then love their work, and their work will make them free.

Thus for Sorel reliance on the organized worker was not only a practical necessity, insofar as workers alone possessed the requisite raw power to destroy all the wasteful components of the system.[1] It was also a moral imperative, insofar as freedom could have no meaning without public action.

So far, Sorel conceded, the action of the workers had never really amounted to anything: their strikes had always left them defeated. But this was explained by the fact that they had resentments rather than goals. They knew what they opposed, not what they favored. There was nothing to inspire them, to move them beyond their rage. What was needed therefore was a unifying, inspirational force for a massive revolutionary push toward their fulfillment.

One way to move the masses toward the goal of the just society had been Lenin's. Lenin had rationally considered the strength of the capitalist bastion to be stormed. He

1. In Sorel's eyes, it was not merely the bourgeoisie which was useless. He proceeded to ask what, in a socialist society, "will become of the thinkers, the men who have no place in the line of production? They reveal themselves as auxiliaries—or more often as parasites—that society should expel as energetically as possible so that it may reach a clearer idea of the nature of work. Nothing, in sum, should be claimed as a right that does not correspond with work. And work, from the socialist point of view, is something of a man that is part of the products in the inception of which he has directly participated."

counted his battalions, tabulated his resources, allocated his funds. And, steeped in the problems of logistics, he weighed his forces against those of the enemy. But Sorel would have nothing to do with organization. He deliberately ignored all problems of timing, scheming, and planning. More than that, he made a positive virtue of unpreparedness. Thus, although he knew that the workers' organizations lacked financial resources, he claimed that this was all to the good. Rich unions, inevitably wedded to the status quo, would not wish to make irrevocable decisions. Forever calculating gains and losses, they would merely strike for defined, limited objectives. But what was necessary, Sorel claimed, was a single, undefined, unlimited general strike. It was necessary to put an end to the scattered operations of the workers and to initiate a single, irreducible assault. Society was to be purified and the worker was to be rejuvenated by an unpremeditated, sudden spectacular act. A truly total commitment was called for.

To generate it the old rational appeals had to be abandoned. Rational manifestoes, instead of preparing men to act with spontaneity, make them reflective. To raise men to the heroic plane, it was imperative to rouse their irrational drives. In practice, Sorel noted, this had always been done by myths—the greatest movers of men. Myths, he knew, have an organizing function all their own. They make us bear up in times of crisis: when we are born and when we die, myths sustain us. They make the mysteries of life comprehensible, and thus bearable. They allow us to pull ourselves together, to direct our action economically.

In his first book, *Contributions to the Layman's Study of the Bible* (1889), Sorel had shown his awareness of the activating potency of mythology. Contemptuous of the shallowness of the life of the bourgeoisie, he argued there for a return to the heroic life whose principles, he felt, had once been embodied in Christian scripture. But it became obvious to him that the apocalyptic Christian myth of the Kingdom of God was no longer potent. Did anyone still truly believe in the return of Christ and stake his life on it? And how much more effective, he asked, was the newer ideology of the Enlightenment, the myth of liberty, fraternity, equality, and, absurdest of all, progress? Was anyone still truly moved by this cluster of ideals?

It was evident that if men were to be moved, they had to be given a new faith. Because no purpose was discernible in nature, because neither God nor History guaranteed one, it had to be fabricated by man himself. Now that the older myths were exhausted, men would have to formulate their own.

Given the character of the need, it was virtually self-evident to Sorel what kind of myth would rehabilitate industrial man. It had to be a cataclysmic myth which once and for all spelled the total end of the present system, which would finally shatter an already decaying capitalism. It had to be a grandiose vision of the total paralysis of all existing forms of industrial production. Thus he formulated a myth which accommodated all the accumulated anticapitalist resentment of the masses—the myth of the general strike. This new myth of the general strike was, in his language,

> . . . an organization of images capable of evoking instinctively all the sentiments which correspond to the different manifestations of the war undertaken by Socialism against modern society. Strikes have engendered in the proletariat the most noble, the most profound, and most moving sentiments that it possesses; the general strike grips them all in a harmonious picture, and by bringing them together, gives to each one of them its maximum of intensity; appealing to their painful memories of particular conflicts, it vividly colors all the details of the composition presented to consciousness. We thus obtain that intuition of Socialism which language cannot give us with perfect clearness—and we obtain it as a totality, perceived instantaneously.

Sorel proceeded to make clear that the specific ingredients of his myth would be utterly irrelevant to its value. Like all myths, it had to be accepted as a totality, not as an aggregation of reasonably connected particulars. It was, as he said, impervious to analysis. Furthermore its mysterious nature would itself make it fascinating. Its very lack of clarity spoke in its favor; susceptibility to analysis would in fact destroy it.

"We must beware of too much strictness in our language," Sorel wrote, "because it would be at odds with the fluid character of reality; the result would be deceptive." To help men get in touch with reality, he wanted to strip them of their deceptions. It was precisely this determination to return to the world of reality which made him value ideas in terms of their effectiveness alone. Ideas, not excepting his own, he considered to be illusions valid to the extent that they could deepen our sensibilities and *move* us. He thought it not inappropriate to characterize the ideas we have about society as "social poetry." The truth or falsity of such poetry, even when it went under the name of Social Science, was utterly irrelevant: the intensity of its effect alone mattered.

In taking this position, Sorel sought to eliminate every vestige of historical determinism from socialist theory. Whereas Marx had kept volitional and rational elements in a state of precarious balance—always inviting the question why men had to do what was inevitable anyway—Sorel put full stress on action. He rejected Marx's sense of fatality and insisted that, at least in society, we are free to construct *any* scientific formula and proceed to act on it. The proof of its validity would be in its success; and its success depended on its social appeal, or perhaps on the power of an elite to make it appealing when it failed to validate itself spontaneously. Thus Sorel did not invalidate Marx's economic determinism; he merely dismissed its claim to finality. He thought of it in pragmatic terms, as a working hypothesis, as a symbol system, as social poetry, as myth. He was quite indifferent, therefore, to its specific content. Myths, in the final analysis, could be appreciated only in reference to their ultimate effectiveness.

Even if the workers were never to envisage what it would mean concretely to engage in the great general strike, in total revolutionary action, this would make no difference. What counted was the capacity of the myth to fire the imagination, to lead men to action. The test of its soundness was its organizing capacity, its capacity for solidifying the apathetic, the shiftless, and the unconcerned—and then moving the masses to revolt. If experience showed the myth to succeed, that would be all that was necessary. It was made valid neither by reason of its content nor by the moral value of its aim, but by its practical efficacy, by the energy it liberated. Should violent revolutionary action fail, this could not occasion despair, for failure would merely demonstrate that the action had not really been motivated by the myth of the general strike. Failure could never invalidate the myth; it could only justify a renewed attempt to make it work—to try again with more courage, persistence, and confidence.[2] By revealing itself to be compelling enough to move men to uninhibited action, it would finally vindicate itself.

Just as all discussion about the intelligibility of the myth was beside the point, so was discussion of the ultimate goal toward which men were to be directed. "The end is nothing," Sorel wrote, "the movement is all." He could be as indifferent about general objectives as about matters of tactics. He would not deign to analyze or define the end result, for he maintained, quite consistently, that all verbal analysis must be reflective and critical. It exposes social plans to critical scrutiny; it raises distracting questions about the

2. This approach is by no means peculiar to Sorel. Gandhi upheld the myth of nonviolence on the same ground, telling his followers that if their love (a concept as boundless as that of violence) failed to melt the bayonets of British soldiers, this was no argument against love. What was needed, he said, was simply more love. Similarly the believer will not be led to doubt the true Church because of the failure of the historical church.

relative value of their parts; it encourages talk of priorities
and compromise. By entailing debate, all analytical activity
inspires movement toward the very kind of bourgeois parliamentarianism Sorel was determined to eradicate.

It is evident that Sorel would have damaged his position
had he rationally considered the justice of either his end or
his method. Given his certitude, all he could consistently
counsel was an undiluted, immoderate, public activism. All
he could consistently promise was the public release of
private passions.

The ground for his resolve to foster nothing but indiscriminate violence was the depth and finality of his moral
vision. It was his moralizing in wholly otherworldly, idealistic terms. The next step in the development of man, so
Sorel believed, would bring about a fundamental improve-
ment over his present condition. The future society would
be qualitatively different from the present one. Sorel's
vision of a future in which nothing would be wrong—and a
present in which everything was wrong—justified whatever action might lead away from the present. If the present
embodied the very ideal of corruption and the future the
very ideal of perfection, it surely became legitimate to take
any steps whatever to move ahead. In fact, one could not
possibly make things worse. To be violent under such
rarefied conditions was to engage in a purified, idealized
violence. Thus Sorel insisted that his Violence must be
distinguished—not in its practical effect but in its essence—
from conventional violence. It had nothing vindictive or
sadistic about it, for it did not stem from resentment. Unlike the violence done by the French state to Captain
Dreyfus, it was not directed toward any predetermined
end. It did not operate under the guise of law, in the name
of justice, or for "reason of state." Beyond good and evil,
it transcended everything merely human and political. It
was a pure construct existing in a mystical realm.

Sorel's own repeated breaks with various political movements merely serve to underscore his awareness of the fact
that when violence is employed by actual, historical ruling
groups—by individuals who share conventional human
traits—it is bound to become corrupted. Thus the Nazis
ultimately made clear that Sorel's mystique of violence inevitably amounts to mere barbarism in practice, that, in the
hands of mere men, it is bound to become profane.

It was Sorel's pervasive moralism, then, which kept him
from seeing any redeeming features in contemporary society.
He truly believed that the most valuable members of society
had nothing whatever to lose: humiliated and brutalized,
they were being treated as mere commodities, objects, or
animals. He realized at the same time that such "men," having been deprived of their humanity, were potentially the
most dangerous of all. They inhabited what for them was a
state of nature—that is, the industrial, urban centers of
Western Europe. The worker, it seemed, really did have
nothing to lose but his chains. Not conceiving of worse
situations—such as the one, for example, in which inmates
of German concentration camps were to find themselves—
Sorel simply fixed on the proletariat. The fact that he was
wrong in this, that he was parochial and dated, may cast
doubt on his judgment, not his logic. His logic, to be sure,
was bound to be irrelevant in all those more or less moderate
situations in which the conflict between the private man and
the public man remains conveniently unresolved. But by the
same token, it does acquire relevance in extreme and artificial situations. Insofar as men are actually dehumanized,
insofar as the fiction of Kafka and Orwell becomes reality,
Sorel's case for the rehabilitation of violence suddenly becomes applicable. Thus while it needs no stressing that his
moral fervor mistakenly made him identify his own world as
worthless, it provided him with a logical tool that remains
relevant in time of total crisis, relevant when the state of
nature has been deliberately established.

But when our social situation is not an extreme one, Sorel's glorification of mass action and of whatever myths might serve to incite it will serve to deliver the masses to society's mythmakers, or at least to those in society able to hire the mythmakers. If Sorel failed in propagating his myth, or if his myth lacked in inspirational potency, others could try to remedy the defect: strategically placed propagandists could become the creators of myths and the founders of the new public order. They could scientifically redesign Sorel's myth and keep putting it to the test, thereby purifying it until it might at last become utterly inscrutable, until public language could truly become the nonlanguage of Naziism.

If Sorel's moralizing can lead to such conclusions, this is because it fails to accept the state as a dual order whose public sector is properly balanced by the private. Sorel, it is true, was not indifferent to man's private sphere. Indeed he felt so deeply about its degradation that he aspired to make the whole of it public. The amplitude of life which Nietzsche had encouraged for the private man, Sorel was prepared to make public. He was set to transform Nietzsche's ferocious activism into a public spectacle. Expecting men to become free in public, he associated freedom with violent action. He was thus driven to convert a political order concerned with using public means for private ends into one concerned exclusively with public ends. That is, by making freedom a single *public* end, he deprived men of their various private ones. Whereas Nietzsche's morality preserved the tension between what was natural and private on the one hand and what was artificial and public on the other, Sorel invited the two to blend. For him the ultimate end of the state became not freedom to pursue diverse interests—a policy which, in practice, entails all kinds of restrictions—but simply Freedom. He thus idealized a state which was, in its totality, an artificial contrivance. And since he withheld every possible rational standard for judging such a state, he delivered it to whoever could in fact contrive to operate it. The practical consequence of his logic was to betray his morality to the men of power. Having given full moral credit to potency, Sorel ended by making morality impotent. Had his moral fervor been more restrained, or had he permitted institutions to deflect his passionate nature toward the private sphere, Sorel's life and work would not have illuminated the unavoidable pathos of our political condition—the tension between our private ideals and our public duties.

The End of Discourse: Fascism

With the intellectual productions of Sorel, one stream of thought about the proper goals of politics began to thicken. It slowly became filled with the tangible stuff of politics, with the twisted gear of political trials, party battles, and street fights. It acquired the sweaty and often bloody smell of actuality. Increasingly turgid, it lost its speculative character and fused with political life itself. It became personal and programmatic, aiming to intoxicate, infuriate, and animate. Its authors were men enlisted to plan spectacles and create effects: propagandists, journalists, professors, ministers of justice or of education—all bureaucratic servants of power. They wrote to deify and to desecrate. They wrote manifestoes, white papers, slogans, manuals, banners, and posters. Their language became the rhetoric of political operations: declamatory, repetitive, ceremonial, conspiratorial, noble, or foul—depending on need and circumstance.

Much effort has been expended to provide students of political theory with an understanding of the new rhetoric—the products of Mussolini, Stalin, Hitler, and their apologists, the massive work of Carlo Costamagna, Vincenzo Gioberti, Alfred Rosenberg, Dietrich Eckart, Joseph Goebbels, and a phalanx of less able technicians. But the study of their productions is essentially futile, for their work is immune to analysis, not even pretending to rationality. To be sure, historians can discuss its genesis, properly making us circumspect. Moreover, behavioral scientists can assess its practical utility, instructing us, should we become interested, how to improve its effectiveness. But while we can rationally do all this with the new language, we cannot tell what it means. It must be *felt* to be understood, and truly to feel it is to be moved by it. Not only would its authors disdain all other criteria; there are none. Its function, in the final analysis, is not to elucidate, to reveal the relation between things; it is to produce effects.

This much had already been intimated by Sorel's doctrines. But while these are generally thought of as specifically Left Wing, they may yet be seen as coupled with the ventures of the Right. Sorel, we should recall, had attempted to unify private interest and public interest, expecting violence to renew the workers' sense of group solidarity. An irrational myth was to weld the working class into a unified organic social force. Yet whatever social organism Sorel nourished, he had nourished it in behalf of individuals. That is, the invariable point of departure for his planned political irrationality had been the individual. It is this fact which invites us to place him on the Left. Two of his compatriots, Maurice Barrès (1862–1923) and Charles Maurras (1868–1952), gave the same impetus to a politics of irrationality; they too wished to overcome the tension between the private and the public. However, because the starting point of their thinking was the social organism, not the individual, they tend to be seen as occupying the Right. There would seem even more reason for this classification: Sorel was violently the revolutionary; Barrès was violently a Bonapartist defender of strong government; Maurras was violently the counterrevolutionary. But the conventional labels conceal their common dedication to violence—and the bliss to follow it. It is their activism that makes them ideological companions. Together, they lead us further into the nonpolitical, nonphilosophical world of totalitarian autocracy. While the less intellectual Fascists who followed them can only be understood in terms of the universality of their denials, the ruthlessness of their hatreds, Sorel, Barrès, and Maurras jointly reveal the positive ground on which the nihilism of the century took its stand. If they hated, they also loved. In fact, it was precisely their passionate longing for order, simplicity, and harmony which released their massive animosities.

The intellectual differences between them fade in the light of their shared hostilities. They were at one in their opposition to the precarious settlement of the Third French Republic. They agreed about the stagnancy of the French economy, the venality of its financiers, the corruption of its press, the softness of its army, and the foulness of its private life. The prevailing political institutions, they agreed, were incapable of bringing order into a public life rife with conflict because it was devoid of meaning. What France lacked, in a word, was grandeur.

Convinced of the decadence of French society, what did they believe to be the highpoint of its health? The extreme Left and Right were strikingly unanimous in their respect for the social arrangements of the pre-Revolutionary epoch. To overcome the specific technological and economic problems of the twentieth century, especially man's great loneliness, they pushed for a neomedievalism, arguing for the renovation of the institutions of feudal society.

That the conservatism of the thinkers of the Right should cause them to appreciate the socializing function of religion, the family, the feudal estates, and the monarchy is only to be expected. These institutions, after all, were the traditional ones. What is more significant is how profoundly the Left was also tied to tradition. After all, Sorel had recognized the workers' association as the vehicle for human fulfillment, perceiving that it represented a new form of the medieval guild. Backing it because it satisfied a need for fraternity, he discounted the possibility that men might merely join to improve their economic lot. Like all associations—like feudal corporations, estates, universities, and monasteries—it satisfied not a rational desire for more abundant consumption but, as Sorel saw it, man's need for belonging. It was not man's rational calculation of private benefits that made him gregarious but his very nature.

This perception—one to be echoed by British guild socialists as well as by American sociologists, anthropologists, and psychologists—related the Left and the Right in an even more basic way: throughout the entire century, from Fourier on, it pushed both extremes toward a sentimental romanticism. Rebelling against an atomized society whose members are related by political compromises, economic contracts, and mechanical contraptions rather than by social bonds, the extremists were led to lay claim to a lost patrimony, hoping to recapture the spirit, if not the reality, of an ideal past. They were led to the exaltation of forgotten crafts, agrarian virtues, local dialects, tight-knit villages, and provincial graveyards. They venerated age and shade, and they developed an affection for the stability and obtuseness of custom. They evoked a love for things small in scale—the cozy shop, the tiny parish, the diminutive name. Commemorating the natural rhythms of the season with which the peasant is in tune, they elicited a fondness for the simple life rooted in the soil of the provinces.[1] And as they preferred the unwritten agreements sanctioned by past usage to the legislative enactments of the present, they exposed all formal politics as artificial efforts to tinker with man's natural order.

While they thus disclosed the sentimental substance of their ideal, they revealed the range of their great antipathies. Feeding the nostalgia of the uprooted, the dispossessed, and the alienated, they defamed the parliamentary forum as

1. This evocation is the reverse side of the toughness of the social thinkers for whom life must be "real" and "practical." It is noteworthy that even Freud—who geared most his life to what is certainly one of the most artificial of man's machines, the clock—revealed this side. In 1922 he wrote Ferenczi: "Something in me rebels against the compulsion to go on earning money. . . . Strange secret yearnings rise in me—perhaps from my ancestral heritage—for the East and the Mediterranean and for a life of quite another kind. . . . Instead of which—we shall meet on the soil of sober Berlin." Freud clearly preferred the life of Vienna to that of hard-boiled, egalitarian, commercial Berlin; American mobility, he noted, made him constipated; and he repeatedly yearned for an idealized Rome and a romanticized Mediterranean.

well as the free market. They were contemptuous of all mobility, competitiveness, individualism, and intellectualism. For them the Jew readily became the natural incarnation of evil. And since Jewish behavior was characteristic of the behavior of all men in the society atomized by the French and the Industrial Revolutions, since what was untrue of the Jew as Jew seemed so emphatically true of modern man, the anti-Semitism of Sorel, Barrès, and Maurras could become creditable ideology.

Believing that man was primarily an animal moved by social sentiments, that the noxious doctrines of individualism had destroyed his nature, but that conformity to a scientific understanding of his real needs could yet restore his rightful condition, these writers supported efforts to recapture the lost meaning of life. They made their contemporaries aware that somehow they had been cheated in a very fundamental sense—not merely by military defeat, economic depression, unequal law enforcement, or intolerable working conditions, but by the political system itself. More than that, they encouraged men in the belief that simplicity and wholeness could be restored. Politics could be transcended.

In 1870, at the age of eight, Maurice Barrès watched French troops who had just been beaten by the Germans retreat through his native village in the province of Lorraine. The memory of defeat was to agitate his imagination for the rest of his life. Determined to reject the reality of French impotence, discrediting his very experience of it, Barrès devoted his life to reaching beyond experience for a more durable foundation. He dedicated himself to the task of revealing that French timidity and sterility did not express the real France, that behind the France that suffered defeat there was the authentic nation, uncorrupted by outsiders, unified by sentiment, making common cause.

To Barrès this nation was the true embodiment of the soul of France. He variously characterized it as "a hereditary ideal," "an ancient cemetery," "a common possession." It provided the organic environment for the solitary individual whose exquisite sensibilities were probed by Barrès' novels. To protect man in all of his exotic preciousness, Barrès gave him social support. The individual could never be upheld by the rationalist humanitarianism of Kant, the constitutional legalism of English Whiggery, or the appeal to abstract justice of those who were defending Captain Dreyfus. Man had to be rooted in historical reality; he had to be disciplined by the glorious heritage of the French nation.

The ultimate symbol of all that Barrès cherished, it becomes clear retrospectively, was the cemetery. He summoned young Frenchmen to retreat to the provinces, to walk among ruins and shrines, to return, at last, to the soil. Buttressed by their venerable past, their natural energies would be liberated.

But although Barrès gave poignant expression to these sentiments, he did not succumb to them. He did not treat them as indubitable doctrines, but, in a modern scientific spirit, as merely useful propositions. What distinguished his romantic nationalism from that of Fichte, Herder, Treitschke, Carlyle, and Kipling was his indifference to the truth of his vision. It did not matter to him whether or not a glorious national tradition had actually existed. It was enough that, like a scientific hypothesis, it could be postulated and put to the test. If it turned out to touch, move, and unify the public, it would do exactly what was expected of it.

Barrès saw the mystique of nationalism as one to be self-consciously expressed in language and reinforced by ritual. He thereby moved the creator of language, the poet, into the center of the public arena, permitting him to become the mover of men. Thus the artist's private vision could emerge as the basis for public policy. The test of its legitimacy could become the capacity of those in power to make it effective. The moral basis of legislative acts was therefore not whether they reflected various interests none of which could lay final claim to truth. Instead, it was whether they could effectively activate the masses. The activators themselves, the myth-makers who operated the levers of political power, did not have to have faith in their myth in order to get others to have faith in it. It was sufficient that they had the will to use their myth, to put it to work. Proceeding, then, in the spirit of science, one could discover what conditions—what specific language, myth, and ritual—would be conducive to self-sacrifice, social solidarity, and self-fulfillment.

Charles Maurras sought precisely the same ends. The spokesman for L'Action Française, a movement dedicated to the overthrow of republican government and the establish-ment of a monarchical dictatorship, he never ceased conspir-ing against the Third Republic. After the fall of France in 1940, he advocated what can only be called neutralism, denouncing with equal vigor the resistance of De Gaulle and the synthetic puppet regime of the collaborationists. His life-long obsession was order. Like Barrès, he was prepared to back whatever myths might re-establish order.

Although he remained an agnostic until just before his death, in the end Maurras committed himself to the Roman Catholic Church. He was indifferent about the truth or falsity of its doctrines, but appreciated the atmosphere created by its rituals. Convinced that the nation bolstered by the Church was the supreme manifestation of individuals and that the individual was wholly fulfilled when the nation was vibrant and impregnable, he was prepared to use whatever means might create such a nation. The end would justify all means, for there was no creditable standard above the nation-state. The nation's needs were final. Its morality transcended human morality. Its wrongs were only apparently so. Its action—against, for example, Captain Dreyfus—had to be judged in terms of a higher ideal; the integrity of the nation. All subsidiary interests had to be pulled together and then directed toward the enhancement of the nation. And its interest, according to the mythology of nationalism, was solely the intensification and expansion of its essential uniqueness. In practice this would require the liquidation of all domestic impurities and the waging of imperial wars to test the collective stamina of the populace.

Because all antagonistic interests would be unified in such a state, there would be no politics—politics being necessary only when one sought to *prevent* the permanent settlement of the conflicts between private interests. The new state, by providing final solutions, would thus overcome not merely the specific contradictions that technology and the rise of the masses had introduced; it would put an end to the very absurdity of the human condition. It would effectively terminate the interminable bargaining, negotiating, and compromising we think of as politics. It would put an end to discourse.

At various times and with different accents, Sorel, Barrès, and Maurras acclaimed both violent change and the constancy of tradition, both the virtues of militancy and the calm routine of the peasant, both the artificial productivity of mechanized industry and the natural rhythms of the countryside. They might have considered and designed institutions to preserve a maximum of both. But instead, they saw undiluted action as necessary for attaining undiluted repose. If violence, revolution, and conspiracy did seem to be at the center of their polemics, this was deceptive. For however much they cried out for conflict, they saw it merely as prelude to harmony.

But as they felt frustrated—as peace would not come— they pushed with a truly terrible fury toward the trouble-free rustic life in which man might be reabsorbed by nature, in which the tension between private ideal and public reality would at last be resolved. So fully did they commit themselves to the means of unmediated, direct action that the distinction between means and ends could lose relevancy altogether. In fact, for one blinding historical moment, violence could become all. After that it would be revealed that the extreme Left and Right shared a yearning for the quiet of the cemetery, the crematorium, the tomb.

With their indiscriminate enthusiasm, they gave rise to the new fraternity of the dead. If we stay with them on the surface and ignore the messy human stirrings beneath, we might momentarily behold Dachau as purification center, Stalingrad as heroic battlefield, and Hitler's Berlin shelter as stage of self-sacrifice, seeing in these the realization of an ideal.

But it remains for the historian to peel away the surface and look beneath the purity of these ideals. The historical record enables us to see a truly pathetic residue of human moderation, mitigation, and reasonableness. Where all was expected to be clean, pure, and undefiled, political man broke through and corrupted. The conflicts repressed on the surface reappeared in perverse form below—among both the oppressors and their victims. As the historical record makes clear, there was pervasive deception, temporizing, and evasion. The history of totalitarianism is one of secret plots and counterplots, backstair politics, pay-offs and intrigues, furtive maneuvers to evade, rescue, and shore up. There was nepotism, graft, and perfidy. The administrators of Fascism and Naziism were a seedy and sordid lot—unheroic types far removed from Roman arenas or Teutonic monuments. They were frail and afraid, obsessed by fears of disloyalty and disaffection. They operated a ruinous economy, an unfocused military machine, and an inefficient industrial system. They supported a black market in luxuries, armaments, and human beings. The typical communication was the dry, official memorandum—supplemented by the sly gesture or the knowing grin of complicity. In this behavior, ironically, there was the semblance of politics and of discourse—manifestations of a human urge to bargain, negotiate, and compromise.

Nor were the victims of Naziism capable of embracing a nonpolitical perspective: they also bargained. Hoping to achieve compromises, Jews in position of authority—presidents of congregations, chairmen of ghetto councils, or teachers of classes—implemented orders to select some from

among their charges for extermination. In this the ultimate
in pathos is exposed, for men were compelled to dehumanize
themselves. They could choose between being murdered
and extinguishing the conventional procedures of politics.
While death was their reward in any case, they chose speech
and politics. Bargaining with human lives, failing to save
themselves by direct action, they too turned out to be confused and inefficient. Master and subject, each in his own
way, engaged in dirty politics. Thus in an obscene parody
of political conduct—that is, in the sheer inefficiency of
totalitarian regimes—an irrepressible humanity stood revealed. It therefore becomes not unreasonable to conclude
with Thomas Mann that there was "hope beyond hopeless-
ness, the transcendence of despair, not its betrayal."

The vestige of political theory in the movements of
Italian Fascism and German National Socialism discloses in
crystallized form what was often merely unshaped and vague
in the polemics of Sorel, Barrès, and Maurras. What remained abbreviated first in the conventional literature of
nationalism and later in the practice of Communist regimes
was fully spelled out by Fascist rulers. Their pronouncements
may properly be looked upon as a direct repercussion of
their struggle for domination. Neither their policies nor their
institutions were meant to appeal to reason. In the phrases
Mussolini had Giovanni Gentile draft for him, "Fascism was
not the nursling of a doctrine worked out beforehand with
detailed elaboration; it was born of the need for action and
it was itself from the beginning practical rather than theoretical." And in the words of Hitler's official theoretician,
Alfred Rosenberg, the ideology of Fascism was a "mystical
synthesis or activity of soul." As such, it necessarily had to
remain immune to philosophical scrutiny. Its distinguishing
characteristic was its tendency to put every position in terms
of unqualified, absolute extremes. It endlessly repeated conclusions which public discourses would of necessity have
qualified. The conclusions it affirmed were wholly subjective,
that is, beyond public verification. It thus eradicated the

distinction between private vision and public discourse, between ends and means, and it converted all means— whether the torture of a platoon of war prisoners or the heroic self-sacrifice of the solitary individual—into an end. It sought to vindicate every experience as an intrinsically exhilarating one, useful not for some postulated purpose but in and for itself.

This ruthless drive toward the total fulfillment of every possibility is an expression of the ominous effort to give sanctity, all at once, to life and death, forcing their reconciliation in fact where, as long as human language attaches values to experience, they remain irreconcilable in theory. The positive themes of Fascist rhetoric, compulsively reiterated, all testify to this central contradiction—belief in the possibility of experiencing death in life and life in death. The texts and speeches of Fascism consistently reveal the aspiration to produce a practical fusion of polarities, to overcome the various dualisms men postulate to help them see the meaning of their experience:

Thanatos	Eros
rationalism	sentimentalism
individualism	fraternalism
mechanism	organicism
complexity	simplicity
technology	primitivism
reason	volition
formality	spontaneity
law	personality
Apollo	Dionysus

As we reflect on the concrete meaning of each of these ultimates, we should recognize how the practical effort to bring about their union was bound to obliterate the ground between them—the ground on which we have traditionally revealed our capacity for charity, forbearance, and compromise. To make room for the extremes, to eradicate everything else, inevitably produced the apparent contradictions of Nazi behavior. Thus the most refined rationalism—the rationality embodied in law, in military hierarchy, and in economic and technological planning—was employed to sustain one of the major convulsions of the century. At the center of the Nazi holocaust, in the quite creditable person of Adolf Eichmann, there was the bureaucrat methodically coordinating railroad time schedules to route undesirable elements to extermination camps.

Eichmann's position symbolized the great effort to abandon middle ground on which private men expressing their antagonistic desires might meet and disarm one another, and this whether they come to fulfill their desire for life or for death. His behavior revealed that dehumanization lies precisely in this: in suspending language and politics as instruments for mediation, as links between polarities. Relying on language and politics as devices for making public policy, we express and preserve our civility. To be sure, language deprives us of public victory. But while it does justice to none of our private ideals, it does a measure of justice to the ideals of all men. Howard Nemerov has put it more concisely: "Civilization, mirrored in language, is the garden where relations grow; outside the garden is the wild abyss."

Recommended Reading

SOREL: ORIGINAL WORKS

D'Aristote à Marx: L'ancienne et la nouvelle métaphysique (Paris, 1935).
Reflections on Violence, trans. by T. E. Hulme and J. Roth, intro. by E. A. Shils (Glencoe, Ill., 1950).

SOREL: SECONDARY WORKS

Gray, Alexander, *The Socialist Tradition* (London, 1946), Chap. 15.
Lytle, Scott H., "Georges Sorel: Apostle of Fanaticism," in Edward Mead Earle, ed., *Modern France* (Princeton, 1951), Chap. 16.

BARRÈS: ORIGINAL WORKS

Scènes et doctrines du nationalisme (Paris, 1902).

MAURRAS: ORIGINAL WORKS

Mes idées politiques (Paris, 1937).

FASCISM AND NATIONAL SOCIALISM:
ORIGINAL WORKS

Darré, R. Walther, *Neuadel aus Blut und Boden* (Munich, 1935).
Eckart, Dietrich, *Ein Vermächtnis* (Munich, 1937).
Gentile, Giovanni, "The Philosophic Basis of Fascism," *Foreign Affairs*, Vol. 2 (January, 1928), pp. 290–304.
Hitler, Adolf, *Mein Kampf* (New York, 1943).
† Rocco, Alfredo, *The Political Doctrine of Fascism* (New York, 1926).
Rosenberg, Alfred, *Der Mythus des 20. Jahrhunderts* (Munich, 1938).
Trevor-Roper, H. R., ed., *Hitler's Secret Conversations, 1941–1944* (New York, 1953).

GENERAL SECONDARY WORKS

Arendt, Hannah, *The Origins of Totalitarianism* (New York, 1951).

† Berlin, Isaiah, "Political Ideas in the Twentieth Century," *Foreign Affairs*, Vol. 28 (April, 1950), pp. 351–85.

Cassirer, Ernst, *The Myth of the State* (New Haven, 1946), Chap. 18.

Curtis, Michael, *Three Against the Third Republic: Sorel, Barrès, and Maurras* (Princeton, 1959).

Earle, Edward Meade, ed., *Modern France: Problems of the Third and Fourth Republics* (Princeton, 1951).

Stern, Fritz, *The Politics of Cultural Despair: A Study in the Rise of the Germanic Ideology* (Berkeley, 1961).

Viereck, Peter, *Meta-Politics: The Roots of the Nazi Mind* (New York, 1961).

† Unabridged in *Sources in Twentieth-Century Political Thought.*

III. THE DOCTRINE OF QUIETISM: MICHAEL OAKESHOTT

The writers whose works supported the convulsive activity of Mussolini and Hitler were at one in denying that a transcendent moral truth or reason should inhibit man in his quest for self-fulfillment. Their joint intellectual premise was skepticism regarding ultimate ends. But because they believed, on practical grounds, that individuals would cooperate to build their secular utopia only under the spell of a mythology, they counseled the acceptance of myth. If God was dead, men with the power and the talent could construct a synthetic god and use it to entrance the masses. Thereby the masses might be driven to accept the destruction of the present order and the establishment of a radically new one; they might be induced to overthrow the tradition of politics and establish an apolitical, totalitarian regime.

The same skepticism regarding ultimate ends has informed the work of Michael Oakeshott (1901–   ). But this has not meant that he has found himself impelled to counsel the establishment of a new order by revolutionary action. On the contrary, his stance has been that of stoic resignation to worldly experience. Thus one might disdain the idealist, show contempt for abstract rationality, place a premium on political practicality, stress the existential facts of earthly life, assert that this world is indeed, as Oakeshott has declared, the best of all possible worlds—one might share this cluster of preferences with the supporters of an unmitigated activism and yet refrain from counseling action. What distinguishes Oakeshott's work is precisely his quiet acceptance of political things as they are, or at least as he believes them to be in England. Indeed, he accepts them so profoundly that his favorable disposition toward the heritage of English liberty emerges as his general theory of politics.

At bottom Oakeshott's concern has been with the protection of liberty. The greatest threat to it, in his view, is the result of our political failure to attend to man in his concrete setting. Man must be conceived of as a creature who thrives only in a communal context, who flourishes only in the midst of traditions and habits. He is properly governed, Oakeshott believes, when he can remain secure in the knowledge that nothing in his future will disturb his conventions, rituals, and gestures. Shaded by familiar landmarks, he finds that peace which is his birthright. What exists—what exists most durably and unconsciously—is also right. Man's liberty lies in his claim to the historically established order which surrounds and supports him.

The right order of things is forever threatened by the political rationalist, Oakeshott's major ideological target. Appealing to an abstract ideological system, the rationalist disrupts the conditions given and sanctioned by experience. Ignoring the restraints of historical reality, he commits himself to his ideals, and, becoming enchanted by them, transfers his affection from the burdensome realm of history to the airy realms of theory. "Indeed," Oakeshott wrote in *Experience and Its Modes* (1933), "the attempt to find what is completely satisfactory in experiences is so difficult and dubious an undertaking, leading us so far aside from the ways of ordinary thought, that those may be pardoned who prefer the embraces of abstraction." Thus Oakeshott at once (1) indicts the great system builders, the rational planners who formulate abstract programs, (2) ironically exonerates their affection for Rationalism, and (3) defends an antiprogrammatic, tradition-centered politics.

In the name of liberty, then, Oakeshott stands opposed to the rationalist. His wrongs are multiple: his action is socially pernicious; his temper bespeaks his immaturity; his love of doctrine reveals his failure to see the limits of philosophy.

Enamored of his system, he proceeds to put it into practice. As he does so, society as it exists in all its inscrutable ways becomes his victim. Ignorant of man's love of settled ways, he does violence to human nature. Disregarding the actualities of social life, insensitive to the stubborn material on which he works, he becomes reckless, righteous, and ruthless. And here it matters not whether his convictions are those of the Left or the Right; their artificial character makes them offensive to man's natural institutions.

In psychological terms the charge against the rationalist is that he craves certainty, rushes to conclusions, and then acts presumptuously. And just as his conduct reveals his psychological imbalance, his doctrine, whatever its specific content, reveals his fundamental failure to grasp the limits of speculative activity, of rational philosophy.

Philosophy, Oakeshott points out, always pushes onward to get in touch with the whole. It seeks to transcend the specific value-impregnated judgments that are offered by the fields of history, natural science, and the practical science of governing human affairs. Not satisfied with merely practical coherence, philosophy seeks always to unify and order experience under comprehensive categories. It is a pursuit that "requires us to renounce for the time being everything which can be called good or evil. . . ." It seeks to move us beyond the world of values and language, beyond practice and history, thereby liberating us.

This activity, Oakeshott made clear in a brilliant introduction to Hobbes's *Leviathan* (1947), is as glorious as it is futile. Oakeshott can thus admire the mature arrogance of Hobbes, his "tone of confident finality." He can see Hobbes, above all, as the creator of a system, one which was conceived "with such imaginative power that, in spite of its relatively simple character, it bears comparison with even the grand and subtle creation of Hegel." But magnificent as such attempts at total comprehension may be, Oakeshott concludes, they are ultimately of no avail. We must, at the end, "recognize the final triumph of inconsequence." There can be no arrival, no salvation. While we can gain a measure of coherent knowledge, the comprehensive knowledge for which philosophy strives is denied us.

The *prudent* political philosopher will stop short of "comprehension," as Hobbes himself did when he compromised his system and made practical prescriptions. By so doing, he submits to the requirements of political life. He sacrifices the purity of his system for the sake of practical gains, for the sake of our marvelously complicated, densely textured existence. To bear up in our everyday life, it is enough that things appear coherent, that they appear to make sense. What our practical political life demands is not "comprehension," in short, but coherence. To be sure, those thinkers and statesmen who help make our life coherent—more properly, who help reveal the organic coherence of life to us—will not enable us to attain salvation. But they will grant us a measure of peace. They will enable us to keep our balance.

Oakeshott views our public enterprises not so much as foredoomed to failure as impossible of attaining success. For us there can be no redemption. In this world we cannot overcome the tension between the real and the ideal, and all efforts to do so, no matter how gallant, will but deepen our predicaments. We must acquiesce in our fate. Unable ultimately to comprehend our condition, tolerating the absurd appearance of our conventions, we must make our peace with the world.

Neither physicians nor metaphysicians can really cure our disease. Politics can provide makeshift arrangements, but provide no fulfillment. At best it can lead to armistices, maintaining a precarious peace. It may perhaps lessen the damage created by men who passionately, immoderately seek justice by attempting to make the political order conform to their vision of health. In any event, all that politics can do—all it must do—is to help us "keep afloat on an even keel."

Because there is no known chart for our voyage, we must

make our way in the light of experience. Having knowledge only of particulars, we must guide ourselves exclusively by them. We must remain in touch with the actual currents of life. Certainly we would be ill advised to withdraw from the world, design a new chart, and then see if it might somehow guide us into port. Abstract reason will lead to shipwreck. Being ignorant, we must rely not on Reason, according to Oakeshott, but on Tradition.

Of our statesmen, the avoidance of disaster demands immersion in history. It is their task to remain sensitive to its promptings. They must get to know the history of their country, stay in touch with it, and faithfully conserve it. To discover what to do in politics, they must take their bearings by prevailing conventions. The proper—indeed, the only— political activity consists of carefully amending "existing arrangements by exploring and pursuing what is intimated in them." History reveals the range of possibilities and pre- scribes the limits of sound action. And political wisdom consists of acting within the range of the given with respect for the possible.

What public morality there is lies embedded in the established order of institutions. Oriented by the moral consensus and the institutions which express it, the true statesman will contribute simultaneously to the true liberties of the individual and to the survival of society. Thus the acceptance of the moral consensus is dictated not by some standard of right and wrong but by prudence.

Prudence insists that we steep ourselves in history, acknowledge its complexity, and remain aware that, in the final analysis, it teaches us no lessons. Since there are no ultimate standards to inform our action, since there is no transcending Truth in reference to which our political con- duct is to be judged, we must stay true to "municipal knowl- edge, not universal," to those specific traits of ours which are irreducible to general formulas.

Because abstract reason can provide no authority for political action, it is mischievous to apply science dogmatically to human affairs. Ruling is an art, not an applied science. As an art, it is a discipline which cannot be taught the way a merely technical discipline is taught, by the memorization of rules. It must be transmitted or imparted, as all matters of taste and style are. The most devoted study of cookbooks, to use Oakeshott's illustration, will not make a true cook. Practical knowledge is not technical knowledge; it is knowledge of how to perform, how to improvise within established limits. It is the ability to exploit existing possibilities, "to make a friend of every inimical occasion." But the occasions, it must always be remembered, are the existing ones.

In agreement with other philosophical idealists, Oakeshott believes that there is an inner logic to every situation and that the proper approach will disclose it. Thus there is a natural order of things which sound political action can preserve and enhance. The point—if indeed there is a point to anything—is to save appearances, to shore up, to preserve and conserve man's precious estate. This can be done only by confronting practical problems directly. Politics being neither a natural science of human behavior nor an applied science of social engineering, the statesman must deal with specific problems. He can no more rely on a deductive behavioral science of "political man" than on an abstract theory of historical development, such as that of dialectical materialism. He must deal with our difficulties piecemeal, not wholesale. The political disasters of the twentieth century have all been due precisely to his failure to attend to specific problems, to become overreaching and pursue ideals.

Should we have to appeal to general standards as we make public policy, we must draw these from our traditional way of doing things. We must see our norms in "the manner in which people have been accustomed to go about the business of attending to the arrangements of their societies. . . ." Tradition, custom, and prejudice yield as much in the way of generalizations as we may safely accept.

Insofar as we operate within the community consensus,

we prevent resentments from arising in the first place. In the well-managed society, men will not feel underprivileged, envious, and alienated. They will therefore not be tempted to design rationalistic models of social life. According to Oakeshott, rationalism—not mindless activism—is the weapon of alienated men. Where prudent statesmen govern, men remain integrated and adjusted, playing their roles peacefully. Such a society is balanced and stable; if it moves at all, it moves to approximate that harmony which is already embodied in its history, in the organic totality of its life.

Oakeshott's opposition to political rationalism is clearly not offered as a universally relevant political theory; it is essentially, and not unintentionally, parochial. It is addressed to the well-ordered society able to dispense with both idealism and the politics generated by idealism. It is appropriate to the well-balanced community in which accommodation is always possible. In such a society there are no irreconcilable elements, and the mood is necessarily such that inequalities do not create resentments. There is a pervasive consensus and no suspicion that men, in privacy, engage in unseemly conduct. In such a congenial society the idealist who dreams up utopias and offers them as rational alternatives will be unknown, for idealism is a function of unstable societies.

It is the stable society which Oakeshott's work effectively vindicates. Indeed, it rationalizes a way of life with which it would be unbecoming not to sympathize—especially when its historical tradition fortuitously happens to be the one to which heart and reason give their unforced assent. Yet at the same time, his doctrine loses in relevancy where history and tradition are ambiguous, where there are conflicting traditions to which men think it proper to appeal, or where the range of conflicting traditions is too narrow to make public life tolerable. Thus to be instructed, however subtle the homily and genteel the voice, to be attentive to tradition, is not always to get clear counsel. Nor is the counsel necessarily harmless, for traditions differ. To be sure, Oakeshott's approach must remain appealing enough when offered in a society committed to civil politics, gentlemanly manners, and controlled conversation. Where such a consensus exists (leaving altogether open the question whether it in fact exists in Great Britain or elsewhere), the discipline imposed by history may well be preferable to that imposed by the loyalty to absolutes.

Nevertheless, the loyalty to absolutes can also serve to emancipate, especially where the social order does not resemble Oakeshott's image of English society. It may emancipate from an oppressive tradition and an oppressive history. Moreover, it may free men from the rule of activists who accept Oakeshott's premise of skepticism—but simply shrug off his conclusion. The activist, too, has placed his faith in his feelings and his tradition. Mussolini, Stalin, and Hitler all believed their policies to be in tune with reality; they simply sought to give their subjects those opportunities which conventional reason and conventional politics repressed. To do so, they sought to exploit a popular malaise and to apply serviceable techniques—including effective ideologies—to engineer consent. Their reliance or rationality was thus not unrelated to *their* feeling that a tradition had been violated and must be re-established. As tradition dictates moderation for Oakeshott, so it dictated ruthless action for them. Oakeshott assumes that the tyrannies of the modern age found their inspiration in rational constructions. He is critical of reason in politics because, he holds, men have been sacrificed to rationality, to abstract ideas. His criticism presupposes that ideology was no mere façade for the power-strivings of a Hitler or a Stalin. He discounts their opportunism, their own shrewd sense of what is feasible and practicable. He assumes that for them the ideology was not merely one of the levers of political power but an actual ideal.

Generalizing this view, Oakeshott holds that civil life is threatened when we distinguish between means and ends, proceed to articulate the ends, and then engineer consent on the ends we have articulated. We are threatened by the rational planner, the policy scientist who, indifferent to the community consensus, to its habits and prejudices, imposes an abstract order. The result, he believes, is the destruction of liberty.

But in point of fact, liberty is endangered not only by the rationalist who, having separated means from ends, speculates about the ends and then acts in their behalf. It is also threatened by the activist who, disdaining reason just as much as Oakeshott, follows his impulses. It is endangered by the "great simplifiers" who remove complications and contradictions and resolve to *force* the fusion of the ideal and the real, insisting, in unspoken agreement with Oakeshott, that the divorce of means and ends is the great scandal of the age. They, too, act in obedience to feeling and tradition, though radically different ones from Oakeshott's.

Thus whether one recommends a policy of revolution or a policy of tranquillity is truly a matter of feeling, or of historical accident. The choice follows from one's feeling, a feeling conditioned by a national heritage which may, but need not, demand the exercise of reason. Merely to stress submission to tradition is to deprive oneself of that reason which makes it possible to distinguish between competing views of what constitutes a well-ordered society. It suspends the dialogue which enables us to discriminate against some traditional restraints and in favor of others. To stress only practicality and realism, as Oakeshott has, is to make the choice between political activism and political quietism but a function of one's disposition.

Oakeshott's own preference for moderate, piecemeal action testifies to his profound trust either in the good sense of his compatriots or in the durability of the institutions compelling them to remain so sensible. Counseling calmness, he expresses his fondness for the settlements achieved by past revolutions. He expresses his conviction that plans designed to accord with ideological preconceptions must change a just establishment, and will therefore tend to injustice.

It is thus Oakeshott's very provincialism which protects him from the charge of being indifferent to justice. Failing to tell us what is just, he is confident that his fellow citizens will know well enough what he means. Given his restrained audience, he is not worried about being misunderstood. He has, after all, meticulously addressed himself to his neighbors, shaping his idiom to their cadences. Speaking softly, he has conversed with those who cherish their England and need not think up schemes for changing it. He has not strained to be overheard by outsiders who appeal to man's speculative intellect to produce changes. He certainly has published sparsely, and hardly anything abroad. Thus he has not been haranguing outsiders whose experience reveals conditions threatening survival and whose sense of injustice alerts them to intolerable social arrangements. If the calmness of his reflections is disconcerting, it is because other thinkers share his mood even though they live in neighborhoods more troubled than his.

Recommended Reading

† Oakeshott, "Political Education," in *Rationalism in Politics and Other Essays* (New York, 1962).

  † Unabridged in *Sources in Twentieth-Century Political Thought*.

IV. SOCIETY AS FACT AND NORM

It is possible to look on the whole range of contemporary Western political theory as an ideological reaction to the real (and alleged) aftereffects of the French Revolution—the democratization of politics, the shattering of society, the atomizing of the economy, and the leveling of culture. Thus European thinkers as diverse as Tocqueville and Marx, Nietzsche and Comte, Freud and Mannheim, Sorel and Weber, or Jaspers and Eliot may be brought under the same conceptual roof: their work may be analyzed as the repercussion of the disintegration of the pre-Revolutionary feudal order. Even more is involved in entertaining such a perspective. The paternalistic state of Bismarck may be seen as a concerted effort to pacify and order the masses; the activism of Fascism may be seen as a desperate drive to renew the meaning of our common existence; and the thrust of Marxism may be seen as an endeavor to convert the irrationality of an individualistic economic system into a harmonious, new community. Even the amalgam of American political thought and practice may be subsumed under such an analytical scheme: what makes it explicable is precisely the American *escape* from the French Revolution; that is, even if Americans were not born as free and equal as Tocqueville had dramatically maintained, the assumption may yet prove to be fruitful for purposes of analysis and understanding. In sum, what we believe or fail to believe and what we do or fail to do may be comprehensively ordered by recognizing our hankering for a lost community.

Yet to see all contemporary thought and action in this

light would be to deprive ourselves of distinctions. It would be to treat political writers merely as ideologists who have passively responded to the tendencies of a post-Revolutionary era. What would still remain of interest for the student of political philosophy is an understanding of the various proposed political alternatives. After all, political thinkers have continued to offer competing visions of the just state, and this in the face of a widespread disenchantment with utopian schemes. They have reacted not only against the revolutions of the eighteenth century but also against an optimistic revolutionary faith.

Their acceptance of pessimism, skepticism, and "realism" has had at least one significant effect. It has pushed a good number of theorists—economists, psychologists, and sociologists—to ground their policy proposals in what they believed to be the observed facts of "social reality" or "human nature." Skeptical regarding all results of philosophical discourse, they have felt compelled to advocate their reforms under the aegis of empirical science. Thus, although their case for the reconstruction of a sick, maladjusted, or unbalanced society may have sprung from their personal revulsion to social disorganization, it has nevertheless been offered as if based on "the facts of social life"—or, more precisely, as if based exclusively on phenomena so patterned as to be manageable by the methods of empirical science.

Their attempt to justify reform proposals solely by appealing to empirical science for authority is a procedure so evidently fallacious that the point need not be labored. At the same time, their basic fallacy should not prevent us from considering their positions. While norms cannot be derived from empirical science, empiricism serves both to chasten us by defining limitations and to prod us by revealing possibilities. And while it cannot finally validate any conclusions about what constitutes the sane or the rational society, it can outline the tense, contradictory, and tragic character of our own existence. Thus even if we should prefer social conflict to stay unresolved lest its resolution be utterly conclusive, even if we should reject all final definitions of social health, the analyses offered by the English pluralists, by Erich Fromm, or by Elton Mayo—all thinkers presuming to operate empirically—may enlarge the range of our understanding.

The Reality of Groups: English Pluralism

In the period preceding the First World War, Europe witnessed a burgeoning of concerted intellectual interest in assorted institutions which might be reconstructed so as to protect individuals—individuals who seemed increasingly lost in the mass, debased by the division of labor, and exposed to manipulation by an unrepresentative state. Thus it was widely felt by various kinds of syndicalists and socialists (as well as by sociologists, psychologists, and criminologists) that the emergence of the sovereign nation state under conditions of industrialism posed a threat to individuality by destroying its natural social habitat. The state was seen to reinforce conditions under which men, while technologically interdependent, became emotionally and intellectually estranged from one another. Society had become a mere aggregation of individuals; men were no longer members of a true community. If they were bound together, it was not by their natural ties, but by artificial devices: an ascending industrialism, a centrally controlled economy, and a legal order which made all coercion appear legitimate. These conditions being deplorable—on the ground that they were not natural to man—how could the individual be rescued? And how could a genuine public purpose be restored?

The first task, it seemed, was to reintegrate and resocialize the masses. Given the view that an unmitigated individualism is as reprehensible as statism, that the former would indeed lead to the latter, it became reasonable to argue for a plurality of associations. Poised between the individual and the state, such a social pluralism might enable

96

man to develop his true potentialities, to find and to be himself. Intermediary associations would provide a sense of community while shielding their members against undue state power.

Not surprisingly, this line of reasoning was to lead to a renewed appreciation of the pre-Revolutionary landscape dotted with innumerable groups. The desire for a new social pluralism could make it tempting to plead for reorganizing productive units in the image of the medieval guild, for redesigning communities in the image of the village, or for reforming the social system generally in the image of an obviously "functional" regime. The modern world being so obviously "dysfunctional," the lost feudal world of guilds, corporations, churches, monasteries, universities, municipalities, and estates could take on the attributes of a utopian society. By reintroducing individuals into it, wholeness might be restored.

To guarantee the rights of individuals, it seemed essential to fortify the rights of private associations. Small, close-knit groups, so it was held, constituted man's true communities. Since the modern state had grown large and imperious, it now became appropriate to dismantle it, or at least to have it do no more than (1) foster, within its own boundaries, those small groups which alone preserve the habits of self-government and (2) administer the remaining public order so as to keep the peace between the coexisting groups.

These views were to find particularly cogent expression in English political thought. Prompted by their respect for individual freedom, a number of English thinkers had been aesthetically and morally stirred by what they saw in their social and industrial environment. They grew indignant over the ugly and degrading effects of industrialization, especially its inhuman discipline. They witnessed and proceeded to document the gradual concentration of economic power and the concurrent loss of individual autonomy. A seemingly laissez-faire economy that was postulated on individualism actually encouraged the exercise of power by a social class performing no intelligible social function.

While all this seemed clear to the critics of the ascending state, they did not feel that the state itself might be employed to assert individual rights against an increasingly concentrated economic order, for they looked in particular at the developments taking place in imperial Germany. There a nationalistic and militaristic state socialism circumscribed individual freedom just as effectively as an economic elite had done elsewhere. Their impulse remained consistently to protect the individual against the corrupting influence of monolithic power, against whatever force threatened to entangle and destroy him, whether political or economic. Because power was always subject to abuse, they felt that the very possibility of its unified exercise must be made remote. Because the existing state was increasingly the instrument of the dominant class ruling in its own interest, the neutralization of the state became imperative. And because the state was increasingly unrepresentative and irresponsible, it had to be fragmented—that is, pluralized.

In behalf of the dignity of the individual person, then, but aware of his fate when an unrestrained minority has the power to mechanize work and organize the market, two generations of English pluralists attacked whatever political theory presumed to justify an exploitative capitalism. Today, no single political thinker stands out as the foremost representative of pluralist theory. All that may be said is that the ideas of a number of diverse thinkers momentarily converged, and that at the point of convergence they gave coherent form to a doctrine diminishing the significance of the state while enhancing that of the group. Frederic Maitland, John Neville Figgis, Arthur J. Penty, and S. G. Hobson were followed by Harold J. Laski, R. H. Tawney, and G. D. H. Cole—and all of them were prepared to challenge the theories that bound individuals and groups to the state. It did not matter to them whether the theory defined the state as the embodiment of the general will, as legally omnipotent, or as the highest manifestation of disembodied reason. Rousseau, Austin, and Hegel—none of them escaped the onslaught of the pluralists.

On the one hand, the pluralists reacted against nineteenth-century liberalism and utilitarianism, which had placed the individual in a social vacuum, abstracting him from his associations and making him the sovereign calculator of his interests. Here the pluralists realized that such a detached individual was all too quickly coerced and reintegrated by Bentham's sovereign legislator and by Austin's positive law. And on the other hand, they reacted against continental idealism, in particular the Hegelian doctrine that the power now being exercised by the real state gave mere intimations of the all-powerful ideal.

Exposing the pretensions of German idealism, of the Austinian theory of sovereignty, and of Spencer's defense of a laissez-faire state, the English pluralists sought to direct attention to the social reality and the political facts which philosophy and jurisprudence had generally begun to blur. They found philosophy out of touch with historical experience; it appeared increasingly artificial, contrived, and "unrealistic." Determined to remain empirical, they revolted against the prevailing fictions, in particular against the fiction of state sovereignty. Trying to hold fast to political reality, searching for the durable basis of existing but neglected individual interests, the English pluralists aspired towards a theory which took its bearing by the observed facts of political life, the most fundamental of which was the group nature of all politics. Beneath the fictions of philosophy they rediscovered man's associations. As soon as one inquired what really aroused and commanded the individual's interest and loyalty, one saw a plurality of groups. And the modern state, it turned out, was not to be found among these. Neither the positive state of idealism nor the negative state of classical liberalism ever satisfied genuine human needs. Men were far more inclined, it had to be recognized, to feel obligated by their club, their church, or their union than by the sovereign state. When opposed by the cluster of these groups, the state failed again and again to prevail. Did not the labor unions engaging in the French postal strike of 1908, the South Wales miners' strike of 1915, or the Norwegian general strike of 1916 actually share in sovereignty? Did not the policies of the churches affect the real constitution of society? History could be enlisted to show that conflicts between groups and the state were not necessarily resolved in favor of the state. Groups effectively preserved their prerogatives; they fought the state, modified it, parceled it out.

Rousseau's, Austin's, and Hegel's theories were all put into jeopardy by the rediscovered facts. These facts, of course, buttressed the value assumptions of pluralist thinkers, so that the very history which was uncovered by their scholarly work could also be appreciated. Thereby their case could be both historical and moral, both empirical and normative. What existed behind the façade of British life was fortunately as it should be. It therefore remained for political theory merely to stress and nurture a concealed reality, to call attention to the associations which the liberal state had unjustly relegated to the periphery because, like the church, they represented a vanquished enemy, or else because, like the trade union, they represented new economic interests. Theory could advance under the guise of history.

This general appreciation of the significance and reality of groups was given unintended support by the scholarship of Otto von Gierke, the German legal historian. Ironically, his work was a contribution to German nationalism: it was an effort to revive institutions native to Germany and to repudiate the alien doctrines of Roman law. Roman law had regarded the corporation as a legal personality which owed its existence exclusively to state action. Against this, Gierke's scholarship showed that the source of law was actually not the omnipotent state but men acting through groups. He urged that the corporation, having flowered without state aid on German soil, is an irreducible entity, not a creature of the law, not a fictitious personality made or unmade at the pleasure of the state. He saw it as a living organization with its own will and consciousness.

Although there certainly was no need to react against Roman law in England, Maitland found application for Gierke's ideas. Supported by Gierke's research, he felt induced to refer to the state as but one of a number of associations, and one, furthermore, with no right to preeminence. Thus Gierke's work, which had actually not presumed to attack the doctrine of state sovereignty directly, helped make it possible to perceive the natural autonomy, and therefore the natural rights, of a plurality of disparaged or unrecognized private associations. It became inviting to use his doctrines, as did Figgis, to vindicate the rights of the church or, as did Laski and Cole, to defend various economic groupings. Should group and state ever come into conflict, the question of whom to obey could therefore be an open one: it could become legitimate to side with the group which represents us against the state.

The belief in the representative nature of the group, as opposed to the state, was based on two premises. A voluntary association, it was believed, would naturally enlist the interests of those who established and maintained it. And furthermore, as R. H. Tawney was to argue, its managers would be professionalized and hence socially responsible. When given freedom within that association which we value because it encompasses our day-to-day economic and productive relations, when given freedom where it matters, we can be counted on to participate energetically in politics. We will cease being estranged from one another and from the public order generally.

Whatever label we might attach to it—industrial democracy, economic federalism, functional corporatism, occupational representation, or guild socialism—the new confederation of self-regulating, harmoniously coexisting groups would emerge out of the old state. The old state would grow into a passive coordinating authority, merely acting in response to

group desires. Sound public policy would emerge without
independent state action; it would be the automatic result
of the free play of group interests. The state would lose that
primacy which idealist theory had postulated. Since we respond, in point of fact, to various subnational associations,
regions, and productive units, sovereignty would be divisible
and our allegiance to the state contingent and qualified. Thus
English pluralist thinkers argued what American statesmanship—insisting on bills of rights, on a separation of power,
and on federalism—had concluded more than a century
before. They affirmed that the state could have no inherent
natural right either to impose upon its governmental com-
petitors or to oblige us to obey the law of the state for the
sole reason that the state had enacted it. These conclusions,
so it seemed, were dictated by the data of history. The facts
yielded a definition which, used didactically, could also be
a summons for social reform.

Although the advocates of pluralism had taken a fresh
look at society in the name of realism, they ultimately succumbed to new fictions. For one thing, they ignored the
complex reality of group life and thus never considered the
possibility of group tyranny over individuals. To them it
appeared that existing groups necessarily represent our purposes and functions, realize our values, and thereby make
our freedom meaningful. They depended on a human rationality and interest in politics which experience hardly bore
out. The notion that groups were truly representative they
failed to subject to empirical analysis.

Moreover, they were so concerned about the abuse of
governmental power that they preferred to risk political
stalemate, inviting what Laski frankly called contingent
anarchy. Having devitalized the state, they saw it as a neutral umpire who would never act on more than a common
denominator of group interests. They saw it as carefully
protecting the law-making prerogative of groups, not as
presuming to take the initiative in the field of public policy.
They viewed government as an agency facilitating agree-

ment, but not as an independent source and initiator of policy. They realized that this might well make for deadlock. But inaction seemed better than action when action might be directed toward the realization of some group-transcending purpose discerned by inspired leadership. Still, by the 1930's, it appeared necessary to some of the pluralists themselves to reintroduce what they had previously banned: a unified purpose above and beyond the will of a plurality of groups. They had rejected such ideas as common good, community interests, and general will. Yet they were to find it scarcely possible to conceive of the political process without the purposeful helping hand of the state—especially as domestic group competition and foreign threats endangered the viability of a pluralistic political order. Thus both Laski and Cole (anticipating Hans J. Morgenthau, James M. Burns, and other American political scientists reacting against governmental fragmentation in the 1960's) were finally driven to recognize needs more fundamental than a vibrant group life. They were to argue both for leadership to crystallize these needs and for a state so equipped as to assure their satisfaction. But for this breakthrough their pluralist theory had left them unprepared. Under the pressures of modern group life, of unprecedented technological and economic developments, their theory grew irrelevant, however appealing the assumptions about human nature upon which it rested.

Sanity a Social Goal: Erich Fromm

The immense popular appeal of Erich Fromm's work—and this notwithstanding serious criticism of its logic—should not be hard to understand. When we desperately desire to change our environment, and especially when we feel that it must be frivolous for social theorists to concern themselves with problems less great than the survival of the species, we become understandably impatient with painstaking, inconclusive empirical analyses. And we become doubly grateful to those who confidently use the language of science to attack social problems. Erich Fromm (1900–   ) has emphatically responded to our craving for answers. He has endeavored to explain the rise of the mass movements of the twentieth century, making the sadistic and masochistic behavior of Fascism and Communism explicable. He has cursed a self-indulgent, consumption-oriented society, pronouncing it sick. He has shown his ardent concern with man's survival in a nuclear era. And, perhaps most attractively, he has used the credentials of science to back social reforms.

It is not surprising that in a scientific age political theory should wear a scientific garb. Using the terms of an empirical science of man, Fromm has challenged a whole range of institutions and beliefs we tend to accept as indubitably given. He has enlisted the categories of psychology for political analysis, and has then proceeded to offer the knowledge his psychological approach has yielded to justify his prescriptions for curing our social ills.

It is a psychoanalytical approach, according to Fromm, which makes it possible to formulate the laws which inhere in our nature. Once these "inherent mechanisms and laws" have been discovered, it should become possible for us to determine the degree to which a particular society actually conforms to them. Moreover, once we know to what extent society represses or satisfies the needs of human nature, it should become possible to make an evaluation. Having psychological knowledge, we know what constitutes social health and social disease: we are able to offer our diagnoses. Because, in Fromm's view, there are "universal criteria for mental health which are valid for the human race as such," we can assess our condition without making subjective valuations. Health—and sickness—can be defined objectively in reference to universal criteria. Some ways of functioning are objectively right. To know these ways is to be able to solve the problems posed by modern life—the problems of economic consumption, industrial technology, bureaucratic management, and large-scale warfare. If a science of man were to arrive at what Fromm has called "a correct description" of human nature, we could regain or achieve our balance. There is, then, a knowable essence toward which man inclines everywhere. And this core of human nature can be inferred, according to Fromm, from the various existing manifestations of our behavior. Making the proper inferences, we can delineate "the laws inherent in human nature and the inherent goals for its development and unfolding."

What, according to Fromm, constitutes man's nature? By nature we are, of course, the kind of creatures who have obvious biological needs. But, in addition, we also have distinct psychological needs. Psychologically we require the opportunity to express the two aspects of our nature: our personal and our communal selves. It is false, Fromm has maintained, to see these dual aspects of our nature as polar opposites, as constituting conflicting goals within us. Where Freud had defined man so as to leave our psyche in a perpetual state of conflict, Fromm resolves our internal conflict. Unlike Freud, he believes it to be amenable to resolution. We should and can be satisfied. Appearances to the contrary, we are not so constituted as to be forever torn between the need to assert ourselves and to join society. Optimistic about our capacity to overcome the dualism Freud had posited, Fromm sees no underlying antagonism between individual and social demands.

If conflict does exist in fact, this is avoidable, for it is due to our environment. Were it not for our deranged social existence, we could live in harmony, retaining our individual autonomy while working with others on necessarily common tasks. A society considerate of our diverse needs would make the actualization of these needs possible. We do not, in any case, have to renounce forever what we truly desire, as Freud had pessimistically assumed. In the sane society we would be genuinely integrated, balanced individuals. However disintegrated and unbalanced we may now be, by nature we are unified beings at peace with ourselves. However much we may in fact experience a rupture within ourselves, knowing ourselves to be out of touch with our true ends, we are essentially all of one piece. If we feel otherwise—split, bewildered, anxious, insecure—this is due not to our nature but the society in which we happen to live. In the just state, then, we have regained our natural wholeness.

Whereas Freud had deemed it impossible, in principle, for us to gratify our instinctual demands in the civilized society, Fromm conceives of society (whether it wears the label "civilized" or not) as capable of satisfying us. Not, however, any society: it can only be a society which meets those psychological requirements which in fact are ours. Removing the obstacles to self-fulfillment, it is one which liberates. And having liberated us, it allows us to be social—social in conformity to our nature and not in conformity to the contrived, synthetic economic and political arrangements which mark our present "civilized" existence. It allows us to discover and realize both our creative and our sociable selves.

Such a society it would be irrational for us to reject. Upholding it as the objective standard for judging alternative existing social orders, it enables us to discriminate. It makes it possible for us to speak with confidence as we repudiate the type of society that threatens to deprive us of our very nature by impairing either our creativity or our sociability. It makes it possible, indeed imperative, for us to reject societies which debase us, which make us into mere objects and commodities and thereby keep us from realizing our selves.

It is Fromm's knowledge of the attributes of individual autonomy that gives him knowledge of the attributes of social health; knowledge of the former would appear to yield knowledge of the latter. For him it is self-evident when men lose their autonomy. An awareness of the wholeness of our nature, a sensitivity to our internal tensions, a look about the modern industrial world, a more general glance at Western history—this, Fromm would have us conclude, will disclose to all but the most obtuse where human autonomy exists and where it is in the process of being lost. He assumes that we readily know what constitutes individual autonomy, or, at least, where it is being effectively destroyed. It is this assumption which enables him to define the proper balance between individual freedom and social restraint. It is this which enables him to testify when freedom and restraint are *duly* proportioned. He can tell us what is proper because too much restraint debases man and too little leaves him so free that he sacrifices his independent, creative self to escape from unwanted freedom. Thus Fromm can define the just state in terms of social health. Furthermore, he can emerge as both social diagnostician and pathologist. Presuming to have knowledge of man's true character, of the laws of human nature, he can tell us both which specific historical society reveals its sanity by conforming to such laws and which specific historical society reveals its insanity by deviating from them.

Indifferent to the historian's concern for the complexity of the actual stuff of history, Fromm has sketched out several "types" of historical society, showing how man has fared in each. His view of history led him to conclude that whereas medieval society was marked by an excess of restraint, modern society is marked by an excess of freedom. In the society which for Fromm is that of the Middle Ages, man was an unfree but secure being. He was "rooted in a structuralized whole" that gave life meaning. But as the medieval system of feudal society broke down, the individual was left isolated and free. He was left to his own devices, unguided and spiritually insecure. "Protestantism," Fromm has noted, "was the answer to the human needs of the frightened, uprooted, and isolated individual. . . ." Under conditions of a capitalism ethically reinforced by Protestant dogma, man was freed from the ties that had given him a feeling of belonging. At the same time, however, he was threatened "by powerful suprapersonal forces, capital and the market." Thus today, man "is free—that is, he is alone, isolated, threatened from all sides. . . . Paradise is lost. . . ."

Capitalism, from this perspective, may be seen as having contributed to man's degradation in a far more basic way than Marx had anticipated. While Marx believed that man was becoming progressively more miserable, he wrongly attributed this misery to economic conditions. The conditions were in fact psychological ones. Capitalist society had actually created a new type of character structure which Fromm has been at pains to delineate. Essentially, the new man is a stereotyped conformist. He imitates advertised fashions and lives up to social expectations. He escapes aloneness by being a reflex of the expectations of others, becoming a victim of a nameless public opinion. He has been leveled, adjusted, and integrated. He has been made a mere commodity in the market, selling himself on an open exchange. He merchandizes ideas, skills, his very personality. Without ever understanding his products, he is absorbed by the endless process of consuming them. He is no longer himself, for there is no authentic self left to be his. "Man does not experience himself as the active bearer of his own powers and richness, but as an impoverished 'thing,' dependent on power outside of himself, unto whom he has projected his living substance."

With overtones that are those of individual psychology, the theory Fromm offers us is that of the mass society. Yet he does not treat the theory as a tool for analysis or a hypothetical proposition. He treats it quite simply as the completed map of the terrain before us, as if it actually depicted the whole of our environment. By thus identifying the modern world, Fromm betrays his moral aversions and affections. By insisting, despite the unyielding ambiguity of history, that the mass society debases man but that a pluralist society would elevate him, Fromm advances a political doctrine. It is as political doctrine, then, and not as empirical theory exposed to countervailing evidence, that his ideas merit consideration.[1]

Reacting against the Reformation, the French Revolution, and the advances in industrialization, those who subscribe to the doctrine of the mass society contend that modern man (that most serviceable abstraction) has become interdependent technologically while becoming estranged socially. The social landscape, once highly pluralized, has been flattened out. The organic bonds of primary and local groups have been cut. There are no guiding values. There is no genuine culture. There is no aristocracy to shape our opinion or discipline our taste. The consequent social mobility, dispersion, aimlessness, and lostness result in our envying our neighbors, in our compulsive search of status. We are forever trying to find ourselves and to learn our roles. Having no sense of self, we search for coherence, faith, and leadership, eagerly turning to whoever promises

1. Two noteworthy studies point critically to the doctrinal character of the theory of mass society: Leon Bramson, *The Political Context of Sociology* (1961) and Joseph R. Gusfield, "Mass Society and Extremist Politics," *American Sociological Review*, Vol. 27 (February, 1962), pp. 19–30.

salvation. Disoriented and anxious, we seek escape, reveal
our ripeness for manipulation, and deliver ourselves to political extremists. Two unhealthy escape routes are open to
us: either we choose the way of "democracy" (conforming
to majorities) or that of fascism (conforming to the will of
autocratic leaders). Neither path can set us free.

Yet it is by no means necessary, Fromm assures us, to
concede defeat. We must overcome our alienation. We must
—and we can—overcome the unhealthy escapes from freedom by uniting the individual "with the world in the spontaneity of love and productive work," realizing a new
relationship which "connects the individual with the world
without eliminating his individuality. . . ." We must move
into "a state of positive freedom" in which man "exists as
an independent self and yet is not isolated but united with
the world, with other men, and nature."

But what can we do to make the study of society something other than a branch of pathology? We will have to go
to work on society itself. In order to realize the values
which, according to Fromm, conform to our true needs, we
must institute a society "centered around the idea of workers' participation and co-management, on decentralization,
and on the concrete function of man in the working process. . . ." We must challenge the mass society and the
bureaucratic state, revitalize democratic pluralism, and re-
establish the small, intimate community. The members of a
plurality of new groupings are to discuss public issues on
the basis of information supplied by an independent agency
composed of leaders "whose outstanding achievements and
moral integrity are beyond doubt." Although these leaders
will admittedly have different views, they will agree,
Fromm feels, "on what is to be considered objective information about the facts." Collaborating with a representative
assembly and an executive establishment, this enlightened
governing body will make the existing political institutions
obsolete. Basing economic policy on man's objective needs,

it will replace the commercialism of modern society—a market system which induces us to want what we do not need. It will rationalize production, distribution, and consumption. And it will do so with the help of a politically conscious and active citizenry. Thus man will have regained the opportunity to realize his potentialities, to live as actively and spontaneously as children and artists do now. Man will be enabled to be himself at last, to be an integrated, fully developed, healthy personality. Finally, in order to fortify the new society which synthesizes freedom and restraint, which encourages free-flowing activity within an organic association, Fromm will have us rely on a religion of humanism, a wholesome faith in human productivity, creativity, and love. This nondoctrinal confidence in man as man is a faith "in freedom as the active and spontaneous realization of the individual self." The new communal synthesis, it should be noted in summary, will be at once natural and normal, necessary and moral.

In his prospectus for reconstructing our shattered social order Fromm does not seek to define the substantive nature of individual morality, to specify the meaning of private virtue. His view of man as productive, creative, and loving is not meant to disclose the nature of the realm of morality itself but, more modestly, to establish the social and political precondition for morality, to provide the social security which allows us to live the good life in our own way. He tells us to act in accordance with our own nature, making clear that we do not do so now. But he does not presume to tell us what form of conduct would be proper. About ultimate ends he remains unconcerned. Prescribing no more than a pluralistic polity, he hopes to create the prerequisites for freedom. At the same time, he leaves open what we are to be free for. The ultimate choice is ours.

The state Fromm would have us establish is one within which we would realize that moral choice, when authentic, is ours alone. In this state we would have an opportunity to "choose ourselves," to realize ourselves, to bring our potentiality to fruition. There is no further directive, no definition of virtuous conduct, for there is no fear that under new conditions fulfillment may be denied and we might fail in new ways. The case is for freedom, for removing the artificial impediments to it. It is made in the conviction that free men will not choose solitude but will, once emancipated, find new forms of association, natural associations rather than our present synthetic ones.

In the new state, economic class relationships will wither while administrative, managerial ones take their place. Fromm has no illusion that we can dispense with superiors and subordinates; he merely insists that we establish our social relationships on noneconomic foundations, or at least not on the foundations made imperative by a capitalistic system of private ownership and acquisitiveness. Once we destroy the capitalist foundation, so Fromm would have us conclude, we are free from meaningless control and regulation. What controls remain will then, by definition, be meaningful; they will answer our genuine needs. The pseudo-rationality of capitalism will be displaced by the genuine rationality of the new "communitarianism."

To sum up: Fromm's political recommendation is presented as if derived from empirical study. It is offered as if based on the conclusions reached by the familiar procedure of postulating a general proposition and putting it to the test by checking it against observed facts, or, less rigorously, examining it in the light of possible counterpropositions. But, as has already been noted, this is not Fromm's method. His hypothesis—namely, that ours is a mass society which breeds such intolerable disease that we resort to irrational cures—is never subjected to the test of counterevidence, evidence which might show that a mass society has manifold implications, some good and some bad for the individual. Fromm, in short, treats the theory of the mass society as if it had been finally confirmed. Similarly, he assumes that the laws of human nature are known and that, in accordance with them, healthy individuals, revering life in all its amplitude, aspiring toward self-enhancement, properly engage in such productive work as they see fit. Thus he manages to conclude that the liberal-constitutional state which checks and directs such work, which curbs political activists, which disperses and restrains the creative power of individuals, is an objectively neurotic one. He can hold that the restraints on action imposed by the cumbersome apparatus for lawmaking found in constitutional democracies is uneconomical: the trouble with constitutional politics, as he sees it, is that it will check attempts to implement the most noble of ideals, including those of Fromm.

Should we continue to disagree about the ultimate needs of man because we recognize that the science of psychology, being empirical, is not a completed science, it remains ever necessary to inquire on what grounds we may legitimately move toward the establishment of a saner society. Fromm's approach will not help us here, for policy recommendations cannot be finally authenticated by an empirical social science. Even the most scrupulously accurate observation of social changes, of man caught up in social processes, can lead but to tentative conclusions.

Just as we differ about the objectivity of human needs, we cannot agree on social health. There is no agreement, certainly, that a mass society must have the pernicious implications for individual freedom claimed by Fromm. The consensus it entails and the sympathies it supports may in fact serve to assimilate the very activist who is driven to assault free institutions as he is unnerved by the frustrating stalemates of pluralist regimes. A mass society, to be sure, is not without coercive features; but it is also not without liberating ones. It has not been demonstrated that the individual is doomed in the mass, nor that he is saved in the world of pluralism. Whatever our longing, society cannot dispense with coercion. If we associate the ideal state with absolute freedom, our disenchantment is assured. Society, whether it be the mass society or the pluralist one, is a coercive institution. Still it may be so designed as to force its members to become civil, talkative, and, at best, discursive. It may be so designed as to keep them from coming to conclusions, even enlightened ones. To this end, it must appreciate conflict over harmony and politics over administration. It must nourish what Fromm's work places in jeopardy and, for that very reason, helps us understand.

Participation as Norm: Elton Mayo

The English pluralists had sought to protect the individual against the irresponsible exercise of state power by vindicating the authority of intermediary association. These associations, so they felt, would rightly shield the individual against the sovereign state. Where theories of laissez-faire economics and utilitarian politics had led to a conception of a thoroughly atomized society—a society so atomized, in fact, that its individual members would be perennially provoked to seek reintegration under a unified state—the theory of pluralism had reaffirmed the natural rights of churches, corporations, universities, and unions. Where the classical liberalism of the eighteenth century placed the sovereign consumer and voter vis-à-vis the sovereign state, and where Continental idealism celebrated the integrated organic state, pluralism focused on the intermediate layer of groups. The pluralists found support for their case on empirical grounds, pointing to the historical fact that men discovered purpose in their lives when involved in associational activities. This demonstrable fact, so they claimed, had been disregarded by the theories of both an atomistic individualism and an organic idealism. The plea for a diversified social order of small-scale groups was based, then, on the conviction that only such an order would do justice to man's genuine social needs.

It was this specific deduction of social policy from psychological needs which was to find expression in the work of Erich Fromm. While the English pluralists had derived their policies from their reading of history, Fromm derived them from his understanding of the laws of human nature. But behind the veneer of empiricism, there was, in both cases, the moral desire to satisfy human needs in the face of their manifest frustration. So strong was this desire that what scientific empiricism itself can never assume was assumed nonetheless: the laws of human nature are known; what man needs in order to be called "man" has been defined. It was this assumption which was quietly introduced to validate the hoped-for society of English pluralism as well as the so-called communitarian order envisaged by Fromm.

The work of Elton Mayo (1880–1949) illustrates how the blending of moral convictions with a scientific empiricism finally leads to reliance on elite rule. It shows how the belief that man's needs are already known can lead to the manipulation of individuals, and thus to the denial of the moral impulse of pluralist thinkers themselves—their desire to enable man to realize his own nature.

While Mayo, a professor of industrial research at the Harvard School of Business Administration, took his bearings by the specific problems of business and industry, he was in fact concerned with the massive dislocations which, in his view, troubled the whole of the Western world. Modern society, he felt, is radically out of balance. It is simply not a *society*. It is but an aggregate of asocial individuals more interested in themselves, their leisure, and their private lives than in the common good. An older tradition, a set of customary beliefs and habits, had been destroyed. Social disintegration is manifest, Mayo believed, in the widespread factionalism of modern life, that is, in the presence of innumerable conflicting interest groups, each failing to understand the other. There is pervasive conflict between economic classes, between groups and the nation, and between the nations themselves. But most important—and this, he said, betrays our basic inability to cope with technology on the social plane—there is the conflict between workers and employers, between the managed and the managers. Self-seeking individuals and groups, incapable of communicating effectively, are in wasteful competition with one another.

Mayo's own large-scale, carefully empirical research into our industrial setting turned out, perhaps not surprisingly, to expose a positive relation between a meaningless social life and low productivity. Having demonstrated a link between social disintegration and nonproductivity, Mayo was able to conclude that human energy was frustrated precisely because the so-called society of the twentieth century is a mass society. It thus became apparent to him that only a well-structured society of a plurality of work teams could provide the conditions for renewed, meaningful productivity. Clearly the isolated individual was not the happy worker. He was content only when his individual efforts met group approval, when his craving for a genuine society was appeased. By nature, man was a gregarious being, questing for status, order, and harmony. He obviously yearned for the solidarity of the close-knit group and rewarded his employer when such groups were provided.

Psychology, so Mayo maintained in his *Democracy and Freedom* (1919), had made "at least one general assertion as to the form a given society must take if it is to persist as a society. It must be possible for the individual to feel, as he works, that his work is socially necessary. . . ." And Mayo portentously added that "failure in this respect will make disintegration inevitable." Thus he sought to make it clear that not only is man's nature violated by the failure to give him social support; the survival of society itself is at stake. The *facts* confronting modern management—worker turnover, absenteeism, fatigue, and, above all, misunderstanding of the goals of management—could now be perceived as *problems*. Mayo could therefore characterize the factual "breakdown of the social codes that formerly disciplined us to effective working together" as "the chief difficulty of our time."

What was responsible for the breakdown of the established society? Mayo credited the loss of community to the twin forces of industrialism and political democracy—or, more precisely, to the way in which we have sought to cope with the impact of the Industrial Revolution, to the way we have politically responded to it.

According to Mayo, we have responded to the socially devastating impact of industrialism by means of artificial political regulations. We have chosen to legislate. As inheritors of the rationalistic tradition of the Enlightenment, we have permitted the positive, interventionist state to impose order from above. The ultimate causes of our joyless work, of the disease of modernism, are our deliberate, calculating, rationalistic efforts at political regulation by impersonal and distant public agencies. Rationalists that we are, we believe we can actually *make* laws, and impose them. We fail to recognize that law, to be valid and binding, must well up from our social tradition. Because it must be the result of unforced natural growth, it cannot be initiated by legislative agencies. Reacting to the interest conflicts that distinguish and bedevil the atomistic mass society, we perpetuate these conflicts by assuming, wrongly, that they inhere in the nature of man, that there is a necessary split between the individual and society. Assuming this, we act so as to foster the very conflict we must try to overcome. That is, we encourage the kind of politics which breeds disagreement and cultivates differences. We desire political solutions—but political solutions are not final solutions at all. They merely preserve the existing conflict of interests.

What, then, is to be done? Without our being quite aware of it, so Mayo pointed out in the 1930's, a remedy is already in the process of emerging. Just how the needs of industrial man might be satisfied is being unwittingly suggested by our nonpolitical economic associations. Modern industrial corporations, Mayo observed, are already "learning to regard themselves as social functions rather than sources of merely national wealth, and are already experimenting in the direction of extrapolitical or world-wide organization." As they consider the common good, as they cease to conceive of themselves as mere profit-making mechanisms and become responsive to the community, they are beginning to reveal the extraneous character of public government. To the extent that they themselves provide welfare and assume the burden of government, it becomes superfluous for public agencies to mediate conflicting interests. The traditional organs of politics, Mayo affirmed, can never bring about a condition of wholehearted cooperation; their very existence implies the need for concessions. The institutions of the well-functioning society, on the other hand, will make it possible for the individual to contribute his all, to hold back nothing. They will make his full participation meaningful.

As our economic enterprises are presently conducted we waste our productive energies, indulging in feelings of group and class hostility. These hostilities, and our consequent underproductivity, arise because of the failure of the existing public order to give our real selves an opportunity to unfold. Present methods for resolving differences have caused our private interests to harden "into emotional antagonisms, instead of developing the rival conceptions, both defective, into mutual understanding."

To eliminate the conflicts which beset us, to organize our technology on a truly scientific basis, we must call on experts, whose scientific knowledge of human motivations establishes their credentials. They are the trained specialists in the discipline of human relations, personnel management, and industrial psychology. These, and not conventional politicians, must operate the new industrial order. A new kind of industrial management, Mayo argued, must be recruited, trained, and then empowered to govern the industrial machine to achieve consensual ends.

The new plant manager will in effect be the agent of rationality, bringing the new society into being. It will be up to him, according to Mayo, to combine men in such a way that their need for shared experience and meaningful work

can be satisfied. It will be his function to administer the
social system, to develop a satisfying communal life.

Because knowledge of "the biological and social facts
involved in social organization and control" is sufficient for
government, the issue of the age is no longer who should
govern and what procedures legitimize his power. That issue
is settled. We must simply ask whether those in control are
scientifically objective, whether they are "aware of the
problems—physiological, personal, social, and technical—
involved in a situation both technical and human." Alert to
man's need for cooperative productivity, informed by a
scientific sociology and psychology, knowing how "to re-
ceive communications from others and to respond to the
attitudes and ideas of others in such fashion as to promote
congenial participation in a common task," the new manager
will be both authorized and equipped to forge fraternal
bonds.

Himself engaged in controlled social experimentation, the
new human relations expert will add to the body of a social
science while at the same time facilitating the progressive
unification of society. His quest requires not the reflective
understanding of history but the will to participate. The
manager as human relations expert knows that until social
science, in Mayo's phrase, walks into adventure, there can be
no progress. To achieve the mastery of human affairs experimentally, he must be taught how to "secure the effective
participation and cooperation of everyone," how "to help
society to unanimity," how to provide for "the maintenance
of spontaneous cooperation."[1] If the energies of individuals
are to be released, an elite of human relations specialists
must be equipped with the knowledge—admittedly not yet
complete—of "how systematically to set about the task of
inducing various groups and nations to collaborate in the task

1. In his *Social Problems of an Industrial Civilization* (1945), Mayo
argued that the universities today overvalue subjects which seduce otherwise able students by offering "philosophy, literature, sociology, law,
economics, and—God save us all—government"; the universities should
develop "manipulative capacity."

of civilization." The new managers must know how to reduce the conflict between worker and employer, between
industry and industry, between nation and nation. They must
rediscover the lost sense of community.

The technique for doing so on the level of the industrial
corporation is that of directly involving the alienated,
apathetic, irritable, or discontented worker in the industrial
process. Mayo stressed that workers be permitted to participate in decision making, to feel that they too are members
of the industrial family. Thus the emerging human relations
specialists are to enable workers to identify with the industrial plant, to find status and fulfillment in it, to recognize it
as the very source of their welfare. For the welfare of industrial man, as Mayo conceived him, was precisely in the
corporation—the corporation not as a self-interested business
enterprise but as a massive work team in which union and
management were one, jointly tackling the "problems" of
industrial management, jointly informing the disloyal or
recalcitrant worker that his failure to participate is really
due to his confusion and misunderstanding, due to his irrational spirit of self-interest.

Enlightened about the nature of the social equilibrium,
the managerial elite must clarify the goals of work, the true
objectives of industry. As long as the mass of men are confused about objectives, they will remain unbalanced, un-
reliable, and irresponsible. The elite must act on the knowledge that this lack of balance is causally related, as Mayo
disclosed experimentally, to the worker's failure to share
the interests of the industrial company. So far, the goals of
management have remained unaccepted because of management's own failure to communicate. The worker has not yet
been given sufficient understanding of his work situation.
Because he finds it difficult to be enthusiastic about an end
he can but dimly see, he will have to be educated. It is up
to the new managers to start being persuasive, to remove the
blockages in the channels of communication.

If only the worker understood, so Mayo contended, he

would not remain opposed to the industrial enterprise. He would quit stalling, and industrial harmony would be reestablished. The conflicts that had created such problems for the politician would be eliminated. Given the techniques of human engineering, it would become possible to escape the politics of liberalism. The social would triumph over the political. Administrators would settle the disagreements which, in the liberal constitutional state, were always left unresolved. Duly enlightened, man would be balanced, steady, and hence productive. "The physiologists," Mayo pointed out, "have found that work can continue to be performed only in a 'steady state.'" And once such a state is achieved, there would be no interruption to human activity.[2]

Having assumed that within industry as presently organized man is indeed unsteady—as evidenced by his fatigue, his absences from the job, or his low output—Mayo had set himself the task of discovering what forces outside the individual might cause his instability. To that end he managed experiments which allowed him to conclude that worker mobility, absenteeism, and restricted output can be overcome most effectively by improved understanding. When all who are involved in industrial production understand their goal, they will work to their physical utmost. Altruistically, they will do their duty. Since they are not basically rational animals forever calculating alternative courses of action, no *specific* end need be furnished to keep them in motion. Indeed, an incandescent vision of endless productivity, like Sorel's great myth, will move them onward. They do not, accurately speaking, understand their activity, for they are not detached from it. Their rationality is immanent in their action. When they sense this unreflectively, fully living their productive lives, their natural needs will be satisfied. To the

2. "Studies on the performances of men or of the laboratory dogs while in this 'steady state,'" Mayo wrote in *Human Problems of an Industrial Civilization* (1933), "give no present support to the business-economic theory of fatigue, gradual in onset, which is related to the depletion of fuel reserves."

extent that they are submerged in the *élan vital,* they will lead—they will truly embody—the perfect life.

Thus Mayo concluded that it was only reasonable to accept "industrial reality." Assuming that man is by nature a productive being, recognizing that industry is the very incarnation of productivity, Mayo held that the unproductive person must adapt to the demands of industry. Industrial reality does not, in Mayo's view, impose burdens which might justify the individual's resistance. To accept the industrial discipline is to satisfy one's true needs. What man truly wants and what is asked of him coincide. As a matter of both fact and norm, only one compulsion is and should be operative in a social group: the "inner compulsion to think and act in a way that is socially acceptable. . . ." In all preindustrial communities, and no less in the good state, "the situation is not . . . that the society exercises a powerful compulsion on the individual; on the contrary, the social code and the desires of the individual are, for all practical purposes, identical. Every member of the group participates in social activities because it is his chief desire to do so."

Such meshing of private interest and public purpose is to be found in the ideal democracy, democracy defined as that form of government in which "the central and peripheral authorities supplement and complete each other—logical and purposive control from above, spontaneous and cooperative control from below." In Mayo's ideal state, the individual will labor without restraints, with full spontaneity and commitment. It will be possible for him "to feel, as he works, that his work is socially necessary." And he will recognize that he only deceives himself when thinking that he has ideas of his own, since, in fact, "they all originate in the social and professional tradition of the community to which he belongs." United with others, enlisted to give his all, he will find no reason for resentments. In the perfect society, Mayo wrote, there would be no hatred or bitterness toward anyone.

Mayo's postulate, one he found uncontradicted by experience, was that beneath all existing discontent there was a true consensual community. There was not merely the familiar consensus which enables us to abide by the rules of the game of politics, which permits us to negotiate our conflicting interests. Beyond this there was a more fundamental harmony of individual interests. Thus whatever conflict we may in fact experience in modern life, this seemed to Mayo superficial. It could in any event be overcome by the human relations expert who, ever sensitive to man's underlying needs, could usher in the good society. He could master the prevailing irrationality, subject all dissidents to social therapy, disciplining them not by external coercion but by reaching them through their groups, applying social pressure until, at last, unanimity might be achieved.

Those thinkers who defined the exemplary state as one within which public authority would properly devolve on a plurality of groups had been initially concerned with individual freedom, with private rights. They expressed their confidence in the kind of voluntary, representative association which enables individuals to find personal fulfillment. They hoped that the public realm could become one in which a plurality of groups would naturally complement one another. For this public realm little government would be necessary. The role of government would be limited to preserving that equilibrium which, at best, would always emerge spontaneously. The resultant natural equilibrium, its parts in amiable competition with one another, could be granted independence from external controls. Expressing the fundamental harmony of its organic parts, it would not have to be checked by either the sovereign individual or the sovereign state.

To translate this ideal into practice under modern industrial conditions, it was evident enough, the postulated natural unity which Mayo had assumed to exist could not be counted on to emerge automatically. In the face of unnatural and hence intolerable conflict, the ideal would have to be energetically instituted. Thus, as group anarchy was recognized as intolerable, order would have to be created. Policy would have to aim at integration so as to restore the presumed natural health of the body politic.

Mayo's work shows that when the sole aim of public policy is to integrate what is presumed to be disintegrated, to make healthy what is presumed to be diseased, we cease to call on the statesman for proposing, weighing, and reconciling alternative ends. Instead we ask the technician to move men as painlessly as possible toward health. Thus the logic of those thinkers who sought to have public authority devolve on society as a confederation of groups was to drive them— insofar as they were as rigorous as Mayo was—to advocate an elite-governed society. If they were to be unequivocal and conclusive, they would have to introduce a benevolent autocracy. They would have to acknowledge that as long as groups threatened to serve conflicting private interests, it would remain necessary to have social pathologists and social therapists on hand.

Yet for the thoroughgoing advocate of pluralism, prepared to accept modern industrial technology, the expert would not merely be on hand; he would operate the levers at the very center of society because he alone, ever sensitive to nature's objective dictates, could diagnose disease and restore health. Assuming possession of objective knowledge of man's natural needs, he would be prepared to manipulate individuals in order to enable them to satisfy these needs. Mayo's readiness to act on his empirically untenable assumption—the assumption that the elements of social health are known—led him to elitist conclusions unexpressed in the writings of other pluralists. Indeed, it led him to contradict the very aspirations of pluralist thinkers, their sincere hope that the individual will be emancipated when industrial associations at last become self-governing.

Recommended Reading

ENGLISH PLURALISM: ORIGINAL WORKS

Figgis, Neville, *Churches in the Modern State* (London, 1913).

Laski, Harold J., *Studies in the Problems of Sovereignty* (New Haven, 1917).

Tawney, R. H., *The Acquisitive Society* (New York, 1920).

Cole, G. D. H., *Self-Government in Industry* (London, 1920).

Cole, G. D. H., *Guild Socialism Restated* (London, 1920).

ENGLISH PLURALISM: SECONDARY WORKS

Ulam, Adam B., *Philosophical Foundations of English Socialism* (Cambridge, 1951).

Gray, Alexander, *The Socialist Tradition: Moses to Lenin* (London, 1946), Chap. 16.

Coker, Francis W., *Recent Political Thought* (New York, 1934), Chaps. 9, 18.

FROMM: ORIGINAL WORKS

Escape from Freedom (New York, 1941).

The Sane Society (New York, 1955).

FROMM: SECONDARY WORKS

Schaar, John H., *Escape from Authority: The Perspectives of Erich Fromm* (New York, 1961).

MAYO: ORIGINAL WORKS

The Human Problems of an Industrial Civilization (New York, 1933).

The Social Problems of an Industrial Civilization (Cambridge, 1945).

The Political Problems of an Industrial Civilization (Cambridge, 1947).

MAYO: SECONDARY WORKS

Bell, Daniel, "Work and Its Discontents," in *The End of Ideology: On the Exhaustion of Political Ideas in the Fifties* (New York, 1962), Chap. 11.

Bendix, Reinhard, *Work and Authority in Industry* (New York, 1956), Chap. 5.

* Excerpts in *Sources in Twentieth-Century Political Thought.*

V. THE ORGANIZATION AS END

So stylistically different are the works of V. I. Lenin (1870–1924) and Max Weber (1864–1920), so dissimilar were their vocations, that it is hard to see how the achievements of these contemporaries can be mutually complementary. There certainly was a profound distinction: whereas Lenin sought to impose order in practice, Weber remained satisfied to understand it in theory. This difference remains crucial even though Lenin had an irrepressible urge to theorize and Weber clearly yearned for power and action. Still, a unifying theme is undeniable. Fundamentally both were preoccupied by the need to manage and organize intractable human elements; both were troubled by spontaneity, irrationality, and random behavior, one as maker of history and the other as its student. Both reacted against disorder—Lenin in the great hope of disciplining the mass of men so that they might be led to a new and indescribable utopian regime of freedom, and Weber in the knowledge that freedom was a thing of the past and regimentation the fated wave of the future.

The Apotheosis of Strategy: V. I. Lenin

Lenin was pre-eminently a man of action. When in exile, he conspired; when on the sidelines, he fought to get to the center; when not commanding and organizing, he schemed how best to do so. His writings—memos, polemics, tracts, letters, platforms—were fully dedicated to revolutionary action. Yet to recognize that the body of his thought was but the by-product of his deeds is not to dismiss his theories.

Revolutions, as Trotsky once observed, are always verbose. The stretches of inaction, waiting, and exile provide ample time for debating options, sharpening doctrines, and refining plans. The basic decision to overthrow an old order having been made, there is always a surfeit of time to discuss its implementation. Hence arguments are spun out to logical conclusions with the result that specific problems tend to be seen in the light of extreme possibilities. As there is time for discussion there is time to reflect on the ethics of violence. Yet such reflection is not so much on alternative ends as on alternative means. The intellectual wrangling and infighting merely concern techniques and their justification. The revolutionaries direct their language and the traditional institutions of politics—conferences, congresses, debates, resolutions—toward organizational alternatives; they turn them toward logistics and tactics, toward social engineering. The resulting political theory is necessarily practical. It is oriented toward specific kinds of action, its promises and limits.

But however much Lenin's strategy was adapted to the needs of the hour and the opportunities of the moment, it always took its bearings by a theoretical position. Opportunistic as Lenin's conduct was, it found its rationalization in the Marxist theory of history as a dialectical movement from capitalism through socialism to communism. And Lenin embraced the theory in its totality. On a verbal level he operated within it throughout his life. Whatever he did, he did in the name of Marxism. Whatever the substance of his beliefs, he professed to accept (1) Marx's doctrine of history as conflict between classes, culminating in the triumph of a classless society; (2) Marx's interpretation of the state, including the liberal-constitutional state, as the instrument of the dominant class; and (3) Marx's view of modern industry under capitalist auspices as necessarily exploitative, as insufferably humiliating and degrading to man. He considered the theory of Marx as being at once true and powerful, powerful precisely because true. Rather than to probe its foundations, Lenin put it to the only test which the theory itself accepted as validating belief: its practical efficacy. The proof of its validity could only be furnished pragmatically, by its success as an intellectual weapon in the quest for power. Appealing to it as he acted—and Lenin's appeal to Marxism was as obstinate as it was tedious—he succeeded in vindicating it precisely to the extent that his tactics led to victory. If Lenin thus added to Marxist theory, it was insofar as he contributed tactics—not new moral insights or ideals.

To understand what has aptly been called Lenin's operational code, it is necessary to recollect Marx's radical critique of the prevailing political order. In the theory of liberal-democratic constitutionalism, the state rests on a consensus which makes the results of negotiation among conflicting interests tolerable to all. Reliance on the techniques of politics, on election, debate, and compromise, makes it possible to avoid violence for the resolution of conflict. A degree of well-being, or at least prospective well-being, promotes that spirit of forbearance toward one's opponents which makes the system workable. This theory conceals a social reality which, according to Marx, must outrage the morally sensitive. In point of fact, the liberal state is but a *special* group representing and serving but a *special* interest.

Reiterating this view, Lenin saw the state as tool of the ruling class and hence as necessarily unrepresentative of the various conflicting interests in society. Whatever the pretense, these interests are beyond reconciliation. Their economic bases differ, making some in society the exploiters and others the exploited. Since there is an objectively existing division in society, all merely political efforts to bridge it are superficial. In fact the politics of a liberal society is necessarily repressive, and the "legality" of the liberal state is but an attempted legalization of its repressive measures. To these measures general public assent is gained by social and economic pressure. Politics is thus but a façade behind which the really consequential economic decisions are made by the class in power in its own interest, and in opposition to the interests of the unrepresented proletariat.

Lenin's opposition to the liberal state was not, however, merely based on its unrepresentative character. To put an end to conflicts of interests—that is, to bring history as a conflict between classes to its conclusion—it will not do simply to give the proletariat a voice in decision making. From the Marxist perspective the politics of liberalism is an essentially futile activity. Within the liberal political order the existing constellation of economic interests is always assumed to be rational and is, at most, subjected to periodic rearrangements. There is a kind of superficial shifting about, a periodic maneuvering for political office, but the status quo is not thereby meaningfully altered. As Lenin put it, "To decide once every few years which member of the ruling class is to oppress and suppress the people in parliament— there you have the real essence of bourgeois parliamentarianism." Attempts at reform from within would thus not really change anything. But such reform would be pointless in an even more fundamental way: the resolutions of conflict in parliamentary assemblies are never final. Indeed, the entire system is contrived so as to keep conflict in suspense;

hence it never puts an end to repression. Its laws are discriminatory, and participation in the decision-making process is participation in discriminatory action. To put an end to discrimination, to achieve the true, uncompromised, final emancipation of all discriminated-against interests, the entire political order must be repudiated. The state will therefore have to be seized and converted into a liberating instrument.

To act on this analysis means stripping away the political façade and ruthlessly dealing with the social and economic interests operating behind it. Just as the liberal state is the repressive dictatorship of the bourgeoisie, so the forces of freedom will have to become the repressive dictatorship of the proletariat. There is no shirking the mandate of history. The forces of freedom will have to capture the command posts and communication centers, and they will have to proceed to eradicate the last vestiges of traditional politics.

Under the new dictatorship it will then become possible for the state gradually to move out of politics into conflict-free administration. State officials will be reduced to the role of simply carrying out instructions as "moderately paid 'managers.'" This in itself, according to Lenin, will lead "to the gradual 'withering away' of all bureaucracy, to the gradual creation of a new order . . . in which the more simplified functions of control and accounting will be performed by each in turn, will then become a habit, and will finally die out as *special* functions of a special stratum of the population." By the transcendence of specialization man will regain his wholeness, his integrity. As class antagonisms are neutralized (to use language which fails to evoke the reality of expropriations, labor camps, terror, and purges) the state will become truly representative. And at that moment it will automatically cease to be repressive. Its laws will cease to be discriminatory insofar as they will sustain the existing society in its entirety, sustain it as an undivided, harmonious unit. Whatever the new nonpolitical "state" will then do will necessarily be liberating. Its actions will have a merely administrative character, implementing not special interests but the general consensus. In the precommunist state, governmental laws are obeyed from sheer habit, or because the people know that compliance can be coerced. The people need not have knowledge of the soundness of the laws, only of the penalty for disobedience. In the new communist society, however, administrative regulations will be obeyed because the people know that compliance is reasonable; they will obey freely because they know the regulation is sound. As legally sanctioned exploitation has been eliminated, as state power to subject one part of society to the interests of another has become inconceivable, the members of society will quite simply "observe the necessary rules of life in common"; they will "observe the elementary conditions of social existence," and they will do so "without force, without compulsion, without subordination, without the *special apparatus* for compulsion which is called the state." To be sure, individual men will inevitably commit "excesses." But this will be spontaneously taken care of—not by political agencies but by the people themselves, who will act as naturally as anyone who simply "parts a pair of combatants or does not allow a woman to be outraged." With unforced innocence, the people will live up to Engel's celebrated vision:

> In a communist society, where nobody has one exclusive sphere of activity but each can become accomplished in any branch he wishes, society regulates the general production and thus makes it possible for me to do one thing today and another tomorrow, to hunt in the morning, fish in the afternoon, rear cattle in the evening, criticize after dinner, just as I have a mind, without ever becoming hunter, fisherman, shepherd, or critic.

The rest is tactics. Until total freedom is obtained, total control is imperative. There can be no room for politics to negotiate chunks of freedom in exchange for moderate restriction. It is all or nothing.

How was the great promise of natural freedom to be fulfilled? It was always perfectly evident that the overthrow of the traditional political order would not simply come about by itself. Yet beyond the counsel to engage in revolutionary action wherever economic conditions seemed most ripe, there was nothing in Marxist thought that prescribed what, specifically, had to be done. On the whole, Marx was close enough to the Enlightenment to trust the process of history, confident that history would progressively "unfold." Of course, Marx had known that this could not happen spontaneously: men would have to exercise their free will. Still, in this blend of determinism and volition there was nothing paradoxical. Marx assumed that when economic conditions were such as to clarify in the minds of men what their lives amounted to, they would freely decide to act. Determinism and freedom were thus altogether compatible. Theoretical imperatives and practical action were joined.

But as Lenin sought to put theory into operation, he drove a wedge into the Marxist system. Whereas both Marx and Engels had believed in the inseparable unity of theory and practice, Lenin was perfectly willing to let theory take precedence: after all, *he* knew the theory was sound. Giving theory an independent status as guide to action, he would not have to wait on the sidelines until economic changes and technological development had educated the immature urban working class. He would not have to wait for unmistakable signs of the rationality of the masses. The masses would not need to gain the full theoretical knowledge which, according to Marx, comes at that precise moment when its conversion into action is automatic. And because they could be animated before they quite knew what they were doing, even underdeveloped countries (such as Russia) and unenlightened social groups (such as the peasantry) could be impelled toward revolution.

Lenin's impatience, then, led him to sever Marx's deterministic theory of history from its specific practical provisions. His belief in the rightness of the revolutionary ideal drove him to act in its behalf. But far more than his idealism was involved, for his sharp sense of practicality compelled him to acknowledge that history was not working out as predicted. Experience deprived him of his trust in the natural process of history. When history is not consciously directed toward its predetermined end, so Lenin recognized, all sorts of compromises are made and the attainment of the end is indefinitely postponed. Lenin perceived that the masses would actually be satisfied by halfway gains. They would readily succumb to the economic temptations held out to them by an advancing industrialism organized under a capitalist economy. Instead of triumphing over the middle class, they would join it. Instead of retaining their consciousness as exploited workers, they would acquire trade-union consciousness, settling for higher wages, more leisure, and better working conditions. Losing sight of the revolutionary purpose, they would conclude an armistice with the parliamentary state of bourgeois democracy. Seduced by material comforts, they would be cheated of real victory.

Once such facts were recognized, Marxist theory was put in jeopardy. Marx, it should be recalled, had postulated that economic changes would create such miserable conditions that the masses would ultimately gain rational insight into their true interests. He held this was most likely where capitalism was at its most mature, hence at its most oppressive. He therefore believed that the industrial proletariat, not the peasantry, had to be the vanguard of the revolution. Lenin, however, saw that the industrial proletariat simply did not possess that knowledge of its conditions which would force it to perceive the consequences of a compromise with capitalism. It was not as rational as Marxist theory postulated.

In closer touch with events, more realistically attuned to them, Lenin thus effected a profound revision of Marxist theory. He shattered its unity. For Marx, material conditions made the masses intellectually aware of their true interests. Experience gave them knowledge; economics determined their consciousness. But Lenin could have no such illusions.

Not only did the industrial proletariat lose sight of ultimate goals; it was also irrational in its pursuit of immediate objectives. Even its revolutionary fervor tended to be impulsive, expressing instinctual feelings rather than a clear vision of historical necessities.

Yet Lenin did not permit himself to be embarrassed by the irrationality of the masses. On the contrary, he prepared to welcome the raw human energy which they provided. Moreover, he could now enlist the peasant, whom Marx's theory had to discriminate against. The Revolution of 1905 had taught Lenin how useful the peasantry could be. He therefore incorporated it in the mass base he knew to be essential for the success of a revolution.

The practical problem became that of channeling the spontaneous revolutionary outbreaks of the masses. For Lenin this required not the elimination of irrationality but its rational control by a skilled and enlightened governing elite. If the masses were unclear about their mission, if they failed to grasp their true interest, an organizational apparatus would have to act as an educational force. It would be the task of the organization to protect the masses against their short-range interests. Thus it was no longer material conditions which would make the masses aware of their long-range interests. It was the Party. And the Party itself would consist of an elite driven not by economic need, determined not by economic, material conditions, but by its understanding of the ultimate imperatives of history, its devotion to the ideal of the stateless society, and its recognition of the need to overthrow the political order. While there could be no dictatorship *of* the proletariat, there might be one *for* it.

For Lenin, this implicit case for elitism had a double utility. Not only did it slough off the economic determinism of Marx and thereby free Lenin's hands for political warfare; it also eliminated the sentimental notion that an unguided proletariat would somehow display the heroic

qualities which in themselves would insure victory. In his
polemic against Karl Kautsky, who defended a socialism at
peace with the traditional political order, Lenin candidly
saw the masses as "downtrodden, backward, ignorant, in-
timidated and disunited." He deprived Marxism of its romantic image of a heroic proletariat, an image even Sorel had
cherished. The movement toward total freedom, in Lenin's
view, would not spontaneously follow from the removal of
bourgeois road blocks. The direct emancipation of the
masses, in their present ignorant condition, would only
prove to be disastrous. Because the masses were simply not
made of the stuff Marxists permitted themselves to assume,
a new discipline would have to be substituted for the old one.

If Lenin had doubts about the masses, this implied his
unacknowledged distrust of the notion that the economy
was the instrument shaping their mentality. Having lost
confidence in the economy as the governing force, Lenin
was compelled to replace it with the Party. The Party—more
precisely those who controlled it—would have to be the
governors of men. But once Lenin had abandoned the economic determinism of Marx, he was left with nothing but
the unchecked drive for power on the part of the new
rulers. Ignoring determinism on the one hand, and repudiating the checks imposed by liberal constitutionalism on the
other, Lenin made room for the most thoroughgoing control
of society. Autocratic oligarchical rule could become legitimate because it alone was left to usher in a realm of total
freedom. Since the consciousness of the proletariat could not
be trusted to lead it to the proper kind of behavior, the
Party had to assume leadership. It had to have the power
to defend the revolutionary enterprise against all opposition
—the more ruthlessly the more reasonable the guise in which
opposition appeared. It had to discipline and channel the
energy of the masses and, at the same time, be the very
incarnation of rationality. Where individual action remained
irrational and spontaneous, organizational action would be

responsible. The Party was obliged to control the irrationality of individuals manifest in their willful, erratic behavior.
Its very structure—a well-articulated division of complementary functions performed by specialists—had to reflect
its rationality. And its capacity to manipulate the ever
maturing society outside was to guarantee the continued
rationality of the historical process.

Vis-à-vis the external world, the leaders of the Party had
to practice the art of statesmanship. Self-disciplined, they
had to retain a flexible, nondoctrinaire attitude toward the
world, a willingness to do what one could under given conditions. No laws of history were available to decide specific
cases; experience could provide no abstract precepts. "Every
period," so Hegel wrote and Lenin explicitly agreed, "has
such peculiar circumstances, is such an individual state, that
decisions will have to be made in it and out of it." Marxist
theory provided a coherent intellectual scheme of historical
development, but no timetable. Nor could it teach those
imponderable political skills which conservative political
theory has always found endearing. The new statesman must
therefore keep himself from becoming intoxicated by the
abstract rationalism of either the Right or the Left. Attuned
to social reality, he must be able to invigorate majorities—
and yet be ready to follow them. The masses may well be
erratic, but this cannot justify deserting them when they
become restless and express their impulsiveness. On the
contrary, the statesman will stay in touch, balancing the
strength of their impulses against what he knows must be
done. His will be a politics of improvisation and flexibility,
not of doctrine. His art will consist of maintaining social
cohesion so as to maximize performance. It will consist of
requiring no more than can be delivered—but demanding
everything that can be delivered. Thus while it may be
necessary to submit to public opinion and hold the reins
loosely, prudent leadership will tolerate what freedom it
must, but no more than necessary.

Under modern conditions of mechanized industry and mechanized warfare, such statesmanship was bound to be ineffective without a bureaucratic apparatus to provide intelligence for decisions and insure their efficient implementation. If a large-scale political experiment was to succeed, authority and work would have to be coordinated on a hierarchical chain-of-command basis. Functional specialization would be unavoidable for the creation of a new economy. If only to maintain the necessary secrecy, the organization would have to remain strictly limited in its membership; it would have to recruit its own leaders. Control over the complex, far-flung activities of the state required a tightly disciplined group of reliable, tested, and hardened professionals. As Lenin made clear in *What Is to Be Done?* (1902), merely to launch the revolution they had to be specialists in revolution, and in nothing else. It was necessary for them to be skilled in revolutionary action and to be fully devoted to it. As became apparent after 1917, theirs was to be a loyalty to function, to the job well done. Their organization would subsequently coordinate and integrate them; whatever they lacked in comprehensive vision, their organization would supply. Through the rationality and scope of the organization it would be possible to overcome individual limitations and thereby to master a hostile environment, to gain power over man and nature.

In Lenin's eyes the Party was essentially a power apparatus so structured as to facilitate control. Its sole concern was to assure that the most appropriate means would be used to attain the predetermined end. The end being fixed by the dialectic of history, the Party would be preoccupied by the means. It would suffer from no distractions and give itself fully to the task at hand: to implement decisions promptly and efficiently. It could aim exclusively at domination, the measure of its success being precisely its capacity for liquidating opposition and creating consensus. As it eliminated conflict and established peace it would automatically bring the communist ideal of the harmonious society to fruition.

To sum up: Lenin's political theory was a strategy for action based on his estimate of concrete opportunities for the seizing and holding of power. It was based on no model laid in heaven. Lenin did not intend to build the new society, as he put it, "on the basis of truth, justice, or the equalization of labor, etc." Such ideals, he wrote, are entirely subjective, whereas his are founded in objectivity:

> My ideals concerning the structure of the new Russia will be nonchimeric only when they express the interests of an actually existing class whom the conditions of life compel to act in a definite direction. By adopting this point of view . . . I am by no means justifying what actually exists; on the contrary, I am pointing out in this very actuality the deepest (though at first unseen) sources and forces of its transformation.

The justification for the Leninist strategy was the belief in the certain validity of the interest of the proletariat—not its generally expressed interest, for gearing strategy to this would result in mere conservatism, but its "deepest" and barely visible interest. It is this ideal interest which Lenin took it upon himself to discern; for him it constituted the only authentic morality, the only legitimate basis for action. "We deny all morality taken from superhuman or non-class conceptions," he wrote in 1920. "We say that our morality is wholly subordinated to the interests of the class struggle of the proletariat. We deduce our morality from the facts and needs of the class struggle of the proletariat." What had to be done was prescribed by the process of history, history rightly understood. History, interpreted by those who have the power to make their interpretation prevail, demands action. And it is action which in turn validates the interpretation of history. Victory in revolutionary activity thus certifies the theory; success provides the credentials for the activist.

But the activist, Lenin realized, could not be the man of the masses. Lenin's practical realism—a realism which lies also at the core of the contemporary theory of constitutionalism—had made him pessimistic about the rationality of the mass of men. At the same time, it had also led him to see that their irrationality could be redeemed by the rationality of the organization. Thus mass interests could in fact be entrusted to the organization. Confronted by the obtuseness and willfulness of ordinary men, and knowing what constituted their salvation, Lenin was led to elitism. To save the Marxist vision of autonomous men, to assure it of survival in the face of modern technology, he established and vindicated an autonomous organization.[1]

An elite of professional revolutionaries, so Lenin hoped, would protect the true interests of the working class. It would consist of educated members of the bourgeoisie who had a comprehensive view of the imperatives and final objectives of history. Trained intellectually, they would be able to perceive the long-range results of the practices of liberal-democratic regimes. They had the time and inclination to see consequences to which the masses were blind. Committed to ideals, they would remain revolutionaries, whereas the worker would be seduced by material benefits. The clarity of their views was due to their rational understanding of the end of the process of history; it was not determined by economic forces. Thus Lenin reintroduced the very idealism banished by Marx, though he confined it to the ruling elite. The worker, Lenin was compelled to say, is driven by experience—by the hard experience of the as-

---

1. The sequel is instructive: it was finally to become possible to give even ideas autonomy, though they were the ideas of the Party. In *Marxism and Linguistics* (1950), Stalin was to declare that the new ideological superstructure "becomes an exceedingly active force, actively assisting its [economic] basis to take shape and consolidate itself and doing everything it can to help the new system finish off and eliminate the old basis and the old classes."

sembly line, of the coal mine, of poverty. The elite, however, is oriented by ideals. It is detached from the economic order, operating independently.

Having been compelled to make a case for organized inequality of power, having found it indispensable to concentrate rationality and power at the top, Lenin did not proceed to ask whether the new elite might seek to achieve ends of its own, exercising power not in behalf of the overriding revolutionary purpose but simply in behalf of the organization. He did find it necessary to argue for the ideological indoctrination of the new masters, but provided no independent source of power for the indoctrinators. Thus he simply failed to consider what might occur when a well-armed governing body, checked only by its own sense of right, operates with genuine detachment.

Lenin, in any event, had detached the ruling group from economic conditions—from those pecuniary interests which channel the energy of capitalists. At the same time, he had not, of course, reattached it to the institutional forms of liberal constitutionalism—to those devices which force politicians to be sensitive to the will of their constituents. He thus liberated the Party. The Party could become self-seeking without either economic or political restraints. In an underdeveloped part of the world, operating on a populace deemed less than rational, it could exercise power solely to maintain its own viability. It could systematically aim at survival and consolidation, securing its place as a self-replenishing and self-authenticating autocracy. As Trotsky perceived in 1904, in Lenin's model for leadership "the organization of the Party takes the place of the Party itself; the Central Committee takes the place of the organization; and finally the dictator takes the place of the Central Committee."

If these trends were ultimately to be softened and checked, this could be done only on the ground that the new totalitarianism did not really facilitate organizational survival, that constitutional procedures had to be accepted because dictatorship threatened to calcify the military, scientific, and industrial establishments. Constitutionalism was demanded not by the imperatives of justice but by the imperatives of survival. And about the conditions of survival, one requires not the testimony of political philosophers but of the specialists in group solidarity and organizational viability—the new men of social science.

The Theory of Bureaucracy:
Max Weber

By arriving speculatively at conclusions to which Lenin
was driven in practice, Max Weber spelled out some of the
purely logical implications of elite rule which remained un-
elaborated in political practice. Encumbered neither by
Marxist rhetoric nor by practical considerations, Weber provided an ideology of modern organization in its purest form.
Where Lenin's polemics were blunt and personal, Weber's
writings were formal, dry, and detached. Engaging as his
work is for sociologists, it barely enlists our interest as purposive, political beings. By all appearances, it was above the
battle. But this aloofness nonetheless gave his analyses an
authenticity which remains impressive. Free from abuse and
invective, his abstract scholarly studies cannot readily be
discounted as subjective. They reveal his incredible intellectual range and help account for the universality of his
impact on modern sociology.

At the same time, they do not altogether conceal his
position. For while he depicted the relentless standardization
inherent in modern life—reacting to mechanization in the
late-romantic mood of Spengler, Jaspers, and Marcel—he
repeatedly revealed a nostalgia all the more poignant for
being controlled. His model of mankind's future, his prophecy that we are all becoming integrated components of an
ultimately global social apparatus, implied a past that all
decent men would feel compelled to honor, even though it
was no longer possible to regard it as a rational alternative.
Thus while he outlined the future with calm detachment,

he did not lack moral perception. Scientific objectivity did not preclude moral commitment. It is the quality of this commitment, and not Weber's descriptive sociology, which ultimately engages the student of political philosophy.

Man's autonomy was threatened, Weber found reason to believe, by the developments of mass technology and mass society. These developments were so comprehensive as to overshadow all ideological conflicts between agrarianism and urbanism, between welfare state and laissez faire, between equality and hierarchy, between Left and Right. Under changing technological conditions, the only really relevant problem became that of organizing one's life in the most rational manner. And this question is necessarily one of techniques, of efficient and economical administration. To raise it is to pose the issue of how to bring order and rationality to our mismanaged existence. Our new problems, in a word, are managerial.

In Weber's eyes it could make no difference whether one liked the new order or not. Opposing it would be opposing the momentum of history. Because of our determination to harness machine power, because of our dedication to large-scale industrialism, bureaucratic management has become inescapable. It is an organizational necessity, demanded by the very logic of endless production for limitless consumption. The rationalization of production *means* (1) the standardization of work tasks, (2) the scheduling of the rhythms of work, (3) the division of labor, and (4) the physical meshing of men and machines. The use of machines in the mass production of uniform goods requires both division of the work process and continuous control over the separate tasks created. It requires the fragmentation of labor under integrated control. To remain free from disturbances and friction, the industrial system neutralizes all manifestations of idiosyncrasy and entrepreneurship. It reconciles conflicts. It transforms individual irrationality into over-all rationality. And to enable it to do so over a period of time and over a large geographical area demands a hierarchically structured control apparatus. So as to integrate variously skilled work teams at the appropriate moment and place in the productive process, a management capable of making the plans and the schedules must impose a work discipline. Those who perform these functions constitute a hierarchy of specialists. Such a regime entails inequalities, but these are based not on inherited status or inherited property but on competence duly certified by educational institutions designed to be of service.

There can be no question about the superiority of this new social system over all others. It is only natural to assume, as Weber did, that "the whole pattern of everyday life is cut to fit this framework. For bureaucratic administration is, . . . always from a formal technical point of view, the most rational type." It has advanced, Weber wrote, precisely because of its "technical superiority over any other form of organization":

> Precision, speed, unambiguity, knowledge of the files, continuity, discretion, unity, strict subordination, reduction of friction and of material and personal costs—these are raised to the optimum point in the strictly bureaucratic administration in its monocratic form. As compared with collegiate, honorific, and avocational forms of administration, trained bureaucracy is superior on all these points.

What unites all the human members of the system is their joint recognition of its needs—not any loyalty to a transcending ideal. They maintain the system not for self-aggrandizement, personal wealth, or private pleasure. On the contrary, they are dedicated to the system, loyally contributing to its maintenance. The ultimate criterion for the decisions they make is the successful perpetuation of the productive process. The policy makers up and down the hierarchy are most interested in the self-sufficient goods of efficiency and economy. They are concerned with means and techniques. Their power, in other words, is validated by their ability to maintain smooth operations. Should they fail, they do not reconsider the validity of the ends but the utility

of the means. Thus those who formulate the rules for the
new industrial society are as indifferent to ends as those
who obey them. For the managers as well as the managed,
all ends infinitely recede. Every concern with ends, even
personal gratification, becomes a kind of stalling, an irrational diversion from the need to keep the system going.

What is efficient, functional, or rational is determined by
the system as an autonomous force. Rationality is defined in
reference to organizational needs. The organization itself
provides the standard of rationality, and men are led to
conform to it. Thus just as rationality inhered in the Party
for Lenin so it inhered in industrial organization for Weber.

It is not hard to see why this approach discards politics
as an instrument for containing conflict. Whatever conflicts
of interests may appear in the new society, they can be
resolved objectively, for they are *technical* ones about
appropriate means. The over-all end being fixed, all seemingly political questions are seen to be really administrative
ones. Man's alienation from politics is perfectly explicable:
the age of ideological controversy has come to an end. The
fundamental problem of man's place in the social order is
scientifically settled by those who master the complexities
of modern existence. The individual's competence—measured by his ability to serve the productive process—fixes his
place in the hierarchy. And this place is rationally deter-
minable by testing his actual or potential performance. To
administer such tests and allocate the work force requires
not politicians but a bureaucratic elite skilled in the tasks of
planning, scheduling, and administration. The function of
leadership is not to introduce new goals but to coordinate
and adjust.[1] The end being set, politics truly is administra-

1. Where Weber saw personal drive and magnetism being gradually
routinized, Joseph A. Schumpeter was to see the erosion of the risk-taking
spirit of the capitalist entrepreneur. In his *Capitalism, Socialism, and
Democracy* (1942) he concluded that we would inevitably meet every crisis
by further rationalization, consolidation, and socialization. Like Weber, he
was certain that individualism, competition, and eccentricity are doomed.

tion, and statesmanship is the application of administrative science.

This organizational model—this grandiose metaphor—emerged when Weber asked what, ideally, is likely to follow the unimpeded rationalization of the work process. The fact that such a model conforms to no historical state, that it is but an idealized projection, did not deprive it of formidable analytical utility. Because it pushed trends to unrealized conclusions, it actually made Weber aware of new relationships and showed up the superficiality of orthodox distinctions.

Weber's approach made clear that capitalism and socialism, whatever may be the appearance, are not antithetical. Capitalism was an arrangement for utilizing scarce natural and human resources in the most efficient manner. As Weber analyzed capitalism, it was in its very essence a rationalistic system. It stressed the need to calculate the consequences of action, to take them quite literally into account. It made the countless commercial transactions of suppliers, producers, distributors, and consumers coherent and orderly. To master its intricacies, and Weber saw this as clearly as Lenin,[2] required specialists—technicians in finance, law, and management. And specialization of course implied the hierarchical division of labor into superiors and subordinates.

There was finally no reason to believe that our public life would be different when organized under the label of socialism. Weber saw bureaucratic behavior as generally characteristic of modern society, not as the peculiar attribute of any special system. The central rationality, standardization,

2. Lenin consistently respected the organizational acumen of the members of the bourgeoisie: they had "connections, habits of organization and management, knowledge of all the 'secrets' (customs, methods, means and possibilities) of management. . . ." The revolutionary elite, he wrote, would have to learn about the intricacies of administering a complex industrial society. Communist control of the state would then require capturing not the capitalist outposts but merely the strategic center.

and precision promoted by capitalism would remain quite unaffected by socialist aspirations. Even more: if socialists desired to utilize natural and human resources in the most efficient manner, they would in fact have to carry the rationalist premise of capitalism forward. For they criticized capitalism precisely because it "wasted" resources. Did they not see it as beset by "internal contradictions," by "class antagonisms?" What socialists really wanted, so it appeared, was a refined form of capitalism, a society whose internal harmony would make it, in psychological terms, more "human" and "sane" than the capitalist order. Such a society would indeed not need to be governed; it would only need to be managed. Making explicit what was implicit in capitalism, the socialist order would be the very embodiment of rationality.

If socialism would merely make explicit what was already implicit in capitalism, the difference between the two could be only formal, not substantive. From the point of view of the individual worker there could be no meaningful difference under socialism: the units of production would still be bureaucratically organized. One might institute a system which, to use the language of Pareto, ensured the circulation of elites. But one could not eliminate elites; one could not free oneself from government by an oligarchy of the competent.[3] In any case, no revolution would unshackle the working class. All talk of revolutionary overthrow of the existing order was thus futile and sentimental. If we seek to realize our ideals under modern technological conditions, the substance of our ideals will not matter: our means will certainly pervert our ends. We may endeavor to equalize the burdens of life or to push toward some millennial realm of absolute freedom. But the more concerted our drive—that is, the more rational, the better planned, the more efficiently

---

3. Weber's case was elaborately reinforced in Robert Michels' *Political Parties: A Sociological Study of the Oligarchical Tendencies of Modern Democracy* (1915).

executed—the greater the likelihood of our disenchantment. In place of equality and freedom, we will have introduced hierarchy and constraint. In the light of this analysis, political action advancing ideals becomes either naive or demagogic, for whatever we do will ineluctably move us toward a more tightly meshed economic and industrial organization.

As Weber conceptualized the new rationality, as he projected its implications and ramifications, he clarified its gains and losses. With restrained irony he showed what price we would have to pay for it. This did not mean, of course, that he had any more affection for the future state than Tocqueville had for equality and its attendant resentments, or than Freud had for civilization and its attendant "discontents." Men who are unable to escape history need not feel moved to cheer it. Depicting the new system, Weber in fact betrayed his own liberal instincts for all that it displaced: improvisation, spontaneity, entrepreneurial talent. His elucidation of the crystal palace of bureaucracy, it is clear, was inspired by his passionate attachment to nonbureaucratic order. His very preference for freedom made him the thoroughgoing analyst of organizational imperatives.

There can be no question where Weber himself stood in the battle between individual freedom and organized rationality. In 1906 he wrote that the modern industrialized quest for material satisfaction was incompatible with democracy and individualism. It would lead to a "benevolent feudalism," to "welfare institutions":

> Then man will move into the house of servitude. At the same time, the increasing complexity of the economy, the partial governmentalization of economic activities, the territorial expansion of the population—these processes create ever-new work for the clerks, an ever-new specialization of functions, and expert vocational training and administration. All this means caste.

Those American workers who were against the Civil Service Reform knew what they were about. They wished

to be governed by parvenues of doubtful morals rather than
by a certified caste of mandarins. But their protest was in
vain.[4]

But his distaste for routine, standardization, and regu-
larity no more kept him from filling in the details of his
bureaucratic model than it kept George Orwell, for example,
from giving a full (and equally ambivalent) account of the
despotism of *1984*. In view of Weber's theory of knowledge,
this was no wonder. He considered it impossible to provide
an analytical blueprint for a social group without first identifying with it. To understand society, he insisted, we have to
reject the detached view of the physical scientist and see
our subject matter sympathetically from within, much as the
novelist does. We must share the experience of the society
we seek to understand, be genuinely taken in by it, be won
by its ideology. Only then can we push the prevailing possibilities to their logical conclusion.

Yet this surrender to one's subject matter was never to
be unconditional. One participated with mental reservations,
that is, with a sustained commitment to a methodological
relativism. The social scientist, Weber argued, had always
to maintain his ties with the discipline of social science.
Failing this, he would lose himself in the morass of history,
surrendering to the impurities of actual politics. And this
surrender was disreputable because the stuff of history and
politics was obviously made of the very opposite of all ideals:

4. Speaking at a meeting of an academic political club in 1909, Weber
revealed his personal position with equal clarity. "It is horrible to think,"
he said, "that the world could one day be filled with nothing but those
little cogs, little men clinging to little jobs and striving towards bigger
ones. . . . This passion for bureaucracy . . . is enough to drive one to despair.
It is as if in politics . . . we were deliberately to become men who need
order and nothing but order, who become nervous and cowardly if for
one moment this order wavers, and helpless if they are torn away from
their total incorporation in it. That the world should know no men but
these: it is in such an evolution that we are already caught up, and the
great question is therefore not how we can promote and hasten it, but
what can we oppose to this machinery so as to keep a portion of mankind
free from this parcelling-out of the soul, from this supreme mastery of the
bureaucratic way of life."

history showed man forever struggling for power, compromising and defiling his ultimate values. Nor was it proper to consider the process of compromise itself, that is, politics, as an acceptable ideal—though it necessarily was the raw material of sociology. To understand man's worldly affairs, then, required both perceiving the impurity of politics from the point of view of the participants *and* returning to the domain of social science. Thus it would be possible, Weber believed, to become implicated with one's subject matter and yet maintain objectivity. The student of society would not have to favor any specific kind of social order, whether it be equalitarian or hierarchical. As scientist he could suspend judgment, his sole concern being the scientific task of projecting probabilities, of constructing a plausible conceptual model of a social system. He would thereby display his love not for any substantive regime but merely for the procedure which made him temporarily loyal to the object of study and permanently loyal to his scientific discipline.

Requiring moral neutrality within the field of science, Weber imposed no moral imperative outside of it. The individual remained wholly free to choose, as Weber himself stubbornly chose to resist the march of history. Thus the citizen or statesman was not constrained by the historical processes social scientists had revealed. He might well feel moved to attempt more than what appears possible. Conceivably, if graced by the exceptional leadership gifts Weber called "charisma," he might break through and achieve a kind of triumph. And should he be denied victory, he would yet have preserved his moral integrity. In any case, success at the price of integrity would not be worth having.

Weber himself was certainly prepared to defy what he, as social scientist, had characterized as inexorably fated. He was quite prepared to consider playing the role of the romantic hero alone against the system.[5] He clearly understood

5. How far Weber carried his romantic individualism is shown by the advice he gave the Kaiser when, in 1918, the armies of imperial Germany were doomed. Weber urged him, just before his flight to neutral Holland,

the pressures of organized life and accepted them as part of the necessary order. Moreover, he envisaged no rational, objective alternative. But still this did not mean that he, as individual, had to submit. There remained the utterly personal, subjective alternative: one could stand up to the system. As an act of will, one might make one's own "value judgment," disdaining both a God-given moral order and the logic of history.

Thus Weber defiantly shielded individual value judgments against the onslaught of organized rationality. For him, private opinions became moral absolutes beyond mediation, beyond reduction to politics. One had simply to embrace and assume responsibility for them. Placing them out of reach of all discussion, they acquired dignity by their very irrationality. After all, they—and nothing else—revealed the human impulse. And they were authenticated by the integrity and courage of the individuals who affirmed them. They merited all the more respect insofar as they were asserted in opposition to all that which reason, embodied in positive science, showed to be so obviously imperative. At the very center of his position, then, Weber preserved a realm of irreducible personal freedom. He thus upheld a moral order in which individuality counts for something.

But he knew that he did so in a void: having placed all reason on the side of history, there was no reason left to sustain him. As he chose, he chose wholly on his own, unsupported and unreduced by the tradition of rational discourse. Separating scientific objectivity from personal value judgments, he left himself with no rationality in the field of public action. To be sure, public action could continue to be rationalized. Moreover, it could be understood scientifically: science could lead us to understand under what conditions we are likely to make particular decisions; it could tell us how "realistic" our choices are—how likely their

---

to go to the head of his troops and seek death in no-man's land. And with General Ludendorf he argued in all seriousness that, for the sake of the honor of Germany, the general ought to offer himself as a war criminal.

attainment may be in practice. But the authority of reason could reach no further.

Weber's pessimistic outlook was premised on the proposition that modern history in the form of technology and bureaucracy would run its course. He made his prognosis after having asked toward what kind of state prevailing technological and organizational tendencies are likely to lead when undeflected by public policy, when left to follow their natural momentum. If he was driven to despair, this was because he rigorously excluded the possibility of the *use* of technology and bureaucracy for purposes external to them— that is, for humanistic purposes politically formulated. He saw bureaucracy absorbing the whole of life: politicians would *naturally* be turned into administrators, private law into public law, entrepreneurs into coordinators, private enterprise into public projects. He arrived at these sweeping conclusions by employing the familiar method of isolating one set of factors in the welter of available ones and inquiring which way they tended. Just as Tocqueville had speculated in the early part of the nineteenth century about what was likely to happen when equalitarian tendencies found their fulfillment, Weber asked what would happen if the rationalization of the economy found its fulfillment.

It is scarcely necessary to note that, for analytical purposes, Weber's question turned out to be an extraordinarily fruitful one. It opened up vast new realms for sociological exploration and synthesis. But where its hypothetical character was forgotten, where Weber's speculative construct was accepted as an essentially accurate picture of the totality of modern life, it was bound to emerge as a conclusion, as a political doctrine. It could then become a *position,* as it did in the work of polemicists who have used Weber's analysis as an argument against rationality, planning, and bureaucracy.[6]

6. Similarly, it has been easy to use Orwell's *1984* as argument against state planning, ignoring the fact that it is a novel seeking, if not altogether successfully, to make a new range of experience comprehensible.

Indeed, Weber himself acted as if his model were something more than a purely ideal construct. Had it been merely that, Weber could not have made it the ideological foundation for his prophecy, as he did in 1918 when he addressed students at the University of Munich on "Politics as a Vocation." Supported by his knowledge that modern civilization was an increasingly worthless venture, he esteemed the kind of political leader who, when up against it, would take his stand, proclaiming "I can do no other," and then stake his future (and the resources he controlled) on his private conviction. Had Weber's system been merely an analytical model, it could not have justified his bleak vision of the future of mankind: "Not summer's bloom lies ahead of us," he said, "but rather a polar night of icy darkness and hardness, no matter which group may triumph. . . ." When unconstrained by the formal language of sociology, Weber identified his model—which, after all, was but an abstraction of historical reality—with the *whole* of the future. For him it exhausted all possibilities. He examined and perceived no countervailing tendencies, so determined was he to discover what one perspective, rigorously applied, might yield in insight. He had engaged in his analytical labors, so he himself testified, "to see what I can bear." Like Nietzsche, Henry Adams, Freud, Michels, Spengler, and Kafka, he looked for the worst, and he found it. Overwhelmed and tormented by his vision, he then saw nothing else, retaining merely his indomitable poise, his weary sobriety, his stoic detachment.

Weber's specific contribution to our knowledge of the social facts of modern life grew out of his imaginative construction of abstract "types." Brought to bear on our environment, these were to connect the most scattered phenomena, establish new relevancies, and thereby expand the dimensions of our understanding. Although he was far from unique in his basic method, he employed it with an extraordinary combination of rigor and flexibility. As his method gave coherence and respectability to the work of others, it encouraged the most diverse adaptations and imitations. Certainly the theory of private and public administration, of industrial management, of economic development, and, more generally, of modern social organization pervasively reflects Weber's influence, if not his final desperate judgments. Social scientists have refined and qualified Weber's model, applying it to political parties, unions, hospitals, government bureaus, and military units. On the most abstract level they have designed typologies to probe the functional relationships of the elements of social structures. However diverse their analytical models, they have sought to discriminate against some social phenomena and in favor of others. Their models have reflected what interested them, or what they believed might lead to unanticipated insights. They have thus been selective—unavoidably so. What remains avoidable, however, is the treatment of analytical schemes—schemes which are, it bears repeating, mere postulates—as final truth. When such schemes are in fact identified as Truth, as the Logic of History, or the Imperative of Industrialism, they curtail political philosophy. To accept them as the verified goals of public action is to delimit the practice of traditional politics; it is to substitute the criteria of empirical social science for those of rational discourse.

To circumscribe the future hypothetically is assuredly a positive sociological good. As Weber's work illustrates, models alert us to the consequences of alternative courses of action. Without prescribing what we are to do, they reveal the gains and losses of possible policies. Yet models may be offered with such authority, they may be made to appear so compelling, that they become the exclusive basis for public policy. When they become the unexamined pictures in our minds, crowding out all other pictures, we are likely to implement what, after all, are merely analytical constructs. We then convert speculatively fruitful postulates into blueprints for action, literally putting them to the test.

To do so is to ignore the necessarily tentative, comparative, relativistic, and even ironical character of social theory;

it is to misunderstand social science and assume that its formulations are conclusive. It is to make an approach to modern life—Weber's model for the progressive rationalization of our existence—into our ideology of organization. Such a misunderstanding results in our accepting organizational developments as our fate. Furthermore it results in our acquiescing in what we believe (perhaps even with reason) to be the consensus of the Western world. By such an acceptance—and this acceptance is implicit in much current sociological theory itself—we unthinkingly ratify a consensus. Since organizations deliver what we *all* seem to want, we accept organizational goals as indubitably valid ones. Less troubled, less thoughtful, and less arrogant than Weber, more ready to choose what we think is fated for us anyway, we sanction the supposedly iron laws of industrial development, doing so both for ourselves and for those who have not yet "advanced" through the gradations of our experience.

Weber's work outlines the utopia (as Weber himself once called it) to which much contemporary social science is resigned as if there were no other. Elaborating on it, social science provides us not merely with an empirically tested body of natural laws of society but also, and more significantly, with a possible conception of society. It thereby offers us, however unwittingly, a full-fledged political theory which merits recognition as such.

This political theory upholds a regime in which political science becomes, at bottom, policy science: its true purpose is realized when it makes policy recommendations based on knowledge of the natural laws of society. Such a science is a natural science of organizational survival. Its practitioners seek to discover how best to preserve the organized social system against the forces within and without that threaten its existence. The ultimate touchstone of specific policies is their contribution to the viability of the system. Put to the test, alternative policy recommendations become increasingly objective. Thereby an authentic social science, in gear with an increasingly rationalized society, becomes a genuine possibility.

What standard prescribes the ends of this new society? The ethic of organizational behavior, in such a regime, is furnished by the needs of the social organization, the organization as a unit of functionally interrelated parts. But while the needs of the organization define the overriding public purpose, individual purposes are not necessarily extinguished. Organizational needs may well be compatible with private claims and the democratic machinery which encourages their expression. Thus it may be true empirically that organizations cannot survive unless they remain flexible, unless the conditions for competition, instability, and innovation are built into them. In other words, the organizational function of conflict may well be recognized. As a result, whole tracts for spontaneity may be reserved; they may be recognized as useful functions of organizational viability. Democracy—at least in the sense of personal participation in the policy-making process—is thus not necessarily doomed. Its admissibility depends strictly on the empirical judgment of whether it contributes to organizational survival.

To accept this approach in public life is to make the functioning system autonomous. Whatever room it leaves for individual diversity, for self-expression, or for the pursuit of private goods, this will be left not because man has inalienable rights but rather because the denial of asserted rights leads to the loss of organizational dynamism, because without reliance on constitutional procedures the organization is likely to calcify. Given this approach, one that has attracted the Soviet heirs of Lenin's party system, decisions regarding the permissible degree of social rigidity and individual liberty are best made by the expert with knowledge of organizational needs. His concern is not properly with the merits of alternative ends but with specifying the conditions of organizational health. He is best able to identify some kinds of individual conduct as healthy and other kinds, in Victor A. Thompson's apt term, as "bureau-pathic." Since he has empirical knowledge of the proper relation between freedom and restraint, his policy recommendations become irresistible. Lest irrationality be admitted, they must be accepted as a basis for legislation. Legislative action which rests on such an empirical basis will, of course, remain as discriminatory in its effects as all legislative action. But it will replace the older ways of discriminating with more "rational" ones—that is, with those demanded by the industrial order of the Western world. The inequalities following from our acceptance of the "irrational" distinctions of race, color, sex, class, status, and property will give way to new inequalites based on aptitude, skill, and capacity to perform. And these, it becomes clear, will be best specified not by seriously interested citizens—those whom Socrates had engaged in discourse—but by the practitioners of the natural science of society.

So far the only explicit delineations of such a rationalist regime are those offered as fictional possibilities. They may be recognized in Dostoevsky's notes from underground, Weber's idealized bureaucracy, Ernst Jünger's Heliopolis, Kafka's literary experiments, B. F. Skinner's life at Walden Two, George Orwell's regime of 1984, Harold Lasswell's picture of the garrison state, or Michael Young's account of the rise of the meritocracy. These are the political fictions of our age. But while their fictional character seems to deprive them of objective validity, it in no way diminishes their speculative worth. If they cannot tell us what we should do, they nonetheless testify about the awesome range of human possibilities.

Recommended Reading

LENIN: ORIGINAL WORKS

What Is to Be Done? (New York, 1929).

*The State and Revolution (New York, 1932).

The Young Generation (New York, 1920) or "The Tasks of the Youth League" (1920) in *Essentials of Lenin* (London, 1944), Vol. 2.

LENIN: SECONDARY WORKS

Gray, Alexander, *The Socialist Tradition: Moses to Lenin* (London, 1946), Chap. 17.

Meyer, Alfred G., *Leninism* (New York, 1957).

Plamenatz, John, *German Marxism and Russian Communism* (London, 1954), Chap. 10.

Wilson, Edmund, *To the Finland Station: A Study in the Writing and Acting of History* (New York, 1955).

Wolfe, Bertram D., *Three Who Made a Revolution* (New York, 1948).

THE SCIENCE OF SOCIETY: ORIGINAL WORKS

Lasswell, Harold, "The Garrison State and Specialists on Violence," *American Journal of Sociology*, Vol. 46 (January, 1941), pp. 455–68, and "The Garrison Hypothesis Today," in Samuel P. Huntington, ed., *Changing Patterns of Military Politics* (Glencoe, Ill., 1962), pp. 51–70.

Mannheim, Karl, *Man and Society in an Age of Reconstruction* (New York, 1940).

March, James G., and Simon, Herbert A., *Organizations* (New York, 1958).

Michels, Robert, *Political Parties: A Sociological Study of the Oligarchical Tendencies of Modern Democracy* (New York, 1959).

Schumpeter, Joseph A., *Capitalism, Socialism, and Democracy* (New York, 1942).

Thompson, Victor A., *Modern Organization: A General Theory* (New York, 1961).

* Weber, Max, "Politics as a Vocation," "Science as a Vocation," and "Bureaucracy," in *From Max Weber: Essays in Sociology* (New York, 1946).

Max Weber on the Methodology of the Social Sciences (Glencoe, Ill., 1949).

Young, M. D., *The Rise of the Meritocracy, 1870–2033: The New Elite of Our Social Revolution* (Baltimore, 1961).

THE SCIENCE OF SOCIETY: SECONDARY WORKS

Gouldner, Alvin W., "Metaphysical Pathos and the Theory of Bureaucracy," *American Political Science Review*, Vol. 49 (June, 1955), pp. 496–507.

Hughes, H. Stuart, *Consciousness and Society* (New York, 1958), Chap. 8.

Wolin, Sheldon S., *Politics and Vision: Continuity and Innovation in Western Political Thought* (Boston, 1960), Chap. 10.

* Excerpts in *Sources in Twentieth-Century Political Thought.*

VI. THE THEORY OF
CONSTITUTIONALISM

It has never been possible for the political philosopher to outline the proper purposes of public policy and public action without simultaneously jeopardizing the content of his message. The very method he uses to advance his case will make it debatable. Knowingly or not, the advocate of a specific political regime always does more than provide us with his blueprint for the good society; he also shows us how to engage in discourse. Simply by involving us in a civil dialogue, he tends to make a case for discussing politics. Thus Plato's *Republic* is not only a model society but also a model conversation. It reveals that those who discuss political matters will never, as long as they remain friends, come to conclusions. Determined to temper all extreme positions, they will never tell us in irrevocable terms what really constitutes substantive justice. Inevitably, the inconclusiveness of the great Socratic dialogues puts under pressure the very conclusions it suggests—but never defines.

It was Machiavelli who had first attempted to institutionalize the moderating, civilizing function of political discourse by making it the very foundation of an actual order. Machiavelli provided a theory for the institutional basis of the constitutional state, a theory which had previously been implicit in the *method* of classical political speculation. But he was concerned with more than a mere gathering of friends interested in talking about politics; he addressed himself to a state composed of diverse groupings, some civil and others not. This state, larger than Plato's Cretan city, he regarded as one properly charged with preserving a peaceful, *in*determinate, open-ended public order.

Such a large, complex public order is to be kept open and flexible, it has been recurrently argued, so that the variety of our private interests might be protected, so that we might freely pursue our diverse professional, aesthetic, cultural, and spiritual goals. While seeking to keep public goals undefined, the modern defenders of constitutionalism—thinkers as various as John Dewey, Karl Popper, Sidney Hook, Reinhold Niebuhr, Jacques Maritain, and Hans J. Morgenthau—have not sought to deflate goal-oriented political philosophy. Committed to perpetuate the political dialogue, determined not to permit our public life to be directed by unrestrained rulers who claim knowledge of the public good, they have certainly continued the speculative quest for political wisdom. But in doing so they have bluntly reasserted an easily blurred distinction, the distinction between public means and private ends. Continuing the speculative quest for political wisdom, they have pre-eminently attempted to deal with the alternative public means for the achievement of private ends. They have been interested in specifying what kind of practical means might preserve a plurality of ends. They have concentrated on the "realities" of power, and hence on the possible and practicable machinery for checking and balancing it, for dividing and separating it so that none who claim title to it can succeed in exercising it with finality. Aware of the presumptuousness of all political arrangements, these thinkers have addressed themselves to the question of how most expediently to guarantee man's private quests for ultimates against the unjust exercise of state power. Even though they may appear to make a plea for unqualified freedom, they in fact aspire to free only *public* man, to provide for no more than his *political* equality.

These thinkers have as a matter of course focused on the public aspect of our social existence, on that comprehensive order within which various private orders have been confederated. Their theory is thus meant to be one of architectonic range, establishing a frame for the whole of society, defining the common will and the public interest.

As the exponents of constitutional theory have delineated its sweeping range, they have also circumscribed its function. As they have made it applicable to our public ventures, they made it inapplicable to our private ones. Ultimately, their concern was precisely with protecting man's private life in the realm of ends. Yet insofar as they recognized that the private sphere will always tend to intrude on the public sphere, they argued that the justification for such intrusion must be subjected to a public dialogue. Consequently their theory embodies a defense of the prerequisites for political discussion: an educated citizenry, a widespread sense of civility, a measure of material abundance, an absence of special privilege, a minimum of resentments, and the forums for debate. These prerequisites, according to the political theory of constitutionalism, alone merit our public support—whatever else we may feel impelled to cherish privately.

Constitutional theory, in other words, will itself dictate no final end, no substantively just political order. It merely allows for the private continuation of the philosophical quest for the good life. It asks how to contain this quest, how to temper it and keep it civil. Constitutional theory does not provide us with blueprints for the just state, only for the state that avoids being unjust. Designed to foster politics as an art requiring the ability to improvise solutions and pacify extremists, it is provisional and relativistic: the state it supports will be prepared to invigorate groups when they are moribund and to restrain them when they become overbearing. Accordingly, it is content with offering specific policy recommendations provoked by practical problems and sanctioned by practical judgments about actual conditions in society. The proponents of constitutionalism will therefore turn to assess the felt actualities of public life, alerting us to the quality and texture of our common existence. Disdaining abstract ideologies, they will challenge whatever movements threaten to impose a final order on public life—whether it is an order perceived by scientists or metaphysicians.

The Sense of Measure: Albert Camus

There would seem little reason to suppose a tie between the ideas expressed in the literature of contemporary existentialism and the central commitments of constitutional theory. The thrust of the existentialist movement, after all, has been toward man's personal experience, toward intensifying our awareness of man's subjective condition. This concern would scarcely promise speculation of political relevance. Nevertheless, the ideas of a number of Europeans generally associated with existentialism—especially Jaspers, Malraux, Camus, and Sartre—significantly reinforce the commitments of liberal constitutionalism. They support skepticism regarding ultimate values, self-determination as an individual right, and whatever practical arrangements are likely to reconcile the individual to his defeats as he struggles to make his values prevail. To be sure, these writers do not address themselves to the specific problem of making a constitutional political order a durable and workable one. But, as the introductory discussion of Nietzsche intimated, they do clarify the imposing psychological demands on those who, in constitutional regimes, are empowered to govern. They stress, moreover, the agonizing choices men must make in public life, revealing the moral burden of all political engagements.

Existentialist thinkers by no means intended to contribute to constitutional theory: their meditations, however diverse in aim, were merely such as to illuminate its character. Thus in responding to the forces of our time they made clear what it must mean in practice to exist without "given" values, to carry on when all public goods are placed in doubt, subjected to scrutiny, and exposed to revision. Under the pressures of recent European history and politics, they trimmed the theory of constitutionalism to its essentials, depriving it of all tinges of Platonism, natural law, and idealism. Without explicitly attempting it, they developed the basis for a cogent political doctrine.

The citizens of Anglo-American countries have been so habituated to the use of political procedures for the reconciliation of conflicting interests that constitutionalism would seem to be second nature to them. It has been far less an abstract doctrine than an obviously working system which guarantees that every effort to reallocate public rights and duties be subject to challenge. For Americans, especially, the case for constitutionalism, if it is made at all, arises amidst a consensus. In fact, it is so pervasively accepted as the true science of politics that it has become the axiomatic basis for political analysis.

But whereas the system of constitutionalism has appeared to Americans as the self-evidently just instrument for achieving a reasonably tolerable public order, continental Europe had to articulate a case for it. What could be taken for granted in the United States, European thinkers had to define in opposition to totalitarian theories and totalitarian institutions. If, then, the political theory of European existentialism is dramatically pointed, this may be attributed to its emergence under the most critical of conditions—in the face of feelings of social suffocation, political coercion, and military occupation. It has a polemical edge, therefore, which American theory is beginning to gain only as Americans are also being put on the defensive, as they too feel compelled to make a case in behalf of their political practices.

To review the work of Albert Camus (1913–1960) as an expression of the case for political moderation is to heighten one's understanding of the range of the issues involved. It is to perceive the promises as well as the limits of liberal constitutionalism as political doctrine. The great merit of Camus' essays is that they show him arriving at his political position with an arresting personal honesty. His stand is demonstrably the result of a conscious weighing of alternatives, of a determination to give full credit to the claims of two kinds of extremists: (1) activists who, following Hegel and Marx, have wanted to be done with philosophy and commence *making* history and (2) quietists who, following Kierkegaard, have leaped to embrace God and resigned themselves to man's afflictions. Thus Camus was to come to his conclusions with a freshness, poignancy, and relevance not always apparent in such other exponents of compromise as Locke, Hume, or Madison.

There was nothing academic about either his work or his life. Born in Algiers of Alsatian-Spanish stock, he was truly exiled from the kingdom: he was attached to the French community of North Africa—itself estranged from the tradition and culture of continental France—and yet not at home in it. His life is indeed a record of attachments and detachments, of restless motion violently halted by his death in a car crash.

But it was more than a life lived; it was one recorded. Searching for coherence in a political world that appeared forever incoherent, Camus remained resolutely reflective, providing us with a body of essays, plays, novels, and stories that earned him the Nobel Prize for Literature in 1957. What is striking about his work, all aside from grace of statement, is the grim honesty of his intentions, his quiet and cool determination not to deceive himself.

As he searched for a standard for public conduct and policy, he did so despite his knowledge that none was finally tenable. Whatever standards for action were offered, they all were removed from the day-to-day business of living. They all were fatally abstract and ambiguous. What we obviously require—given the growing technological resources for abusing the power men exercise over men—is not some transcending ethics but imperatives as unmistakable as "Thou shalt not kill!" We require this clear standard not only to cope with extreme situations, the situations of life and death which preoccupied Camus, but to govern the ordinary affairs of men. The difficulty is patent: Although we can meet the extreme situation with supreme simplicity (we can quite simply exalt freedom as we confront the tyrant, the torturer, or the hangman), we flounder when the question is one not of life and death but of the good life. We then proceed with uncertainty, groping for legislation that might balance conflicting interests, feeling anxious as we are compelled to amplify the existence of some members of society and to restrict the existence of others. Under such conventional conditions, uncertainty is inevitable. As long as the members of society must be partially free and partially restrained, there can be no final party line or legislative program to give us security. In the human community the quest for a final, unambiguous standard for public policy must be inconclusive.

Still, Camus pursued it. The specific observations that color the record of his pursuit derive, of course, from his experience. He included precisely what fell within his extraordinary range of vision. Incorporating the unfamiliar, placing it near at hand, he leads us to appreciate the actual horror of the guillotine, the concentration camp, the massacre of hostages. But more than that, he forces us to see, close up, how the scandals of our time were introduced as the instruments of Justice. Thereby he leads us to understand that a government fit for man must be dissociated from Justice. In concluding—and yet not concluding—that a constitutional regime must operate outside the moral order, his work frames the classic predicament of constitutional theory.

In the essays that make up The Myth of Sisyphus (1943) Camus confronts the irreducible senselessness of our lives and considers how the awareness of our "absurd" existence has perennially led us to adopt policies that threaten our personal integrity. Conscious of our pointless work and leisure, we have been tempted to choose between false al-

ternatives: surrender to irrationality or else defiance of unreason in the name of pure rationality. What Camus seeks to
do, recognizing that civilization flourishes precisely between
these alternatives, is to build a plausible foundation for
mediating between them. By making us see what the respective demands of life and reason are today, he generates a
tension between these extremes, a tension so great that it
exposes the precariousness of the middle ground.

His critical strategy is to observe how various contemporary thinkers have become reconciled to irrationality by taking either the road of Kierkegaard's gnosticism or that of Hus-
serl's phenomenalism: that is, they either hold that the
world's absurdity is to be embraced because it is God's holy
mystery or they immerse themselves wholly in worldly
phenomena. Following either road, Camus maintains, we
end by giving up our civility. Neither of these two roads
allows us to remain intellectually detached; both deprive us
of our ability to retain our specifically human quality, to
stand aloof and outside. When we travel them to the end, we
find that they deny our rational consciousness.

To vindicate our very selves, Camus insists that we first
confront the absurdity of our lives. We must become aware
that in the final analysis nothing makes sense, that our day's
labors will be eternally repeated. And having gained such
awareness, we must resume "the chain of daily gestures."
This is all. In his account of the Sisyphus legend, Camus
sees the absurd hero, as he calls Sisyphus, going "with a
heavy yet measured step toward the torment of which he
will never know the end." Turning to his wretched task of
rolling a rock to the top of a mountain, whence it will roll
back of its own weight, Sisyphus consciously acknowledges
the hopeless character of his fate—and smiles. He is condemned and yet remains in control. His consciousness en-
sures his victory: "One must imagine Sisyphus happy." He
approaches his labor with an irrepressible inner gaiety, with
what Nietzsche had called joyful wisdom. For while his

pointless labor continues, he has defiantly saved his reason, his self-awareness, his consciousness. He is engaged and yet remains detached.

While Camus refrains from issuing moral imperatives, merely reflecting on our condition, he makes clear his conviction that we should accept life's inherent unreason and yet do so rationally. Without deception, we are to go on with our lives—indeed, buoyantly to make the most of them. We are to save our only ultimate treasure, our living selves. The first commandment of *The Myth of Sisyphus* emerges therefore explicitly as a special application of the general prohibition that thou shalt not kill: Do not commit suicide.

But the irrational sacrifice of the self is not the only threat to life. Reason, too, endangers our individuality. This theme was to emerge in *The Rebel* (1951).[1] Whereas irrationalism leads to self-annihilation, rationalism leads to the planned death of others. It is precisely our use of reason to justify our passions which has led to violence, torture, and executions on a scale increasingly vast and horrifying. Just as Camus sees the ultimate problem of private ethics to be suicide, so he comes to see the ultimate problem of public ethics to be murder—the systematic, organized, bureaucratized crushing of collectivities of men. In the name of logic we stamp out life. Our existence being intolerably meaningless, we forcefully inflict meaning upon it. If our existence is rationally incomprehensible—or, rather, if we cannot demonstrate its inner rationality—we tend to impose some rationality of our own making. Recognizing no order, we are driven to *make* order and break all those who will not fit it.

But how can we meet this threat to our existence? Only if we keep the meaninglessness of our lives ever present before us, according to Camus, can we avoid being sacrificed

---

1. *The Plague* (1947) is best seen as the narrative, dramatic counterpart of *The Rebel*, just as *The Stranger* (1942) is best seen as the counterpart of *The Myth of Sisyphus*.

to some abstract rational order. To save ourselves we must be continuously aware of the inevitability of our failure, of our inability finally to impose meaning: at the end, we must compel ourselves to realize, there is nothing but our extinction. It is this full knowledge of our finiteness which alone will keep us from enforcing sweeping social plans. Ever conscious of the limitations imposed by our nature, of our being laboring creatures doomed to exist without *knowing* the reason for our suffering and our death, we will suddenly recognize that our plans are simply ours, that we may not claim to have derived them from God, History, or some transcendent Rationality. To claim such absolute sanction for any of our projects is but a sign of our presumptuousness. Worse, it leads to an ordering and disciplining of our existence in excess of the practical needs of our everyday lives. By acknowledging our limits, we will refrain from the needless stabilization of our common existence, from imposing some abstract meaning on our lives. Accepting such restraints, Camus concedes, may not cause us to lead the best life; but it will permit us to lead the least objectionable one.

Knowing that literally nothing gives rational support to our public projects, that no durable realm of ideals authenticates our policies, we will conform to "the ideal of the absurd man": we will "keep each successive moment before the mind unceasingly conscious." In *The Myth of Sisyphus* Camus discusses several character types who in various ways make this ideal the basis of their behavior—the seducer, the comedian, the adventurer, and the artist. Playing their respective roles, they are committed both to their passions and to human reason, to life and to the limits reason imposes. In behalf of life, passionately determined to exhaust its possibilities, they rebel against reason—and yet acknowledge its necessity. If there is agony in this unresolved tension, this is the agony generated by the refusal to obey our impulses and leap beyond the limits of reason. It is the agony spared those who leave the realm of our finite existence and embrace God,

History, or the Absurd, those who escape man's fate by succumbing to romantic idealism, by transcending the conflict between our rational intellect and our instinctual promptings. This conflict, Camus implies, is characteristic not of life as such (for animals are ignorant of it), but of the life of man. To resolve it is to surrender our humanity.

Indeed, it is to this conflict alone that Camus is fully dedicated. Offering us at once his celebration of life and his respect for rationality, he reveals why our public existence must be a deeply uneasy, ironical venture. Giving us both an appreciation of romantic spontaneity and its containment by reason, dramatizing the necessary inconclusiveness of our common life, he points to the need to remain poised between extremes. He demands both our political engagement and our sustained awareness of its final futility. Our engagement may be pointless; our public action, especially in the light of the intricacies of present technology and international order, may be of no avail. Yet, to be redeemed, we shall have to go about our affairs like one of the minor characters in *The Hoodlum Priest,* a film of the early 1960's. The camera turns to a man who is picketing the governor's mansion to protest against capital punishment. A friendly guard tells him that his picketing won't change the world. He quietly responds that he only hopes to keep the world from changing him.

The prevailing political order may be either too accommodating or too hostile to make our protests effective; it may exceed the bounds of comprehensibility altogether. Still, the authentic individual will assert his moral identity. The futility of our actions cannot discharge us from assuming responsibility for them.

The specific terms of Camus' statement are unmistakably those of continental Europe. Significantly, they are not political. While he commits himself to the preservation of the tension between absolutes, Camus says nothing of the institutions and procedures which might implement his convictions.[2] While he recognizes the mediating function of the seducer, the comedian, the adventurer, and, above all, the artist—all figures loyal to both the rich substance of life *and* the forms which order it—he is silent about the function of the man of politics. And this is no wonder. After all, the public figures of continental Europe (excepting Switzerland) have been more concerned with fighting for the victory of their ideals than with mediating between conflicting ones. They have scarcely engaged in the limited, frustrating work of negotiating and renegotiating in the hope that, at best, men will achieve but a measure of success.

But if the experience and vocabulary of liberal constitutionalism lie outside of Camus' reach, he nevertheless expresses a view which entails a politics of moderation. A clear response to the disease of political romanticism, his work sustains a politics providing for the proportionate success of all participants in public affairs but permitting total victory to none. Such politics rests on the awareness of the inevitability of defeat, the defeat of all participants and all policies. Making every policy maker replaceable and every policy amendable, it preserves nothing except the procedures which insure that the conflict between competing interests will never result in the triumph of one of the parties. A politics of renunciation, it is supported by the machinery that thwarts the man on horseback, the man of the hour, the man of ideals and vision. Jeopardizing all visions of the just state, it deliberately compromises our ideals by treating them as

2. Thus Camus never appreciated as fully as Sartre that political conflicts are not between right and wrong but between conflicting rights. Seeing this at its fullest, aware of the bloodied instruments for securing justice, Sartre has consistently dramatized the repressive, offensive character of politics. (*Les Mains sales* leads to the conclusion that dirty hands are the necessary consequence of political activity. In *Le Diable et le bon Dieu* the "realistic" socialist dismisses his principled, idealist comrade to point a simple moral: As long as evil remains in the world, politics must be a dirty business.) Sartre, too, would seem to have been more theoretically penetrating and practically useful than Camus when he insisted, commenting on *The Rebel*, that we improve our condition only by making practical choices which, of necessity, make us culpable.

our private passions. To keep the public order civil, to reduce violence in the political arena, it relegates idealism to
the sphere of the social. It expects and compels us to follow
our biological, cultural, and spiritual ambitions within the
confines of our private associations, ultimately within our
solitary selves:

> Whatever we may do, excess will always keep its place
> in the heart of man, in the place where solitude is found.
> We all carry within us our places of exile, our crimes and
> our ravages. But our task is not to unleash them on the
> world; it is to fight them in ourselves and in others.

Public conduct, to accord with Camus' view, is not to be
regulated by an absolute ethics, by an ideal code, but rather
by reference to the specific claims of individuals. Our personal needs, not some impersonal, supernatural Truth, must
thus become the touchstone of all policies. Thus Camus
shares the familiar premise of existentialist thinkers that
"existence precedes essence": our existence as concrete
human beings takes priority over all abstract ideals. In
recommending public action, we must begin with man.

Camus' approach, in short, would have us embrace a
political order consisting of a value-suffused private domain
preserved—as far as possible in practice—by a value-neutral
public domain. But to share this position is not to settle all
practical problems; our sense of injustice may well be
aroused by concrete situations. If we are to find a specific
state morally acceptable, we would first have to judge and
accept the moral quality that permeates its private domain.
To approve of the public order, as Camus conceives it, we
must be prepared to approve at least the common denominator of values inhering in the private social order. Our acceptance of these common private values is crucial, for in
Camus' state they turn out to be the only ones which may
influence public policy. The policy maker, after all, is not
properly concerned with any others: to see the public order
as properly free from moral imperatives is to think of the

statesman's proper task as the minimal one of balancing existing interests, not of acting on values transcending those upon
which society agrees. Hence if we are to assess the excellence of a particular state we would have to have knowledge
of the moral condition of its society. We would have to have
knowledge of the excellence of private men and their groups.

But how are we to gain such knowledge? In not finding it
possible to deal with this question, Camus, like all thinkers
devoted to the preservation of politics (and the preservation
of nothing else), leaves us adrift, exposing a problem shared
by all apologists for liberal-constitutional regimes. They
would lead us to accept whatever public policy conforms to
the consensus of men free to define their own morality. They
would lead us to surrender the public domain to whatever
private consensus happens to prevail. We might, of course,
resist some policies by arguing, with Camus, that they are
undesirable because they reduce the tension between extremes of belief, or because they fail to preserve the arena
for meaningful conflict. But in reference to what criteria
should we judge the soundness of the *range* of conflict and
the *range* of agreement? Might we not discover, when confronted by some specific regime, that its entire range of
interests—*all* the interests balanced within it—are parochial,
stale, or brutal? To be sure, we may then plead for maximizing the freedom of competing groups. But as long as
procedures duly allow such groups to compete, to press their
case, and to reach agreement, we cannot judge the merit of
their joint enterprise. Confronted by policies reached in
accord with the niceties of due process of law, we must remain philosophically silent—or become irrationally forceful.

We are not likely to sense this as a shortcoming of the
political theory of existentialism. We have, after all, found
the policies of constitutional regimes entirely acceptable.
That is, we have felt that the range of interests and values
being incorporated in public policy has been sufficiently
wide to enable us to do in common whatever had to be done:
in the past, so we believe, our policies have always been

sufficiently inclusive to meet public needs—whether in the fields of health, housing, labor, education, transport, recreation, or culture. In constitutional states our private ethics has generally made us compassionate and generous. It has kept our aggressiveness and greed in check so that we have endorsed a host of domestic general welfare programs, at least up to a point. Since the ethics of private men could be counted on to restrain us, the theory supporting constitutional regimes has seemed wholly adequate. Relying on a residue of private restraint, we have not been troubled by the cry for public freedom. It is only when our confidence in the restraining power of private morality is shaken that we feel driven to question the adequacy of constitutionalism as a comprehensive political theory.

There is another reason why we are not likely to sense the limits of existentialist political thought, why we tend to be satisfied with its recommendation to maximize freedom in the public realm. This recommendation has seemed to be an obviously sensible one in an era characterized by ruthless totalitarian oppression. Under such conditions the decision to liberate men can encounter no reasonable objections. Freedom then is an unqualified good. But what happens when totalitarian regimes are in fact partially oppressive and partially liberating?[3] In a world that is not *wholly* inhuman, the

3. Two tendencies—the relaxation of industrial discipline and the contraction of the world of genuine common experience—have posed a problem not only for political theory but also for writers who, like Camus, seek to employ literary allegory. Compelling allegory depends on a social order which is fixed; it depends on shared frustrations and shared moral assumptions. When such orders are increasingly private, the writer has a hard time locating and holding his audience. What common experience and aspirations is his work to exemplify? Thus Camus' *The Plague* is effective only to the extent that we are still able to accept the possibility of total oppression: this alone makes Dr. Rieux's determination to resist the plague so reasonable. He is a character who works on a small scale in but one city in which the public objective is well defined: get rid of the plague. But how can *we* react if *we* feel that *we* are actually faced not by the plague but by countless lesser ills? What if there is no common definition of social disease or social health? Once we doubt our ability to make conclusive diagnoses, Dr. Rieux's determination to cure will strike us as less than relevant.

simple plea for freedom lacks sophistication. Lest it lead to action which destroys the good with the bad, it must be focused and moderated.

Thus the political thought of existentialism tends to commend itself (1) when we believe that the morality of private life effectively restrains us or (2) when our public environment is seen as totally oppressive. But this is precisely what is being challenged today: (1) social institutions—family, church, school, workshop, neighborhood association—seem to become increasingly less relevant guides to our conduct and (2) state-initiated oppression seems to be a diminishing threat to our existence. To the extent that this is the case, the literature of existentialism leads us up to the central question of contemporary political action: how to enrich and cultivate our private life. And at the same time it leads us up to the central question of contemporary political thought: how to define the morality appropriate to the private order, how to define virtuous conduct and responsible action.

Camus and other existentialist thinkers have not presumed to provide answers. Having seen men victimized by their illusions, having encountered them in chains, they have assumed that whenever we are truly disillusioned and free we will, as a matter of course, act responsibly. Consciousness of freedom, they have felt, leads ineluctably to responsibility and excellence. If we are reluctant to share this optimistic view of man, the existentialist approach to politics has nonetheless led us to recognize what the success of liberal constitutionalism still conceals—the assumption that whatever clouds there may be on the horizon, private virtue will somehow take care of itself and all is well.

The Freedom to Maneuver:
Reinhold Niebuhr

In extreme situations, when the threat to life is unmistakably total, existentialist thought shows itself at its most impressive. Thus the unqualified commitment to the sanctity of the human person—to man as we find him—sparked Camus' single most effective political essay, his attack, at once practical and passionate, on the guillotine. Yet when more than life had to be defended, when a certain kind or quality of existence had to be defined, Camus, like other humanistic existentialists, was to become equivocal.

The reflections of existentialist thinkers make clear that in behalf of life one might speak with absolute certainty. But in behalf of a particular quality of life, of a specific ordering of man's existence, an ironic tone must emerge and qualify one's prescription. One can plead for human freedom—affirm it and reaffirm it. But no absolute ethics for structuring freedom, for bringing order to one's life, can be offered unconditionally. To recognize this does not mean one must resign oneself to an irrational activism. If final answers are unavailable, or if it is presumptuous to submit them, it still remains possible to defend one's limited short-range choices on the ground that they are likely to accord with one's more comprehensive long-range choices. If one cannot rely on absolute Reason, reasoned judgments can still be advanced. Discourse regarding the rights and wrongs of alternative policies can go on. Indeed, such discourse can become emphatically "realistic"—oriented by practical considerations, by the actual possibilities of political life. It can become thoroughly secular

and at last free itself from all vestiges of idealistic metaphysics and theology.

That the politics and thought of Reinhold Niebuhr
(1892–   ) should reveal this is striking, because he has
earnestly sought to ground his recommendations not in a
worldly, atheistic humanism but in his Protestant faith. What
is striking is that his specifically Christian understanding of
the limits of man and the fragility of his projects should have
led Niebuhr's work to give as firm support to the theory of
liberal constitutionalism as Camus' evident paganism. Pro-
nounced differences remain, but these are easily explained
by contrasts in political environment. Camus barely hints at
the theoretical requirements for constitutional politics,
whereas Niebuhr attempts to provide a full and densely
textured theoretical foundation. Moreover, Niebuhr's pronouncements on policy have been far less astringent than
those of Camus; he has ventured to deal with virtually every
political predicament of the age, ranging from antitrust legislation to nuclear war. This ambitiousness—animated as it
has been by the distinctive qualities of American politics—
has often served to make explicit what is merely suggested by
Camus' essays. Addressing himself more fully and directly
to the actual pressures and cross-pressures of American
public life, Niebuhr has made the nature of both constitutional politics and constitutional theory more comprehensible.

Ranging more widely, he has also become more painfully
aware of the inherent shortcomings of all public policies. He
has become forever ready to make us cautiously take stock,
to have us wait and see the other side of even the most need-
ful human undertakings: concerned with what is realistically attainable, he discusses the conditions for an international political order under the sobering title, "The Illusion
of World Government." Yet while his writing may seem to
arrest us as we seek to move ahead, it may also have the very
opposite effect. Since he views *all* of our projects as inherently flawed, he relieves us of doubt and guilt as we seek

to advance them. Having arrested us with his insistence that *all* politics must be corrupt, he frees those who sense that, salvation or not, political action is mandatory.

"For the good that I would, I do not: but the evil which I would not, that I do," St. Paul cried out, adding that within him there is an element of evil which turns his best intentions into his worst acts. In the tradition of Augustinian theology Niebuhr has reaffirmed that man sins not despite his will to do good but because of it, for sin is a defect at the very center of the human personality: it inheres in the will. In the very exercise of our will, as we seek to define our nature and our destiny, we are involved in sin. Thus we sin not because we are merely human with limited capacities, because the mind is unresourceful or the flesh weak. We sin not because of our undeniable limits but because of our failure to understand and accept them. We have, it is true, the power to choose between a far greater range of alternative courses of action than we concede. But, at the same time, we fail to permit our immense possibilities—possibilities for both good and evil—to be tempered by the knowledge that they cannot be fulfilled in this world. Claiming the power to grasp the infinite, acting in the name of abstractions such as Justice, Truth, Nature, Science, or God, we fail to regard our vision as finite. Our sinning consists of our presumptuous self-seeking. In our self-aggrandizement we convert our subjective wants into objective laws; we identify our personal interests with the demiurge of History and Reason. It is our love of self which corrupts. It is our egoism which taints all our proposals, including those we are pleased to think of as most selfless. "We are not only not as good as our ideals," Niebuhr has written, "but we tend to use our ideals as weapons of prestige, failing to recognize that our ideals are not as good as we pretend they are."

The groups to which we belong, in Niebuhr's view, do not serve to neutralize our sinfulness. On the contrary, society "merely cumulates the egoism of individuals and transmutes their individual altruism into collective egoism so that the egoism of the group has a double force." For this reason, so Niebuhr has concluded, groups find it next to impossible to act unselfishly. Where the individual might still rationally consider the interests of others, where he may transcend himself and even choose the advantage of others over his own, his political groups, his churches, or his countries tend to enhance his natural personal egoism. Seemingly absolving us from responsibility, society makes room for our vanities, for our aggressive wants and irrational impulses.[1] Society inflates our private failings. However pure social action may appear to be, it cannot be moral. As Niebuhr has pointed out, even Gandhi's pacifism mutilated the innocent: his boycott of British cotton resulted in the undernourishment of children in Manchester.

The gist of Niebuhr's case is obvious: to act is to sin. Every agreement reached by man, every act of legislation, leads to some injustice. Man cannot do good without doing evil, and doing good with the help of society merely augments the evil he does. Clearly, then, he must sin—more in society than when alone—as he exercises his will. Human history is consequently a record of man's sinfulness.

If such a record has meaning at all, according to Niebuhr, its meaning cannot be found to be embedded within it. To read meaning into man's secular history would be but a variety of our presumptuousness. Therefore only a transcendent faith not presuming to be based on an edifice of logic and reason can resolve the paradox that our work must come to nothing and is yet of significance. And it is the Christian revelation, Niebuhr attests, which can redeem our otherwise absurd secular venture. Christianity furnishes the most compelling symbols of our daily encounters. It gives meaning and coherence to history.

1. This stands in noteworthy contrast to Lenin's and Weber's view of groups. They saw groups, it should be recalled, as the embodiment of rationality, as highly structured entities giving the individual the instruments, the concepts, the sheer factual information to make his potential rationality meaningful.

As *we* look upon our worldly projects, they do not add up to anything significant; from *our* point of view we are unable to do anything truly worthwhile. In our temporal, finite existence we can gain only relative, partial, contradictory insights. Yet while our efforts cannot have final importance for us, they are nonetheless a precondition for what is ultimately important: the substance of the Christian revelation. Thus what we do can be at once radically unimportant and profoundly significant. Our work, in Niebuhr's phrase, can have proximate validity, providing "proximate solutions for insoluble problems." Life can therefore be good despite its evil. Just as Christ embodies both despair and hope, so can we despair and yet hope.

It is evident, of course, that reason cannot validate this view. Niebuhr does not intimate that it can. Man's intellectual efforts—as tainted as all his others—cannot grasp an untainted final reality: "The canons of logic and rationality are transcended when reason attempts to comprehend the final irrationality of things." If reason is of no avail, what is? There can only be acceptance—or faith. Any alternative way of solving the mystery of human history and its Christian redemption is sin.

By the acceptance of the Christian faith, Niebuhr means the total sacrifice of the self, the complete love of the transcendent. The ultimate norm is "the law" of sacrificial love. This law, Niebuhr has written, is the final resource of justice and "it prevents the pride, self-righteousness and vindictiveness of men from corrupting their efforts at justice." Speaking in 1948 before the World Council of Churches, Niebuhr said:

> One contribution which Christianity certainly ought to make to the problem of political justice is to set all propositions of justice under the law of love, resolving the fruitless debate between pragmatism and legalists and creating the freedom and maneuverability necessary to achieve a tolerable accord between men and nations in ever more complex human relations.

Although the law of love is to act as standard for politics and legislation, it is necessarily a hollow imperative. Niebuhr's position is so formulated that one cannot give content to the law of love without simultaneously violating it. To proceed to apply it to concrete cases, he has made clear, would be to mix one's pride with one's interpretation, hence corrupting it in the very process of clarifying its meaning.

If, then, the Christian revelation cannot be *said* to dictate any specific form of conduct, it liberates its adherents, leaving them free to maneuver in this world as reasonably as they might. But this does not imply they may act as they feel. Merely because they are faithful to an inscrutable absolute, they need not be irrationalists. God's justice may be rationally incomprehensible and incommunicable. But the innumerable ways we put our presumptuousness—our tendency to be overbearing and to force restraints on others—into practice can be rationally assessed. That is, we can make empirical appraisals of the degree of restraint that obtains in specific regimes, and use such appraisals as guides for action. We can enter the world of power and politics and inquire how men have structured freedom, how rigid existing social and economic arrangements actually are. And having done so, we may legitimately press for more freedom and flexibility. Thus we are bidden to act so as to preserve a maximum of maneuverability. We are asked to proceed to structure freedom, forcefully to impose order on it—not to institute a just regime but merely to guarantee the perpetuation of the political process. Because the law of love is for all practical purposes nonprescriptive, because it points out no target as it commands us to aim higher than our egoistic selves, we are simply instructed to frustrate whoever might interpret it. At bottom we are summoned to preserve a system of checks and balances, an institutional framework which thwarts all those political romantics and idealists whose vision of justice threatens to become specific.

Responding to this summons in his articles, books, and

sermons, Niebuhr himself has reflected on the practical problem of ordering the freedom men claim for themselves. Ever since 1915—when, at the age of twenty-three, he was ordained in the Evangelical Synod and became pastor at a small church in industrial Detroit—he has been a passionate participant in public affairs. A prolific writer and forceful preacher, he has vigorously entered the world of power politics, taking sides on the momentous political issues of the day. Joining the Socialist Party, or resigning in protest against its pacificism, or helping to organize Americans for Democratic Action, or becoming active in New York's Liberal Party, he has acted less in reference to any specific Christian dogma than in response to his shrewd understanding of the prevailing conditions of public life. Thus his abandonment of pacifism in 1940 rested on his practical understanding of the specter of Nazi aggression. As his theology has so completely receded to a transcendent realm as to lose all discernible relevance, his realistic sense of politics—his sensitivity to the forces which endanger the perpetuation of politics—has been fully at play, so much so that it has never been difficult for unbelievers to accept his judgments. On practical matters—Henry Ford's labor policy, the Marshall Plan, or racial segregation—Niebuhr has simply been right: that is, he has discerned which forces in American public life were likely, if unimpeded, to monopolize the economy, to congeal society, to paralyze politics, or to block the road to inquiry.

Identifying emergent social, economic, and political power blocs as well as the slogans advanced to reconcile the public to their ascendancy, Niebuhr has tirelessly positioned himself against them. He has thundered in opposition. Essentially negativist, he has been critical of all attempts—whether by politicians, industrialists, educators, or social scientists—to resolve conflicts once and for all. He has challenged not only the specific institutions that threaten to eliminate the precarious nature of our existence by offering salvation in this world but also the whole array of contemporary belief systems that crystallize our hopes—the "isms" in the minds of modern man. In turn, he has condemned Protestantism, Marxism, liberalism, scientism, and educationism. He has rebuked an optimistic Protestantism which presumes to do God's work in society and makes but another social value of its religious faith; he has indicted Marxism for its false promise to redeem a history of conflict in a secular utopia; he has condemned classical liberalism for failing to account for man's capacity for evil; and he has rejected progressive education for its effort to eliminate human defects.

While Niebuhr himself caricatured all these ideologies by focusing merely on their degenerate forms, while he himself has failed to do justice to the complexities of the systems he has denounced, he has at the same time warned about the dangers of simplification, and this perhaps no less effectively by exemplifying what he opposes. Ideologies, he has helped make clear, are unrealistic abbreviations of our complex possibilities. They conceal the ambiguous reality of our nature and our enterprises. Our lives are simply more various, contradictory, and ironic than any ideology permits us to believe. To rely on any fixed system of beliefs is to be forever disillusioned. As emergencies arise, as we see evil breaking to the surface, they throw us off balance. To be realistic —and here, as the discussion of Mannheim's thought has helped clarify, Niebuhr may be seen as aligned with a resolutely "practical" anti-intellectualism—is to be in touch with the actual forces of political life, to trust not the dictates of abstract reason but one's sense of history and politics.

Just as ideologies keep us from appreciating the variousness of our possibilities, the institutions by which we regulate our existence keep us from realizing the potentialities of our lives. In the final analysis they too testify to our vain determination to stabilize our necessarily unstable, temporary existence. Despite historical changes, we embrace and idealize such political arrangements as nationalism and such economic arrangements as capitalism as if they were God-sent absolutes. We read divine purpose into merely human institutions, identifying our social inventions with absolute justice. No political or economic order, Niebuhr has pointed out, may ever be considered just; all are imperfect; none is ordained by God. All institutions are compromises of specific conflicting interests, results of the struggles of groups to gain or keep power. They necessarily reflect our compromises, our always partial victories.

In Niebuhr's view there is no God-given equilibrium of power which can please all interests in society. There is no natural balance of forces which can satisfy all political contestants. Hence there can be no enduring political agreement, for none can be said to express God's will. There can be no real solutions for problems, and no genuine science of politics to discover what they are.

Calling attention to our all-too-human tendency to rationalize our ambitions and give them the stamp of absolute authority, Niebuhr has sought to make us aware of our incredible capacity for self-deception. Like the agnostics of the Enlightenment, whose ideologies he has indicted, he himself has been concerned with setting us free. He has been intent on making us detached, having us take an always larger view. Thus he has clearly hoped to emancipate us from our parochial settlements, asking us whether we are not needlessly confined by our attachments and our pride.

If Niebuhr would seem to be opposed to every form of political synthesis, if he exposes all political thought and action to his sweeping critique, what, in the end, remains vindicated? To what kind of political order can he give his assent?

It is apparent that he has always desired more than undiluted freedom, that he has in fact been prepared to accept whatever social, political, and economic order is necessary to maximize freedom. Recognizing that freedom and order are complementary, that they are mutually indispensable, he has wanted freedom and order in due proportion. Whereas European thinkers from Fichte to Nietzsche had been driven to celebrate an unspoiled freedom, Niebuhr has recognized the need for coercive institutions so that freedom may be duly promoted. Whereas European existentialists had looked upon freedom as an irreconcilable opposite of oppression, crying for unrestrained revolutionary action, Niebuhr has emphasized the restraints necessary to secure freedom in society.

He has appreciated that without the discipline imposed by institutions, without an instituted system checking and balancing our conflicting interests, freedom is destroyed by the very idealism of its most active supporters. He has fully recognized the need for coercion in society. To secure a reasonable measure of freedom there must be a governing force to maintain order, to intervene in society. There must be a power above antagonistic social interests so as to create and preserve the balance among them. This power will not spontaneously radiate from man's private behavior. Social life, Niebuhr has noted, will not develop an ideal balance by itself; it must be consciously brought about. Unaided, social life will not, as he has written, develop a perfect equilibrium of power:

> Its capricious disproportions of power generate various forms of domination and enslavement. Human society therefore requires a conscious control and manipulation of the various equilibria which exist in it. There must be an organizing centre within a given field of social vitalities. This centre must arbitrate conflicts from a more impartial perspective than is available to any party of a given conflict; it must manage and manipulate the processes of mutual support so that the tensions inherent in them will not erupt into conflict; it must coerce submission . . . whenever the instruments of arbitrating and composing conflict do not suffice; and finally it must seek to redress the disproportions of power by conscious shifts of the balances whenever they make for injustices.

As this passage makes clear, Niebuhr recognizes that the just state consists at least of (1) a society of diverse parts and (2) a center of political power to insure that none of the parts will gain the upper hand and put an end to diversity. On the one hand, then, he has stressed freedom and diversity. And on the other he has stressed restraint and unity—a unity which, in Madison's relevant phrase, breaks and controls the violence of factions, a unity which, as Hamilton wrote,

> . . . is essential to the protection of the community against foreign attacks; it is not less essential to the steady administration of the law; to the protection of property against those irregular and high-handed combinations which sometimes interrupt the ordinary course of justice; to the security of liberty against the enterprises and assaults of ambition, of faction, and of anarchy.

A tolerably just state, in other words, will combine freedom and order, making the government strong enough to keep order but not so strong that it may itself emerge as the final embodiment of order. Such a political system will protect the moral freedom of the individual, what Madison had called man's rights. Confining morality to the private sphere, separating church and state, it will deflate all public crusades, all moralistic politics. It will prevent the emergence of every final definition of Peace, Welfare, or Justice, its machinery making certain that whatever definitions do emerge, they remain reviewable and revocable. While balances between freedom and order may be struck, every such balance will be determined by the exigencies of the moment, and be subject to change. In sum, the amending process will be built into the system. Dissent will be institutionalized.

Niebuhr's position leads to a full acknowledgment of the place of power in the liberal society. It recognizes, with John Adams, that power is always pitted against power, and that, since there is no escaping this, we must always ask those who in fact exercise power to validate their credentials. A just society, therefore, is one whose machinery affords the powerless the opportunity to scrutinize and reject the pretensions of the powerful. It will not dispense with the exercise of power; it will not do away with injustice. But it will at least make it possible to exchange one group of power wielders for another. It will provide for the circulation of elites, as the American party system has done so successfully.

There is no guarantee, in Niebuhr's model of the just political order, that men will use public power for good ends. All his state makes possible is the organized and effective criticism of potentially oppressive elites. Thus Niebuhr gives justice no substantive content whatever: justice resides purely in those procedures which provide men with the opportunity to unseat those in power. What is left completely open in Niebuhr's scheme, what has been traditionally left open in American political thought, is precisely the content, meaning, and significance of human freedom. Since the moral ends of the state remain undefined, we get no positive case for some absolutely best regime—but we do get an exaltation of democratic constitutionalism. We are offered the kind of negative stand bound to disappoint idealists who wish to push beyond compromise as an end, who subscribe to some ultimate vision of the public good, who, yearning for a simpler life, shy from the awesome political responsibilities imposed by man's striving for power.[2]

In the end it would seem that Niebuhr's pronouncements on the issues of the day constitute an apologetics, not for a religious code or a doctrinal truth, but for the positive implementation of the negative state. Religious experience may well have given impetus to Niebuhr's political speculations, but it has no discernible, communicable relation to

2. Thus a disciple of John Dewey, Holtan P. Odegard, disparages Niebuhr's vision of democratic constitutionalism by describing it in language recognizable as derisive only by those who happen to share Odegard's distaste for politics: "In this new land, Niebuhrians will establish a democracy actually run by an oligarchy. They will be forever frustrated because morally bound to sacrifice their interests upon the altar of compromise. They will find that power and forces have been 'given' in their land, and they will eternally maneuver to balance them. Their freedom will be rootless, paradoxically united with coercive order into a discordant harmony. And they will tolerate each other only because they are not sure whether they have or have not the truth. . . ." (*Sin and Science: Reinhold Niebuhr as Political Theologian,* Yellow Springs, Ohio, 1956, p. 176.)

them. His eloquent case for the balanced commonwealth, his insistence that *all* claims to power are suspect, has not been logically dependent on any theological system, so that believers and disbelievers alike may readily subscribe to it.

There remains, however, one consideration which might give them pause. To intone, with Niebuhr, that it is unavoidably sinful (or, in nontheological language, presumptuous) to define the standards for public policy is to take a pervasively low view of political life. To stress the inherent evilness of public action is to encourage an indifference to civic duty. Moreover, if men are to relate their political activities to an utterly inscrutable goal, they are in effect left to fend for themselves.

Niebuhr himself, having affirmed that the goals of public action are forever beyond our knowledge, will not pretend to interpret God's design for men. Whatever the theological flavor of his terminology, his dialogue has taken place on a secular level. It has not served to mediate between the absolute insight of the believer and the relative possibilities of this world. Ever mindful of our impulse to translate our private truth into public policy, Niebuhr has abstained from the task of bridging the otherworldly command of God and the quite-worldly pressures of those who seek power. That is to say, he simply has not engaged in a necessarily futile quest, a quest which, if seriously attempted, cannot help but agonize. Where mythology, art, philosophy, and theology have traditionally sought to translate our unfamiliar, direct experience into familiar, common knowledge, where these disciplines have sought to convert private vision into public knowledge—thus enlarging our range of experience—Niebuhr has shrunk back. Rationalizing his self-restraint, indeed characterizing it as a Christian virtue, he has instead fully accepted the range of insights implicit in and given by America's social and intellectual life. So providentially rich has been the American experience, so naturally pluralistic, that it has seemed sufficient for Niebuhr to accept its promise. Having done so, he has merely felt impelled to plead for a measure of freedom for America's multiple interests. He has thus managed to remain poised between an irresponsible cynicism and an equally irresponsible utopianism. Escaping either extreme, he has clarified the rules of prudence and counseled that we keep the institution of politics in good repair. Niebuhr's deliberately negative theology has thus led him to be caught up in the stream of American constitutionalism.

Refraining from articulating the inarticulate insight of the true believer, declining to give meaning to the inexplicable ground of existence, he has kept himself from reflecting on the nature of virtue, excellence, or justice. Sensitive to both the critical needs of the hour and the hazards of idealism, he has instead taken his place in the midst of contemporary politics. Within it he has been farsighted, outspoken, and courageous. If he has provided no theory of politics in the grand tradition, if he has not detached himself from the present, he has nonetheless succeeded in defying the spirit of civic despair.

The Conflict of Loyalties:
Jacques Maritain

Born in Paris, Jacques Maritain (1882–   ) grew up in a religiously indifferent Protestant home. In his early twenties he embraced Catholicism. Throughout his intellectual career—he has taught at the Institut Catholique in Paris, at the Institute of Mediaeval Studies in Toronto, and finally at Princeton University—he professed an equal devotion to Roman Catholicism and the constitutional state. His importance as a political thinker lies in his explicit resolve to come to terms, from the point of view of Catholicism, with the secular democratic regimes of the modern age. Falling back on the position of St. Thomas Aquinas, he has vigorously stated the case for democratic constitutionalism and prudential politics. While his use of theology to explain historical developments has remained unconvincing (it is hard to agree, for example, that the source of totalitarianism lies in the political doctrines of the Enlightenment), he has skillfully adapted the Thomist perspective and rhetoric to the conditions of contemporary public life, thereby partaking in the perennial task of reformulating the basis for the politics of constitutionalism.

Following both Aristotle's and Aquinas' affirmation of man's natural need for the temporal order, Maritain has been determined to give the secular state its full due. Unlike Niebuhr, he has accepted it not as an evil necessary to keep sinful men in check but rather as a positive good permanently grounded in human nature. He conceives of it as one of the agencies constructively helping man fulfill his given nature.

Because Maritain regards the state as justified by "natural morality," he has been able to appreciate political action as intrinsically desirable. For him it has a distinct though limited place in the organization of our lives. The temporal state, although limited because we cannot find spiritual fulfillment in political activity, is thus assigned its proper area of operation, and is given autonomy within it.

The actual diversity of our personal inclinations makes it proper, Maritain has pointed out, that we should pursue the good in highly diversified ways. He therefore upholds a pluralistic society of coexisting goal-oriented groups. In his eyes, the just social order consists of unstable, shifting, overlapping economic, cultural, educational, and religious associations. It is composed of family units and "a multiplicity of other particular societies which proceed from the free initiative of citizens and should be as autonomous as possible." This is the society which must give energy and authority to the institution of government. "The whole dynamism of authority in the body politic," Maritain has written in his major political treatise, *Man and the State* (1951), "should be made up of particular and partial authorities rising in tiers above one another. . . ." At the apex, exercising the power to maintain the law, to promote the common welfare, and to administer public affairs, is the rational apparatus of government, what Maritain calls the state—

> . . . an impersonal, lasting superstructure, . . . an agency entitled to use power and coercion, and made up of experts or specialists in public order and welfare, an instrument in the service of man. Putting man at the service of that instrument is political perversion. . . . The functions exercised by the State are for the body politic, and not the body politic for them.

In thus subordinating the state to the authority of society and yet subordinating society to the lawful exercise of state power, Maritain preserves the distinction between state and society. On one side he places that whole cluster of associations that men organize, join, and reorganize by nature, that they design, quite naturally, in accordance with their various needs and values. And on another side he places the state as a stable, formal, value-neutral frame intended to benefit society.

Given Maritain's distinction between the state as a permanent political framework and society as changeable and heterogeneous, what is the proper role of the state? And what is the role of society, specifically of the Church in society? How should the Church be related to society, and society to the state?

To preserve our freedom to conform to our own true inclinations, we must, according to Maritain, keep society separate from the state. Nature itself demands that the state (defined as a morally neutral agency) be kept distinct from society (defined as a cluster of freely competing purposive groups). Having insisted on the principle of separation, Maritain has outlined its specific consequences for state action, for group life, and hence for Church policy.

It becomes the obligation of the state—as the only agency which, cutting across the special interests of the various groups in society, may legislate in the common interest—to preserve the formal order of society, to protect civil rights by fostering the rule of law. This obligation implies that the state must provide the prerequisites for lawfulness, for civility. It must initially free men from want and economic bondage. It must furthermore enable them to form associations likely to secure their personal freedom. It must, in other words, create and maintain the conditions for the health and welfare of individual persons and their groups, making it possible for them to fulfill their peculiar destinies.

These injunctions may seem to underwrite unrestricted state action in the affairs of society. But Maritain's intent is otherwise. While he sees the state as autonomous, he also sees it as limited to its proper sphere. It is limited by society, for the separate members of society—concrete persons, not hypothetical individuals—are the only bearers of moral consciousness, the only interpreters of ultimate goods. The state may therefore do no more than provide whatever minimum may be essential to preserve a social order of free persons. Its only obligation is the protection of an infinite variety of particular goods. The only public interest—in terms that are not Maritain's—is the protection of private rights; the only function of politics, therefore, is to mediate between these rights, to prevent the triumph of any one claim to authority, to block all concerted movement toward the totalitarian blending of society and state. This mediating activity is the state's exclusive obligation, but it is to be fulfilled without misgivings and with all available resources.

A state whose authority is thus confined may not legislate morality. It may create the ground for public-spiritedness, for civic virtue, but, being morally neutral, it can assume no special responsibilities for the enforcement of any of the doctrines which happen to find support in society. To meet its responsibilities it must give equal treatment to all groups in society, repressing only those which conspire to hinder it in the performance of its proper task.

It becomes, then, the responsibility of private associations, including religious establishments, to engage in moral education. It becomes exclusively the function of society—or, more properly, the plurality of existing groups in society, including the Church—to mold character, for the ultimate vision of the nature of man is vouchsafed only by society, and, within the realm of society, by the Church. If the Church wishes to propagate its doctrine and inculcate virtue (and for Maritain this is emphatically its task), it must address its message to society. It cannot use the coercive instrumentalities of the state to achieve its aims; it cannot legitimately ask for governmental support of any single path to salvation.

Moreover, the Church must scrupulously refrain from transforming the civil *form* of the state. Failure to do so is to invite state intervention in its affairs. As but one group in a naturally multigroup society, the Church must consistently respect the authority of the secular order. To exert its own spiritual force, the Church must—as a matter of principle, not expediency—direct itself solely to society. The state alone being competent to guarantee the religious freedom of individuals, social groups—including, of course, the Church—cannot expect the state to perform functions that are not, by nature, those of the state. They cannot expect it to generate virtue or repress heresy.

Tolerance is thus one of the principles sustaining Maritain's public order. Tolerance of diverse religions, including "erroneous" ones, is axiomatic. Accordingly, our right to religious freedom—that is, freedom to order our private lives in the light of ideals we ourselves embrace—does not rest on the claim that our ideals are divinely inspired. Nor is it merely the result of our power to assert the right. It is ours because the abridgment of religious freedom, as history testifies, would expose the secular state to intolerable strife. It would endanger the very foundations of the constitutional order. But the argument for toleration has additional force since more than public peace is at stake. Those in "error" have the right to express their own formulas for salvation because the state, by nature, is limited in its competence. It is simply not the function of the state to act as the agent of Truth.

Whether or not to tolerate diversity, or to what extent to tolerate it, is thus not a moral issue for Maritain. It is, properly, a political question, and its answer must depend on existing conditions. Thus, in Maritain's view, while the state cannot be expected to judge whether any specific creed is heretical, it may be expected "to judge—always with the institutional guarantees of justice and law—whether a political heretic threatens the democratic charter by the tangible acts he undertakes. . . ." Religious freedom, like all civil rights, is a relative good, but we always have to have as much of it as we can afford, for it nourishes that social pluralism which is the natural basis of the just state. And how much we can afford is a practical question; it has nothing whatever to do with morality, metaphysics, or theology.

Maritain's case for civil rights is derived from his view of a natural law which dictates that moral consciousness finds its source in the individual members of society—persons who, being variously constituted, are characterized by differences of moral sensitivity. They, and not the state, must testify to the soundness of public policy. The state may well release their capacity for good; but it cannot presume to make them good. At best it will provide the preconditions for a virtuous public. Negatively, it will prevent social groupings from enforcing their creeds; and affirmatively, it will educate and, if need be, compel all members of society to be civil—to be tolerant and charitable—in their public conduct.

At the same time, however, the state may not compel the individual to accept its own doctrine of moral neutrality as the standard for his private conduct. Thus the democratic process, moral neutrality, and religious tolerance must be the accepted public creed of the individual person. But it need not be his private one. Ideally, both aspects of his given nature will thereby be preserved—his determinate, circumscribed material self and his indeterminate, incommensurable spiritual self.

The community that does justice to the whole person, to man as citizen and as believer, is therefore a political and a coexisting spiritual order. Within this community the religious believer will find himself playing two roles simultaneously, one as member of the secular order and the other as member of his faith. Acknowledging the authority of the civil state, he will play his role as citizen; acknowledging the authority of his faith, he will play his role as believer. Private faith without public work he knows to be insufficient.

What Maritain in effect demands is our recognition of man's dual allegiance, an acknowledgment of the authority of the spiritual order as well as the authority of the secular order. The individual, of necessity subject to the legitimate commandments of both, can only exist in a condition of tension, of perpetual inner conflict. He is obliged to do right as right is conceived by him and his church; and he must be loyal to the secular realm, which compels compromise and tolerance. He must seek to preserve both his own peace of mind and the public peace. In Maritain's eyes there are no enduring precepts for doing so, but there is a political framework—that provided by constitutional regimes—which at least allows for the perpetuation of the tension, which gives man not peace but the shelter of associations within which he may pursue the good, within which his religious impulses are duly contained and disciplined.

It is to the consciences of men in the social realm that specifically Catholic natural law is addressed. In the first instance, the Christian revelation is directed toward Catholics, not the state. The Church, like all groups, may seek to direct the state only by acting on the rest of society, a society which itself is restricted, however, because the state is properly charged with maintaining its pluralistic character. The Church, so as to make an impact on public policies, must therefore uphold Christian principles in the hope that, as Maritain has put it, this will "make the leaven of the Gospel quicken the depths of temporal existence." In a different metaphor, it will give resonance to what statesmen do —but it will not determine the content of their policies.

Maritain variously speaks of the Church as "vivifying," "illuminating," or "spiritualizing" what men will do in the existential realm. It should be clear, however, that to employ these terms is to refrain from articulating the direction in which men are to move. It is to abstain from attributing specific meaning and content to that part of natural law which is directed to the state, or to men as citizens. To the extent that Maritain engages in a meaningful public dialogue, that he does not merely give impetus to the pre-existing private commitments of the faithful, he is quite simply dedicated to the process of politics—but not to any substantive conclusion at which it might arrive. Having left natural law free from all publicly verifiable content, he betrays his dual loyalty, an irrevocable one to process and a revocable one to substance.[1]

The hollow formalism of Maritain's precepts follows from his belief that the natural law, which does have the eternally valid principles of the True Church as its immutable substantive content, can only illuminate the private realm of the human conscience. All public application of natural law, Maritain has said, must vary with historical circumstances. Experience will have to determine the specific form that Catholic imperatives should assume in any particular situation, for "any application or realization is existential and takes place in time." Application is always relative to given historical conditions. And today, in constitutional democracies, these conditions are such as to admit the optimal realization of the demands of natural law. Maritain's position is unambiguous: there in fact exists a peaceful public arena where men can meet on equal footing to conduct their affairs— those affairs they find it prudent to conduct in common. At the same time, there also is a private arena where men can follow their spiritual calling in accordance with their individual conscience. In this world we have no reason to hope for anything better.

The practical results of Maritain's position must at this point be familiar. They are essentially no different from those of other thinkers who also view man as tragically split: bound to this earth and yet capable of self-transcendence. For secular existentialists such as Nietzsche and Camus, transcendence is achievable by virtue of one's understanding of one's situation—and the consequent realization that one's

1. Hence Maritain's defense of a pluralistic body politic and a morally neutral state would not suffer were he to base it on shared experience rather than on natural law. Why should he not merely ask whoever might disagree with his approach, on what empirical grounds they would base *their* case for elite rule? His logic would remain unaffected, however much the power of his rhetoric might decline.

absurd fate is bearable because nothing so pointless can be serious. For religious existentialists such as Niebuhr and Maritain, transcendence is achievable by virtue of God's grace. In either case, to have given full recognition to man's capacity to transcend his given, suffering, circumstantial self is to brace us psychologically as well as politically.

On the psychological level the existentialist outlook has the effect of heightening our self-awareness. It increases the likelihood of our discovering the various dimensions of our personalities. This enlarged consciousness of possibilities, in turn, is likely to make us more pragmatic, more sensitive to the context in which we act, to the alternative consequences of our policies. Whether we realize—with such earth-bound thinkers as Nietzsche, Freud, Camus, Malraux, or Dewey— that this life and this planet is ours and that we must reverently preserve it or else believe—with Niebuhr and Maritain—that we act under a sacred trust and that we are not free to defy God's creation, we are, in either case, filled with a sense of responsibility. Extending our awareness, becoming aware of what we think and do, we tend to beware, to become wary, cautious, prudent, circumspect— in a word, responsible.

And we tend, furthermore, to value the machinery designed for instilling such a sense of responsibility, that is, the machinery associated with democratic constitutionalism. A system of checks and balances has long been seen as an elaborate device to make us sober and reflective. It presents an obstacle for those impatient true believers who know right from wrong and are ready to impose their vision with enthusiasm. A constitutional system operates as if it had been installed to keep us from acting without thought for the consequences. Protecting voluntary associations, public speech, and the right to crystallize dissent, it promotes the full-scale review of alternative policies.

Insofar as such procedures have the effect of compelling socially responsible conduct, it is no wonder that, in the end, Maritain should have been prepared to celebrate the

American Constitution. However uncritically he turned out to embrace it in his *Reflections on America* (1958), he has been properly impressed by its capacity to frustrate and neutralize. But he has also seen it as a basically flexible, adaptable framework for government, as limiting both church and state, giving each but a measure of authority. He has thereby implied that as long as individuals have that excess of insight and energy which it is unsafe to transform into public policy, the authority of church and state must remain in conflict. To this conflict, Maritain has maintained, there is no humanly foreseeable end. Hence we must reconcile ourselves both to the tension it generates and to the political institutions which keep it alive. We must therefore cherish that statesmanship which does not presume to create anew, which, accepting our natural habitat and our natural inclinations, is content to engage in the intrinsically worthy task of mediation and conciliation.

Faith in Process: John Dewey

If the theory of democratic constitutionalism fails to commend itself, this certainly is not because it is presumptuous in its aims. Not claiming to assure the triumph of public virtue, however defined, its objectives are so modest that it remains unaffected by empirical tests which discredit alternative theories. Making no positive claim for any one social value—giving no special advantage to the well-born, the skilled, or the wise—it is the kind of public order left over after each of the alternative ways for ordering our public life has succumbed to rational scrutiny. In this scrutiny a good deal of what men have long cherished has fallen by the way, but there is the consolation offered by William James's defense of pragmatism:

> It is true that a certain shrinkage of values often seems to occur in our general formulas when we measure their meaning in this prosaic and practical way. They diminish. But the vastness that is merely based on vagueness is a false appearance of importance, and not a vastness worth retaining. The x's and y's and z's always do shrivel, as I have heard a learned friend say, whenever at the end of your algebraic computation they change into so many a's and b's and c's; but the whole function of algebra is, after all, to get them into that more definite shape; and the whole function of philosophy ought to be to find out what definite difference it will make to you and me, at definite instants of our life, if this world-formula or that world-formula be the one which is true.

Acceptance of this kind of practicality has been sufficient to evoke a widespread loyalty to democratic-constitutional government where economic and social preconditions made it workable. But this does not mean that a generally accepted normative theory of democratic constitutionalism has actually evolved. No doubt the pressures for producing such a theory have been appreciable: constitutional government has been threatened on the one hand by romantic activists who wish to remove organizational fetters and on the other by conservative idealists who wish to organize society in the image of some transcendental hierarchy of values. The response to these pressures has not, however, been a systematic defense of democratic constitutionalism. To be sure, we have postulated such elements as political equality, minority rights, and majority rule and then attempted to design meaningful deductive models for democracy. Furthermore, we have reached agreement to support specific public institutions so as to provide a maximum range of disagreement on how to conduct our private lives; accordingly, we have argued that aspiring policy makers must acquire their power through an open competition for votes. But we do not really know (1) how much consensus there must be to keep the politics of democratic constitutionalism alive in times of stress, (2) what the essential ingredients of the consensus are, and (3) how to show that these ingredients conform to our standard of justice, how to demonstrate to reasonable men that they *should* approve of them.

The first of these questions is being increasingly recognized as being properly an empirical one. It is not closed to clarification, as V. O. Key, Jr., has shown in his *Public Opinion and American Democracy* (1961). But what of the other questions? Here we have probed with hesitation. We are uncertain about the procedures for making our answers to them rationally persuasive. The entire debate, what is more, is grossly stimulated by practical concerns, for were we to *know* what kind of consensus is essential to preserve a pluralistic society we could confidently move to perfect our public institutions to realize it.

The work of John Dewey (1859–1952) has an obvious

bearing on these issues. Dewey believed that we may reasonably accept a policy insofar as we accept its probable consequences. By focusing on the consequences, we overcome the theoretical difficulties that have traditionally misled us when we wished to know what course of action to adopt. By following alternative possibilities, by determining what they entail in practice, we can manage to control our primordial craving for some fixed supernatural basis for our decisions. We can then ground our policies in our real interests.

To do so in practice, Dewey contended, we must support the kind of public institutions that compel us to weigh the results of possible policies. This implied a system so designed that it would perforce direct our attention to the ramifications of what we might do. To be alerted to these ramifications we must give the social interests affected by alternative policies an equal opportunity to get a full hearing. In short, we must embrace procedures that make us look toward the widest possible range of results.

For these procedures Dewey found a ready model in the conventions long accepted by the practitioners of empirical science. The method of empirical science, he said, is the obviously suitable one for exploring the effects of our action, for it alone can specify the total context of possibilities. We can become wiser in our choice of goals by applying the familiar scientific method to our social problems. To make practical judgments we must observe and experiment, scrupulously remaining within the realm of experienced reality.[1] What to do can then be settled, not by reference to abstract values, but by reference to the known consequences of our action. The concrete situation within which we find ourselves will

1. Although Reinhold Niebuhr has been a persistent critic of Dewey, he has actually always adhered to this position himself, sharing its virtues and, as will become evident, its difficulties. Niebuhr has obstinately interpreted Dewey's views as an attempt to set up science as a means of salvation. Obscuring that Dewey, too, felt it presumptuous of men to idolize ends, Niebuhr has thus attacked a position Dewey himself repudiated, namely, that science provides final solutions.

yield the answers we seek: it contains its inner logic. We must simply examine it critically, that is, by the scientific, experimental method of empiricism. As Dewey put it, we must apply the method of rational intelligence.

Dewey dismissed the objection that his approach would leave us adrift by doing away with what he called "regulative authority." In *The Quest for Certainty* (1929) he wrote that science itself will give us direction. He believed that "the knowledge of the relations between changes which enable us to connect things as antecedents and consequences" will itself provide morally worthy conclusions. If we reach our decisions as a result of an honest survey of consequences, if we remove all the misleading abstract distinctions between means and ends, individual and society, facts and values, knowledge and action, we will reach conclusions dictated by the inner unity of ongoing experience. To understand this inner unity, according to Dewey, is to know what one ought to do. The situation we sense as a problem, in Dewey's view, contains the moral premises which provide the solution. To extract a moral judgment from a factual proposition we need not introduce a moral premise from the outside.

On these grounds, however controversial they have remained, Dewey was able to hold that moral deliberation and empirical testing should be treated as essentially the same thing. He could therefore advocate that, in order to meet the public problems confronting us, we should start to assimilate the procedures of both politics and philosophy to the procedures already employed to yield knowledge of the physical world. Why not, he tenaciously asked, conduct our moral inquiries and our politics as sensibly as we conduct our scientific inquiries? He felt and argued that if we would only engage in politics and philosophy the same fruitful way we perform the operations of the empirical sciences, we could successfully deal with the manifest social problems thrown up by the Industrial Revolution. In science we agree on rules of procedure that leave the road open to inquiry, that make every hypothesis subject to revision. But in politics and philosophy we still follow rules that allow us to jump to conclusions, to make permanent settlements, to consecrate ideals such as Justice or Private Property. Political institutions as well as philosophical tenets are sealed off from inquiry; they are kept in a petrified condition. Because the only irrevocable imperative of empirical investigation is the negative one, we must reject such procedures as block the continuous testing of tentatively reached conclusions; any number of judgments made in politics and in philosophy, however, are treated as if they were far from tentative. Indeed, the very terms in which they are formulated make them immune to public verification, to testing, to amendment. Just as we still accept economic inequalities as if given by God, by the Laws of laissez-faire economics, or by a sanctified Constitution, so we still accept philosophical absolutes as if there were a realm of eternal verities, as if abstractions like Being, Essence, or Nature somehow had status independent of our needs and interests. We compulsively embrace a static moral and political universe, clinging to bloodless legal fictions such as the Individual, the Family, or the State. As a result we neither see nor solve the dynamic problems of our common existence.

These problems, Dewey stressed, are the living ones inherent in the technological character of modern society. They are created by the advance of science and technology. It was science and technology which, having introduced momentous social changes, had shaken up our traditional routines, leaving our future uncertain while releasing the energy to enrich it. And it could now be science, Dewey added, which can show us how to gear our political institutions and philosophical values to the promise of the future. If our politics was restrictive, legalistic, and sterile, and if our minds were closed, acceptance of the policies prescribed by the method of science would serve to invigorate our public life and open our minds. It was science, systematically applied to social affairs, which could tell us how to proceed and where to go.

Unlike traditional, goal-oriented philosophy, social inquiry based on empirical science comes to grips with reality. It does not indulge in idle, unproductive contemplation. It is therefore only proper, Dewey wrote in *Reconstruction in Philosophy* (1920), to have empiricism replace a barren approach offering only "ready-made principles to be imposed upon particulars in order to determine their nature." We must deflate prescientific systems because they muddle our thinking and, as a result, keep us from controlling the social world. The elimination of the philosophies of the past, Dewey wrote,

> . . . would permit philosophy to devote itself to a more fruitful and more needed task. It would encourage philosophy to face the great social and moral defects and troubles from which humanity suffers, to concentrate its attention upon clearing up the causes and exact nature of those evils and upon developing a clear idea of better social possibilities; in short, upon projecting an idea or ideals which, instead of expressing the notion of another world or some far-away unrealizable goal, would be used as a method of understanding and rectifying specific social ills.

All the past theories about the essence of the individual, the state, or society merely served to obscure our public predicaments—were in fact deliberately introduced to do so. They were advanced to ward off the inscrutable forces of life, not to master them. They were designed to stabilize an unpredictable, fluid environment. By personifying, nonpragmatic thought sought to classify experience and idealize the classifications. Thus it had the effect of consoling us, of merely reconciling us to our difficulties. Only by seeing through its fictions, idols, and personifications, only by revolting against formalism, will we become able to perceive and reconstruct the actual condition of our lives.

In *The Public and Its Problems* (1927), Dewey's most specifically political work, he sought to cut through the conventional fiction of the state to lay bare the underlying pulsating reality. Conventionally, he said, the state is conceived in terms of either its supernatural origin or its ultimate end. But such idealistic conceptions obscure the actual events that make up our public activities, and can therefore provide no standard for conduct. They lead us to attach permanent labels to our experiences, thereby producing intellectual confusion. Thus we falsely distinguish between private and public action by not taking an approach that does justice to an always changing reality, by not defining "the public" as consisting "of all those who are affected by the indirect consequences of transactions to such an extent that it is deemed necessary to have those consequences systematically cared for." However angular the prose, the thought is clear: The traditional distinction between public and private action was to be replaced by a more realistic view of observable transactions. Such a view would reveal the actual flow and counterflow of day-to-day politics, specifically exposing the mundane activities of constitutional conventions, municipal governments, and the "private" affairs of interacting groups in society. It would reveal the dynamic process of public life, of groups struggling to get and keep power. It would indeed show that there is no "public," only an array of competing publics. And finally it would disclose that there is no public interest transcending the interests of the various publics composing the state.

According to Dewey—and political scientists such as Arthur F. Bentley, Pendleton Herring, and David Truman, who have followed his cues in analyzing American politics —this is how things are and, moreover, how they ought to be. For such a pluralistic body politic prevents precisely what should be prevented: the emergence of some fixed end, of some final, irrevocable purpose. It admits of continual experimentation, of ceaseless growth. In Madison's language, it "involves the spirit of party and faction in the necessary and ordinary operations of government," and thereby preserves a maximum of individual freedom.

The form of the state, therefore, will follow precisely the lines intimated by American democratic constitutionalism. We will properly take our bearings by what Dewey thought of as the tenets of Jeffersonian individualism. To promote man's inherent and inalienable rights we must first consider all government as but an experiment; second, we must uphold grass-roots democracy; third, we must make democracy effective by an open-ended educational system; and finally we must not hesitate to make property rights conform to public needs.

The first of these imperatives, as Dewey reaffirmed it, entails a willingness to consider all government machinery as tentative, as merely instrumental for enhancing individual freedom. The second has ramifications on which Dewey dwelled again and again, for like Jefferson he desired to inspire local autonomy, home rule, and decentralized self-government. "Democracy must begin at home," he wrote, "and its home is the neighborly community." It was at the local level, he believed, that we might overcome the social habits derived from a philosophy of an extreme, doctrinaire individualism. At the local level one could re-create man's actual interdependence and recapture a sense of community life. The new community, he intoned, would be not merely an aggregation of individuals; it would be one whose members truly communicate, sharing insights and experiences, giving joint meanings to their separate existences. In it, men would be permeated by "the mystic force" of communication. Insofar as their new habitat would be "bathed in the light that never was on land or sea," they would achieve "the miracle of shared life."

This ideal of experimentalism thriving in the intimate association of men was best realized, Dewey maintained, by an education that habituated children to participate in real projects, to solve actual problems, to engage in meaningful intellectual work. The school would be designed to enable the child to discover his own potentialities, to examine his life by testing it. Not compelling children to adjust to social values or given conventions, the school would liberate them from society's narrow utilities. It would incorporate activities and workshops which would become "allies of art and centers of science and history." The school itself would be characterized by the

> . . . disorder in any busy workshop; there is not silence; persons are not engaged in maintaining certain fixed physical postures; their arms are not folded; they are not holding their books thus and so. They are doing a variety of things, and there is the confusion, the bustle, that results from activity. But out of occupation, out of doing things that are to produce results, and out of doing these in a social and cooperative way, there is born a discipline of its own kind and type.

This new discipline, generated by the education system, would make a new generation of self-reliant Americans capable of mastering the problems of the twentieth century.

Given the potent promise of progressive education, there seemed to be no need to reconsider the merits of the existing political system. In Dewey's eyes the political system obviously worked: such flaws as troubled reformers were due to unregenerated individuals. Thus even while Dewey found himself perennially frustrated in his drive to inaugurate social reforms, he continued to work within the inherited system of American politics. If men were to be led to the radiant, warm community in which their energies could be freely and constructively released, American politics, revitalized by duly educated citizens, could point the way.

Like generations of exasperated but still hopeful Americans, Dewey asked not for a new framework for governing but for an improved citizenry. Participating in a familiar American ritual, he insisted on popular education. Education was to teach men first how to distinguish real problems from pseudo-problems and then how to deal effectively with the real ones.

Hence Dewey drafted no political or economic blue-prints. He argued not for a grand plan but for continuous, pragmatic planning. And to the question, "But who guards the planners?" Dewey gave the answer of classical political philosophy: the system of education. It seemed enough to urge that public leaders—and for Dewey this was potentially everyone in society—be properly educated.

But there remained a practical dilemma Dewey failed altogether to resolve. His educational system, which was to be extended equally to every social class, is an unavoidably costly one. Laboratories necessarily operate on larger bud-gets than lecture halls; permissive discussions are less eco-nomical than one-way lectures—even more so when "educa-tional" television must be rejected. Not only are the expenses enormous, there is understandable resistance to covering them. The interest in nonprogressive education is stubbornly vested; after all, the traditional school caters to the existing economic and industrial organization of society. In the face of these circumstances the difficulty obviously is how to per-suade society *as it is now constituted* to tax itself so as to underwrite what is genuinely progressive education. The only tactic Dewey believed to be available for realizing his ideal was the skillful employment of the prevailing political process, so attached was he to the existing system of con-stitutional government. But it was precisely this system—its machinery for blocking all idealists, for checking, balancing, and decomposing every insurgent group in society—which stood in the way. Given this system of government and the inequalities it perpetuated, Dewey's plan for the reform of education and the rehabilitation of intelligence was bound to sound hollow.

That Dewey's basic Americanism kept him from per-ceiving the need for a new strategy became all the more evident as in the 1930's he sought to reaffirm what he inter-preted to be Jefferson's stand on property. He was able to warn that property had to be socialized if America was to maintain a vibrant pluralistic society of diverse cultural and social groups. He could even use a Marxist metaphor to assert that an industrial organization forcing the employed to become "mere appendages to the machine which they operate" denies the principles of Americanism. But he could point to no leverage for making his assertions effective, for giving force to his exhortations.

It is when the economic situation reaches crisis proportion, as it did during the Great Depression, that Dewey's loyalty to process reveals itself as less than adequate. No doubt his energetic commitment to method, to open-ended inquiry, is attractive when we have the leisure, the patience, and the economic security to await the outcome of rational deliberation. It is attractive, moreover, when we find it possible to live with whatever policy might be enacted. Though displeased by specific decisions, we can bear up when confident that in the long run we will be heard. We can literally afford to wait. But when the political process frustrates groups which are in genuinely desperate straits—ill-housed, undereducated, or misrepresented—it cannot have rational appeal. The spokesmen for underprivileged groups can feel no desire to compromise, to accommodate themselves to the well situated, to engage in the luxury of civil politics. Thus Dewey's political theory, insofar as it simply assumes the existence of the economic and psychological preconditions for a wholesome politics, emerges not as wrong but as thin. As a theory of political action it is of but limited relevance. It is bound to disappoint those who expect it to work in underdeveloped regions, whether these regions are distant or close to home.

The limitations of Dewey's political theory are even more strikingly revealed in his commitment to decentralized government and grass-roots democracy. This part of his position was no mere coincidental nostalgia for the rural Vermont in which he grew up. It grew meaningfully out of his insight that in order to make politics rational, in order to ground decisions in experience, one needed the kind of common knowledge, the kind of consensus, which is most likely to prevail in the compact, small-scale society. The mere *appeal* to intelligence and rationality, Dewey knew, would never do. The various interests affected by public policy had actively to participate in the process of inquiry. They had personally to explore its possible consequences. At the same time, however, it was perfectly evident that in a complex, interdependent, large-scale society men are not likely to participate in politics: the consequences of policies are too remote or too complicated to activate them. Men can scarcely weigh the costs and benefits of decisions, for they cannot relate alternative possibilities to their own experience. To be sure, policy scientists might be enlisted to enlighten the people, to inform them, for example, that the preservation (or exploitation) of wilderness areas is "really" in their long-range interest. But such propagandistic efforts squared as little with Dewey's premises as any other form of decision making by elites remote from the people. Hence Dewey was bound to turn away from the large-scale society.

Yet in doing so he jeopardized the relevancy of his approach. How could his faith in common intelligence, his antipathy toward elite rule, help deal with the unprecedented economic, technological, and military problems of the modern era? To impose Dewey's approach on complex industrial societies—to sanction *only* such policies as result from the participation of interests who have reason to believe themselves to be affected—is to deliver the policy-making process to groups who have the power, skill, and foresight to perceive and act on their own interest. At best, it is to make policy subject to the votes of provincial constituencies—and ultimately those with the resources for swaying them. The result, in any event, cannot be public policy sufficiently inclusive to be considered rational. The result is the very elitism Dewey fought.

An unstated assumption of a consensus on social health, that is, an implicit belief that there is agreement on what facts constitute the problems of society, helped make it easy for Dewey to plead for the application of intelligence. For him the questions could remain those of means, not of ultimate ends: he treated the maladjustments and derangements of society as if they were self-evident ones. He was able to justify his political prescriptions on the ground that they were precisely the ones which could meet the problems posed by the socially disruptive effects of an advancing industrialism. Modern industry had shattered home, family, church, and neighborhood. It had taken men from their farms and their shops, moved them to urban centers, and reintegrated them on the assembly line. These effects of the emergent system were, to Dewey, objectively reprehensible. Whereas he would not define what was right, he knew what was wrong: anything that stunted man's natural growth and imposed a needlessly destructive discipline. If our lives were obviously out of joint, the need was to bring them back into harmony. It was necessary, as Dewey saw it, to recapture a lost harmony. To do so we had to perceive the existing situation as problematical and to proceed to solve the problem; we had to respond to the challenge of industrialism and restore the true community. If Dewey therefore prescribed the small, well-integrated community as cure for our maladjustments, the prescription was simply dictated by the inner logic of the prevailing situation. He confronted the facts, perceived their deranged nature, and counseled appropriate reform. He merely followed his general procedure which asks that we address ourselves to the self-evident problems of our era and seek to make them humanly manageable by experimentally searching for workable solutions.

But what kind of solutions are "workable"? On what rational grounds can we accept them? Dewey's response to this question was that we must consider solutions acceptable if they managed to survive the test imposed by a rational process. Their very survival of the method of empirical inquiry will make them "instrumental" to the removal of some specific troublesome circumstance; they will thus have demonstrated their value.

> If they succeed in their office, they are reliable, sound, valid, good, true. If they fail to clear up confusion, to eliminate defects, if they increase confusion, uncertainty, and evil when they are acted upon, then they are false. Confirmation, corroboration, verification, lie in works, consequences. Handsome is that handsome does. By their fruits ye shall *know* them.

Thus wrote Dewey in his *Reconstruction in Philosophy*. He assumed, of course, that there is agreement on what actually constitutes our "confusion, uncertainty, and evil." This assumption, as reflection on French existentialist thought has helped clarify, does have limited validity: it is tenable in extreme situations, when survival itself is at stake. Dewey, however, treated it as tenable in all situations, including those normal ones which find men dickering not about matters of life and death but about ways of ordering their lives. Since it was self-evident to him just what constituted the nature of social disease, he could counsel that we ought to do whatever intellectually honest inquiry shows we truly wish to do. Surely we would not wish the continuation of our discomforts. Hence we must follow "the lead of the subject matter"—follow it presumably wherever it may lead.

The critics of Dewey's logic have rightly pointed to its residue of optimistic Hegelian relativism and historicism. But in attacking his logic—his untenable effort to ground moral propositions in the facts, indeed, to ground them at all—they have disregarded that Dewey's interest was, after all, not in logic but in experience, most specifically the American experience. In insisting that we ought to follow the lead of the subject matter, he meant the American subject matter. He meant not "wherever" it may lead, but the destinations at which it would normally arrive when prudent, intelligent, reflective citizens were fully consulted. And destinations would be mere points for departure, as the true American had always known. Thus Dewey's wholehearted acceptance of the fruits of the method of science can be attributed to his confidence that those who would handle the apparatus of social technology would be subject to American values.

In seeming to resign himself to whatever the social context might yield, Dewey was therefore neither revolutionary nor conservative—for the American context could be regarded as pervasively liberal: it conserved a revolutionary tradition. On this liberalism there was consensus, and Dewey relied on it. He could depend on it to give moral content and stability to his approach. It made it unnecessary for him to bother about ultimate values. At the same time, it could validate his political conclusions—his countless crusades for the reform of education, the extension of civil liberties, or the guarantee of workers' rights. Furthermore, his case for recognizing man's communal character in an atomized society—his case for socializing our lives—found such a ready response among intellectuals that theory divorced from social context proved dispensable. Dewey could trust the march of history, at least American history. Accepting it, Dewey could in fact make it the basis for a universal ethic. He could conclude that liberal institutions and values would certainly triumph because, as he wrote, the cause of liberalism "is too precious and too ingrained in the human constitution to be forever obscured." Liberalism, he believed, conforms with what is deepest in human nature generally. Our ideals, he wrote in 1939, "are backed by something deep and indestructible in the needs and demands of humankind."

It was thus his parochialism—neither a tough-minded relativism nor a complacent historicism—that enabled him to trust in consequences, that enabled him to say without misgivings that "there is no question of false or true, of real and seeming, but only of stronger and weaker. The question of which one *should* be stronger or weaker is as meaningless as it would be in a cock-fight." In America, at least, the survivors in the struggle for power were simply the good: the group process ineluctably produced desirable results. In America one could argue for "growth" as the only moral end. It was American society, then, which provided the unexamined, trustworthy moral foundation for both the procedures of politics and the procedures of empirical science.

Dewey kept his faith in the inherent rightness of the American consensus, assuming that once it was fully articulated it would make the substantive results of proceduralism morally tolerable. This postulate enabled him to proclaim:

> Democracy is the faith that the process of experience is more important than any special result attained, so that special results achieved are of ultimate value only as they are used to enrich and order the inquiry process. Since the process of experience is capable of being educative, faith in democracy is all one with faith in experience and education. All ends and values that are cut off from the ongoing process become arrests, fixations. They strive to fixate what has been gained instead of using it to open the road and point the way to new and better experience.

The only ethical commandment, therefore, is to enlarge and enrich the realm of experience. Dewey considered the proposition that "growth itself is the only moral 'end'" the heart of his ethics. To be guided by it was to have a criterion for resolving the specific problems of the day. Pressed to decide between alternative policies, one would merely have to ask whether a recommended course would facilitate an expanding life, a greater freedom, a fuller growth. To be sure, desirable freedom had to be distinguished from undesirable freedom. But the distinction could be rationally made. Freedom was desirable when it would lead to even more freedom in the future. For Dewey the question was simply whether a policy will *continually* widen options, open multiple prospects, and release further energies. He therefore considered the politics of democracy moral insofar as it contributes, in his words, "to the all-around growth of every member of society." To the extent, then, that our institutions —our political and industrial as well as educational institutions—reflect the need to keep the future open, to the extent that they facilitate self-examination, inquiry, debate, and amendment, they would be morally good. As the machinery of democratic government would actively subject all public policy to correction in the light of new pressures, new interests, and new values, so it would be a form of government demonstrably superior to all others. Indeed, it alone would encourage the reconsideration and amendment of Dewey's own plans for the reconstruction of society.

Recommended Reading

CAMUS: ORIGINAL WORKS

The Rebel (New York, 1954).
* *The Myth of Sisyphus and Other Essays* (New York, 1955).

CAMUS: SECONDARY WORKS

Ayer, A. J., "Albert Camus," *Horizon*, Vol. 13 (March, 1946), pp. 155–68.
Lewis, R. W. B., *The Picaresque Saint* (Philadelphia, 1959), Chap. 3.
Thody, Philip, *Albert Camus: 1913–1960* (New York, 1961).

NIEBUHR: ORIGINAL WORKS

The Children of Light and the Children of Darkness (New York, 1944).
The Nature and Destiny of Man (New York, 1941).
* *Reinhold Niebuhr on Politics*, Harry R. Davis and Robert C. Good, eds. (New York, 1960).
Moral Man and Immoral Society (New York, 1960).

NIEBUHR: SECONDARY WORKS

Frankel, Charles, *The Case for Modern Man* (Boston, 1959), Chap. 6.
Kegley, Charles W. and Robert W. Bretall, eds., *Reinhold Niebuhr: His Religious, Social, and Political Thought* (New York, 1956).

MARITAIN: ORIGINAL WORKS

Man and the State (Chicago, 1951).

MARITAIN: SECONDARY WORKS

Frankel, Charles, *The Case for Modern Man* (Boston, 1959), Chap. 4.

DEWEY: ORIGINAL WORKS

The Quest for Certainty (New York, 1929).
Liberalism and Social Action (New York, 1939).
Reconstruction in Philosophy (Boston, 1949).
The Public and Its Problems (Denver, 1957).

DEWEY: SECONDARY WORKS

Moore, Edward C., *American Pragmatism: Pierce, James, and Dewey* (New York, 1961), Part III.
Schneider, Herbert W., *A History of American Philosophy* (New York, 1946), Part VIII.

GENERAL WORKS

Barker, Ernest, *Principles of Social and Political Theory* (New York, 1951).
Crick, Bernard, *In Defence of Politics* (London, 1962).
Friedrich, Carl J., *Man and His Government: An Empirical Theory of Politics* (New York, 1963).
† Hook, Sidney, "Naturalism and Democracy," in Yervant H. Krikorian, ed., *Naturalism and the Human Spirit* (New York, 1944).
Mayo, Henry B., *An Introduction to Democratic Theory* (New York, 1960).
Pennock, J. Roland, *Liberal Democracy: Its Merits and Prospects* (New York, 1950).

* Excerpts in *Sources in Twentieth-Century Political Thought.*
† Unabridged, *ibid.*

VII. INTIMATIONS OF
POSSIBILITIES

Before probing the frontiers of contemporary political philosophy, it may be useful to recapitulate. The writings of Nietzsche, Freud, and Mannheim helped make explicit that we confront unprecedented difficulties today when we seek to inquire about the proper ends of public life. Their work showed in compact form to what extent our ideas find their source in our sheer will to prevail, in our individual and collective struggle to survive. These thinkers did not so much reduce ideas to a drive for power, to libidinal urgings, or to historical processes as they disclosed a plausible relation between what we claim to be objectively desirable and what we subjectively desire. After Nietzsche, Freud, and Mannheim (not to trace their analyses back through Hume, Hobbes, Bacon, Machiavelli, to the Sophists), it was no longer easy or persuasive to maintain that ideas have status independent of our desire to give them status. The authority of ideas—more precisely, their public authority—could be recognized as dependent on the temper and location of the men who espoused them.

Recognition of the merely human source of ideas did not, of course, discredit policies recommended on practical grounds—on the grounds that they were likely to enlarge the range of freedom, that they fostered growth and contributed to life. But it did make it unconvincing to recommend them on the ground that they accorded with a timeless realm of ideals, that they were somehow deduced from abstract Truth, Natural Law, or Divine Purpose.

Thus the thinkers who served to introduce us to twentieth-century political thought rationally and coherently expressed the deflation of goal-oriented political philosophy. To have been chastened by them has meant to question the validity of efforts to derive policies from supernatural moral absolutes. To have understood them is to have seen that communicable political philosophy must be unhinged from a transcendent realm of ideals. If then this realm was to be somehow preserved nonetheless, it had to be regarded as detached from both public life and political speech. It had to be regarded as irrelevant both to the governing of large societies and to the dialogue concerned with public affairs.

Public government and public dialogue now had to be seen as morally neutral, concerned only with solving the practical problem of extending the range of personal freedom, of providing the private tracts on which men might continue to quest for ideals. But this operation has not been easy to carry out; indeed, its very desirability has been called into question. The crisis of political philosophy, the decomposition of a publicly verifiable realm of supernatural truth, has in fact provoked a whole range of diverse reactions. In a characteristically allusive way, Nietzsche himself anticipated as much, suggesting in his parable of "The Madman" that word about the new moral void would be slow in spreading. Nietzsche's madman, it is worth recalling, had discovered that God had been murdered, that henceforth there would be no atonement, no comfort, no up or down, only a "straying as through an infinite nothing." Yet the madman also came to realize that his contemporaries had not yet understood what they had done: they had dissolved the eternal verities, but they had not yet left their churches behind.

The belief in the possibility of communicable moral truth may have been shaken; we may indeed doubt that any specific ordering of our common life can finally be validated by some transcendent absolute. Yet, even though logic compels us to distinguish between private affirmation and public discourse, some political thinkers, as has become clear, have sought willfully to obliterate the distinction. Others, believing that history itself would somehow guarantee that the distinction will remain in force, have found it possible to treat it with gentle indifference. Still others have sought to transcend it by using the "findings" of science as if these were sufficient to validate social goals. And finally there have been those who have accepted the distinction and sought to outline alternative strategies for preserving it.

The adherents of the first of these positions (Sorel remains its most articulate representative) met the crisis in philosophy by relentlessly pushing ahead, seeking to provide for fulfillment here and now. They moved to destroy the restraints of public politics for the sake of their private vision: man heroically in action. In a furious drive to activate the public realm, to reinvigorate its sluggish elements, these activists persisted in the pursuit of ends, either refurbishing the old myths of race, national glory, or imperial destiny or else constructing equally meaningless new ones. They held, in effect, that men had been sufficiently contemplative; it was now time to act. They thus sought to bring abstract ideals into touch with reality, to unify theory and practice. Their bent was pragmatic. They argued that knowledge of right and wrong must be seen as a function of activity; moral truth makes itself felt when we are involved in the consequences of our commitments. We cannot know what is good (or evil) for us in the abstract. We gain moral knowledge, they said, when we find ourselves engaged in life, not when reflecting on it. Committed to this outlook, they encouraged an endless, mindless activism, a movement to which Sorel's reflections on violence gave a brilliant rationalization.

The twentieth-century repudiation of deductive reason proceeded on other grounds as well. It was to assume that reason enough had already been embodied in an existing political tradition. Thus the unmasking of human claims to know the nature of justice could lead to an acceptance of habit and usage, an acceptance that was gently articulated by Michael Oakeshott. If abstract theory could no longer validate public philosophy, the historical tradition (at least the tradition of Great Britain) could be trusted to sanction public policy; an inbred reserve would keep individuals from imposing their eccentricities on the common realm.

There was a third alternative response. The hypothetical knowledge of empirical science could be interpreted as sufficiently conclusive to serve as basis for social reconstruction. Empirical knowledge of individual and organizational needs could be used to justify the pluralistic order of guild socialism, the corporate society of Elton Mayo, the harmonious "communitarianism" of Erich Fromm, or the administrative state governed by Lenin's rational elite.

These various justifications of an existing or prospective state may all be seen to share a fundamental hostility toward politics. Not envisaging the politician's role as one of reconciling conflicting claims by creatively widening the basis for agreement, they all place their faith in something other than politics. They either place their faith in a historical process so benign that the politician would at most seek to "attend" to its promptings or else place it in an objective common good which policy scientists would uncover and bring about by the empirical method.

It is against this unpolitical point of view that the proponents of liberal-democratic constitutionalism have taken their stand. They, too, have been skeptical regarding man's capacity to know and communicate the alleged dictates of abstract justice. But when they have been consistent, their skepticism has not led them to remove the tension between the ideal and the real, between man's vision of the good and the actualities embedded in history. It has instead led them to define a just political regime as one which preserves this tension, as one which, striving to keep the ends of life uncongealed, will perpetuate the possibility of politics. For large-scale industrialized areas of the modern world, they have conceived of the just state as neutral regarding ultimate values. They have therefore not summoned it to establish justice, welfare, or happiness, but, more modestly, to make it possible for individuals and their groups to pursue ultimate goods. They have sought to foster the kind of creative politics likely to provide the conditions for the private pursuit of ends. They have seen it as the obligation of the state not to make men virtuous but to keep them from becoming overbearing. They have sought to direct it to preserve just enough peace that individuals might find it possible to carry on their own affairs.

Those who have submitted to the logic of such liberal theory have recognized that if they wish their reflections to remain publicly relevant and meaningful, they must engage in the necessarily interminable task of specifying the conditions for private freedom. They have therefore tended to inquire how much order and what kind of order is essential to maximize freedom. If they have acknowledged the need for coercion, inequality, and discipline, they have done so only conditionally, that is, only to enlarge man's total opportunities, only to keep his future open. They have thus been authentically liberal in the sense that they have aimed at emancipating the individual person, at freeing him from whatever order can be shown to exceed that minimum which he requires to encounter, identify, and develop himself.

The Plea for Freedom

The modern thinkers who seem merely to describe our public fixations and routines, to tell us what it is we are doing, are inspired, in the final analysis, by a basically liberal impulse. They may disclaim morality, but not the morality which initially impels them to give accounts of our pieties, mythologies, and superstitions, of what Edmund Wilson has called our patriotic gore. Their work, however varied, has given rise to a new approach to society—that of impassioned but controlled observation. It has had the effect of crowding and superseding an approach associated with traditional political philosophy.

That is not to say that traditional political philosophy was mainly illiberal. Certainly its conclusions were of all sorts. But insofar as it permitted public policy to be prescribed in reference to an abstract order of Nature or Truth to which only the few were presumed to have access, it defies the premise of liberalism. It is the reliance on a restrictive procedure for validating its judgments which keeps the recommendations of traditional political philosophy from remaining relevant. If its ideals are still to give support to public policy, they must be given a new basis of legitimacy. For contemporary political thought the only acceptable (and hence relevant) ends of public conduct are those asserted by individuals and ratified by public procedures. These procedures alone can give them the stamp of authority.

One practical result of this orientation—as opposed to the teleological one of traditional political philosophy—is that nothing conclusive will really be prescribable for the

public domain, and that public discourse, to remain creditable, will take this into account. Like each of the Socratic
dialogues, it will be offered in provisional terms that admit
of amendments. Its participants will give up all hope for
certainty. By the same token, they will be suspicious of non-
controversial propositions. They will necessarily regard all
social harmony, balance, and order with doubt. Postulating
ends beyond those which are said to be given or practical,
employing an ambiguous language which simultaneously discloses what we do and what we might do, they will look
upon our affairs with the detachment that lends an ironic
quality to their reflections. Whether or not they ultimately
offer constructive programs, their writing will be pre-eminently critical. Its point will be negative; its very style will
put all positive programs in doubt.

This style is the one that today characterizes and disciplines virtually all serious social thought. It is based on an
impulse that sustains the great variety of ways of holding
the mirror up to our social existence. Above all, this impulse
quickens the work of the poet and novelist. But the writers
who use the language of the social sciences—students of
society such as Georg Simmel, Max Weber, Ruth Benedict,
Frank Lloyd Warner, Gunnar Myrdal, Thorstein Veblen,
C. Wright Mills, or David Riesman—no less reveal the ways
our thinking and acting are rigid, repetitive, and predictable,
the ways we in fact "behave." Their kind of unsettling analysis of what is settled is of course equally the aim of such
journalists as Dwight Macdonald, such social critics as are
found on British Labour's angry "New Left," such Marxist
revisionists as have emerged in Poland, or such conservatives
as describe the aridity of the cultural landscape. And insofar
as contemporary analytical philosophy corrodes the verbal
abstractions that have no foundation in human experience,
insofar as it compels us to talk sense, to become specific and
considerate of consequences, it too opens the roads to inquiry and action.

Liberal social criticism has of course assumed various

specific forms. One of the ways to jeopardize (and transcend) given conventions has been to depict, in realistic detail, what is entailed by their projection into the future. Thus, even without constructively spelling out alternatives, utopian speculation can become systematically subversive of the status quo. A notable example is Michael D. Young's challenge to existing educational practices by his delineation of a future society which, while it relies on "merit" as criterion of advancement, still does not escape accepting punitive inequalities. Joseph A. Schumpeter's work may be seen as no less inspired by a liberal impulse. His asking how observable economic tendencies might work themselves out according to their logic—how we might "march into socialism," as he put it in an essay by that title—scarcely conceals the radical thrust of his indictment. Harold D. Lasswell's theoretical construction of a state in which power has passed from specialists on bargaining to specialists on violence similarly serves to make us doubt our actions. And so do those more recent attempts to construct abstract deductive models of democratic regimes by which Robert A. Dahl and Anthony Downs have sought to specify what is implied by the principles of political equality, majority rule, and minority rights. The significance of Percival and Paul Goodman's *Communitas* (1947)—their three illustrated models for ordering the modern city—lies precisely in their revealing the absurdity of our present plans for urban life. Their phrases are cool and dry, but their voice is that of moral indignation. Their writing is as clearly in the tradition of utopian thought as is Aldous Huxley's *Island* (1962). Huxley's work, it may be worth noting, has the merit of going beyond the conventional concern of utopian thinkers. Whereas utopian thinkers have generally attempted to provide merely the conditions for equality, simply assuming that personal health would be the natural consequence of the removal of all irrational inequalities, Huxley has directed his sympathetic attention to a society so constructed that it will actually promote a maximum of physical and psychological health. Indifferent to economic problems, he has been interested in rethinking both the process of education and the institution of the family. He has been interested in freeing man for the fullest use of his natural talents, in planning for health in the light of available medical and scientific knowledge.

The leap into a nonrepressive, scarcely conceivable society—a society in which men (and women) might be spontaneously creative, productive, and loving, leading not the good life but the full life—is similarly made in the work of Erich Fromm, Herbert Marcuse, D. H. Lawrence, and Norman O. Brown. If their utopias have always provoked the civilized to consider flight, they nevertheless have provided us with models next to which our own public life appears cramped and destitute.

Social criticism on liberal premises may finally emerge in less exotic garb. It can assume the more circumspect form provided by Daniel Bell's writings, especially his essay on "Work and Its Discontents" (1962). Taking Marx's insistence on the integrity of man and his products as his point of departure, Bell has urged a broadening of our critical perspective. Marx's view had led to an assault on economic inequalities and economic exploitation: the economy, so Marxists predominantly believed, was the cause of man's alienation from his true self. Bell has pointed out, however, that the idea of alienation has gained a new critical edge. Today it may well be used to expose the dehumanization of the worker not by economic injustice but by the ostensibly efficient way we organize our work. Following Max Weber, Bell has noted that as long as technology is permitted to define the organization of industrial work, it matters not whether the individual labors under communist or capitalist auspices. In fact, he has written, there is little evidence that the Communist countries have sought to reverse the process of industrialism, that they have sought

. . . to explore new combinations of work, to re-examine the engineering process, or to question the concept of ef-

ficiency that underlies the contemporary organization of
work. If anything . . . the workers in the Communist countries are even more exploited than those in western lands.
Technology stands as a "given."

In Bell's view, changes are possible. Production may be
decentralized; work rhythms can be made more interesting;
the worker can be given greater control—perhaps not over
his industry but at least over his immediate shop. "If one
accepts the heritage of the humanist tradition, then the work
place itself, and not the market, must be the center of determination of the organization of work. The fullness of life
can and must be found in the nature of work itself."

This intensive focusing on our particular experiences—on
the richness of concrete existence—has found popular expression in David Riesman's writings. His style, more clearly
than that of other sociologists, reveals that the price paid for
an unwillingness to accept any specific observation as conclusive is an unmitigated moral relativism. He has always
been sensitively in touch with what he regards as the consensus of any particular audience and then, having taken his
bearings by it, has proceeded to reverse this consensus. (He
will, for example, warn a group of nonconformist college
students of the dangers of ritualistic eccentricity, counseling
them against "the ruthless sacrifice of protective prejudices.") As his lectures and essays invariably demonstrate,
he will seek never to come down conclusively on anyone's
side. It is not that all sides are right, but that none of them
is. His rhetoric, his continuous amending of every statement,
is a strikingly precise analogue to the flexible procedures of
constitutional politics. If his mode entails moral relativism,
as it does, it is derived from his dedication to freedom as
highest public value.

This dedication, the resolve to save man from humiliation,
sparks all sociology, anthropology, and psychology that is
secular, humanistic, and existentialist in its orientation. It
provides the analyses which alert us to the subtle degra-

dations imposed by our language and ritual. Because of it, we get the arresting elucidations of inauthentic behavior provided by Jean-Paul Sartre, Simone de Beauvoir, and Albert Camus. We get Fromm's account of loneliness, insecurity, and alienation under contemporary industrial conditions of "freedom." We get Erik Erikson's picture of how we cope with the anxieties generated by modern life.[1] We get Ernest Schachtel's study of the way our potential experiences are devitalized by the barren clichés we have for anticipating them. We get Harry Stack Sullivan's delineation of the rigidities which characterize our social relations. We get Herbert Marcuse's stress on "the liberating function of negation in philosophical thought," on the need "to break the power of facts over the world and to speak a language which is not the language of those who establish, enforce, and benefit from the facts." We get Norman O. Brown's stunningly perceptive diagnosis of the institution of money. And we get Riesman's reports of the joyless work, the obsessive leisure, and the nonpolitical politics of the lonely crowd.

These accounts derive, of course, from an acute sensitivity to all types of coercion. They lead to telling and relevant descriptions of coercive institutions and compulsory practices. They serve to confront us with our oppressively organized environment, to make us conscious of ourselves as irreducible phenomena, as ultimately existing independent of all closed systems, classifications, and blueprints, as beings in process, and always unfinished. They lead us to recognize ourselves as autonomous actors whose role it is to conquer our environment and, whenever possible, to limit our renunciations.

1. Erikson has been particularly concerned with showing that, as we mature in modern society, we are unprepared to meet successive crises. Our education fails to tell us what to adjust to and what to rebel against. We are made anxious by our inability to find out where we belong and who we are: child or parent, boy or girl, man or woman, entrepreneur or coordinator. And since we can gain self-knowledge only in specific encounters, our identity becomes diffuse and we do not get to know ourselves. We suffer from a "loss" of identity.

When these accounts engage us, they help us violate the supposedly iron laws of industry and society; they help us depart from the "tendencies" we are inclined to read into history, society, and technology; they help us transcend the stereotypes of the day and recognize both the partisan nature of our intellectual preoccupations and the sweep of our delusions. They finally help us discover our identity and define our conduct to accord with our discovery. Their function is liberating: they allow us to do what our own nature dictates, not what some external code demands. The postulate that gives unity to this approach to man and society is the belief in the desirability of human freedom. This belief, in turn, gives force to the determination to annihilate whatever institutions or ideologies stand in the way.

For those who consistently subscribe to this approach, the only creditable public ethics is a negative one, a prohibition against treating man as an object. Prescribing no specific definition of public excellence, they insist only that the public realm be opened to all possibilities, all save those which imminently threaten the imposition of substantive justice. Treating man as ultimately incommensurable, they refuse to impose a public morality on his freedom. They offer no new moral insight, no restatement of ideals. They do not seek to propound what makes our common life worth living, for they do not presume that our common life has any value apart from our individual lives.

Although they cannot define our ends for us, their prescription to act in harmony with one's own true nature may well steel us for our encounters with society. Insisting that substantive freedom is impossible in society without endangering our autonomy, theirs constitutes a case for formal freedom, for the procedures holding public coercion to a minimum. They are thus deeply committed to politics as an institution for the mediation of conflict and not the attainment of a public purpose. They give us a politics of sensible moderation and civility—but no ultimate reason for being sensibly moderate and civil.

The Plea for Order

An exclusively liberal approach to public life cannot presume to demonstrate the value of freedom. It does not promise that freedom will lead to social harmony or, for that matter, to the moral regeneration of the individual. Morally, it is hollow, formalistic, and relativistic. Still it does stand for some matters of substance: by vindicating the function of rational criticism it implies a defense of the institutions that keep criticism alive. It persistently intimates that we require more than freedom if for no other reason than to preserve as much freedom as possible.

Accordingly, a good number of the very thinkers whose work has constituted a critique of social harmony, order, and hierarchy have given thought to the need for freedom-buttressing institutions and ideologies. Where they have been iconoclastic, challenging the sanctity of public establishments, they have also moved ahead to provide answers, giving title to new public traditions and mythologies.

As they have rushed in to fill the void their iconoclasm helped create, they have often provided more footholds, more niches for comfort, more secure enclaves for togetherness than necessary—necessary, that is, to realize their own liberal aim of maximizing freedom. Thus D. H. Lawrence not only publicized the sexual conventions of his day; he also prescribed a new cult of final fulfillment. Thorstein Veblen not only portrayed our curious ways of consumption; he also prescribed a technocracy of engineers to ensure functional behavior. Wilhelm Röpke not only exposed the restrictive economic practices of an illiberal welfare state; he also prescribed a decentralized governmental order. Erich Fromm not only challenged the compulsions that lead to fascism; he also prescribed a close-knit "communitarianism." Lewis Mumford not only revealed the dehumanizing congestion of the modern metropolis; he also laid out a blueprint for a new city with quasi-religious foundations. Even John Dewey, certainly one of the most steadfast advocates of procedural-ism, permitted himself to plead for a substantive concept of democracy.

There would seem to be few major contemporary thinkers who, having permitted their analyses to do their destructive work, did not proceed to draft some new blueprint of their own, to start building their own structure, and finally, suc-cumbing to temptation, to fence it off. In these efforts to *structure* freedom they have not consistently adhered to the premises of liberal theory. This does not mean that they therefore are wrong but rather that their reflections have become detached from publicly relevant concerns.

Whenever constructive proposals are based on directly perceived truth, whenever the case for a new order rests on authority not subject to public scrutiny, the common realm of political discourse is compromised and deserted. This departure from liberal theory is manifest (1) when writers adhere to what is essentially a private procedure for vali-dating their recommendations, relying either on an inner voice or on a closed institution whose authority is presumed immune to public challenge, or (2) when they submit a proposal for ordering freedom which would itself deny the possibility of publicly shared rationality, which would vest reason in an elite and sentiment in the masses. In either case they defy the liberal proposition that, to ensure the maximization of public freedom, all groups in society must have the equal opportunity to participate in the definition of order. They imply that some private need, insight, fear, or premonition can sanction the public acceptance of their ideas, that a single source of authority is sufficient. They thus adopt an approach which cannot be consistently enter-

tained by those who avow a loyalty to empirical procedures
and a pluralistic society.

This illiberal perspective may be illustrated today in two
distinctively opposite kinds of intellectual endeavor, two
kinds of escape from the predicament of living in a world no
longer marking the road to salvation. One is Norman O.
Brown's endeavor to reintegrate man on a naturalistic basis
and the other is John Courtney Murray's different and more
complicated one to reintegrate him in conformity to the
principles of both Roman Catholicism and constitutional
democracy.

In his *Life against Death* (1959) Brown has passionately
expressed his hope for giving man fulfillment at last. Using
Freud's psychoanalytical model not only to expose the social
compulsions of the present day but also to provide the basis
for a new paradisaical existence for man, Brown looked upon
our social and economic order as pervasively repressive.
Accordingly, he insisted on the abolition of repression altogether. The total elimination of repression, he felt, would
be tantamount to the resurrection of the body. Reuniting
man and nature, such resurrection would bring about a
Dionysian life of "erotic exuberance." While Brown asked
for explicit utopian speculation, he himself provided only the
vaguest glimpse of the substance of his hopes. In willfully
personal language, he no more than hinted at his ideal state
as an exotic but uncultivated garden.

For disbelievers, Brown's language must appear esoteric,
precious, or whimsical. But they should not conclude that
he therefore lacks a public; they may merely assume that his
public is equally estranged from the tradition of political
discourse, equally alienated from politics. If his idiom is exclusive and private, it appears so only from the liberal perspective which regards the public as pluralistic, as composed
of many interests and many minds. In other words, the
public gained by Brown—or, for that matter, by Lawrence,
Fromm, or Marcuse—is not a genuine public: it is rather

the enormously swollen domain of the private. It is the mass of self-regarding men who reject the demands of an open-ended, unfulfilled public life and quest for unmediated self-fulfillment, for total personal liberation. The unpolitical character of this private domain finds its fullest expression in the cult of the hipster, of Zen, and of the beats—all seeking to discover mystical completion where our public life remains agonizingly incomplete.[1]

In his conclusions Brown deliberately severs all ties with those civil traditions that keep men poised between this-worldly pressures and otherworldly ideals.[2] As a result his final stance suffers from fewer strains than that of John Courtney Murray, for Murray would like both to give unity to man's true nature *and* to preserve the disruptive institutions of the liberal society. In the persuasive prose of *We Hold These Truths* (1960), he thus appears to engage unbelievers in a traditional dialogue, initially accepting the liberal belief in a tolerant, pluralistic social order. In the end, however, he commits himself to natural law as interpreted by the Church. By making the Church the sole authority for the liberalism that he too accepts, he in fact, if not in intent, destroys the foundations of liberal theory.

For Murray, liberal-democratic constitutionalism is dictated not on the ground that human fallibility keeps us from knowing what is good for us but rather on the ground that the good is sufficiently known—and dictates public tolerance. Since this conclusion is the liberal one, it would scarcely seem that he poses a threat to the liberal society. Even those who do not believe that one can deduce principles of conduct from natural law should find it possible to agree.

1. For a review of contemporary novels which give voice to this search, see Joseph Waldmeir, "Quest without Faith," *The Nation,* November 18, 1961, pp. 390–96.

2. More precisely, he severs all ties but one: that of the artist who accepts the pressures of this world and reluctantly attempts to communicate. Brown, after all, expressed his commitment in the controlled form of a published book. The same should be said, with even more force, of the work of Norman Mailer.

The difficulty, therefore, lies not in the substance of Murray's policy but in the process he accepts for formulating it. He favors tolerance of social pluralism because he believes that an ecclesiastical organization of men can know the common good sufficiently to have everyone act in reference to it. But to vest authority for formulating public policy in men, however philosophical their temper and astringent their habits, is to move beyond the limits of liberal theory without doing justice to its basis in experience. Liberal theory, after all, is supported by the historical argument that the good one group of men professes to know today (even if this good be public tolerance) may not be the good it knows tomorrow. It is therefore Murray's vesting of power in a closed group of men who insist both "that there is an authority superior to the authority of individual reason" and that they can know and communicate its dictates—it is this which challenges the liberal society, not the pleasing conclusion at which divinely inspired interpreters of natural law have fortunately arrived.

What is significant in the speculations typified by work as radically diverse as Norman O. Brown's or John Courtney Murray's is that they are offered and read as comprehensive public philosophy, and this even though they have lost title to the claim. Whatever we might privately believe to be the merits of their points, their discourse, despite appearances, is not public discourse. Their philosophy is not political philosophy insofar as the only policy recommendations appropriate for the public sphere are those which have been (or may yet be) publicly legitimated, insofar as the only unchanging consensus, at least in nontotalitarian societies, is on the procedures intrinsic to liberal-democratic constitutionalism.

Yet the loss of appeals such as Brown's or Murray's is not irredeemable. Skepticism regarding ideals merely makes it necessary to reroute their pleas for fulfillment toward the private sphere. Within it, as long as economic conditions make this feasible, their respective visions may well be acted

on. When we are able to federate a plurality of voluntary
private orders within the large-scale constitutional state, we
may well follow the most idiosyncratic of our dreams—the
promptings of sexuality, the call of Zen, the cult of the
hipster, or the voice of God. We may do so precisely because
the constitutional state maintains the conditions that invite
variety. In order to save ideal states such as Brown's or
Murray's, in order to save ideals at all, we are therefore compelled, for better or worse, to treat them as if their advocates
addressed themselves only to the private realm—a task we
will find especially difficult when the offered ideal happens
to be a congenial one.

One final plea for ordering freedom by maintaining a unifying consensus (or at least by not disturbing the apathetic
masses) merits consideration, for it arises from within the
liberal tradition itself. Aware of the difficulties of appealing
to natural law to support what is essentially a religious consensus, recognizing how easily the argument based on such
an appeal loses in public relevance in the liberal society, at
least some contemporary thinkers have sought to give weight
to their case by deriving it from practical, utilitarian considerations. Though their point of departure is theological,
they join hands with social scientists of a distinctively behavioral persuasion. Their procedure clearly testifies to the
triumph of secularism in political philosophy, to the triumph
of the belief that arguments for specific political regimes
must be based on estimates of their probable consequences,
not on the ground that they conform to abstract Truth. But
the pragmatic case for institutions that will foster a religious
consensus merely creates another dilemma: it implicates its
proponents in an acceptance of a society split into a rational
elite and the irrational masses. They thus damage the very
ideal they endeavor to preserve.

Their argument has been made familiar by Rousseau,
Maistre, and Tocqueville: to instill civic virtue and preserve
a civil society it would be imprudent to discard the unify-

ing authority of religious belief. The contemporary brief for
a religious consensus to impose order on the disruptive elements inherent in the liberal state remains essentially the
same:

> The separation of Church from State, of ethics from
> politics, of moral codes from public action—so much a mat-
> ter of pride in Western liberal democracies—may in the
> long run work for the destruction of those democracies.
> True constitutionalism cannot be built on the premise that
> expediency, utility, and practicality are the only foundations
> for political obligation. Democracy depends for its survival
> upon fundamental postulates derived from the Judaeo-
> Christian revelation, and these postulates lose their vitality
> and power in a predominantly secular society. We are living
> today on spiritual capital which is not being replenished.

We will drift and ultimately sink, so the advocates of public
support of religious institutions contend, unless our belief in
the sacredness of the human person, in charity, and in forbearance is anchored in absolutes. To enable us to survive we
must therefore replenish expended spiritual capital and
nourish a religious establishment. Only this will keep public
policy from being corrupted by those voters who favor legislation because of "expediency, utility, and practicality."

What for some thinkers may well have begun as an effort
to defend religious institutions on the ground that religious
revelation is true ends here on an eminently practical note,
one more pleasing to the modern temper. To maintain free
institutions, the question runs today, what must be the range
and intensity of the public consensus on ultimates? Having
been formulated in this way, the question can at last be
dealt with by the social sciences. As they proceed to frame
an answer, they deliberately and unavoidably submit to the
evidence of history. As a consequence, they enhance one's
theoretical understanding, revealing functional relationships
that casual observation—or mere "insight"—could never
verify.

Such an approach cannot, however, provide a sufficient

foundation for policy recommendations. Even if history's answer is that a measure of consensus (or perhaps a measure of apathy) is the prerequisite for a stable democracy (and this, as V. O. Key has shown, is far from certain), we still need not accept it. The answer is derived, after all, from surveys of nations which, in terms of liberal constitutionalism, are far from perfect—however "advanced" they may be. It is derived from nations burdened by material scarcity, psychological deprivations, punitive educational institutions, and inequalities of opportunity. Under such imperfect conditions, consensus (or apathy) may indeed be a prerequisite for political stability. It may well be functional. But were we to confine our policies to what has proved to be functional, we would be accepting empirical generalizations not to illuminate the past but to shape the future. The hypotheses of social science would become political doctrines. In other words, the harvest of empirical studies comparing more or less developed nations cannot finally say anything regarding the legitimacy of the functions of any prevailing political structure.

It follows that where the theoretical models of "mature" nations or so-called stable democracies are said to provide policies for political development, they serve didactic purposes. Although social scientists committed to them write in a dry and neutral language, their work betrays an affection for the degree of consensus (or apathy) necessary to maintain stability or at least the degree that characterizes the "mature" nations. Inviting us to diffuse it on a global scale, they assume that what we have is necessarily exemplary. To them, a disparity between ideal and practice does not indicate malfunction; it indicates the need to trim the ideal to make it conform to existing tendencies.

Such contemporary political theory constitutes a commitment to the status quo—to a situation so structured (1) that the masses will be kept from corrupting politics by remaining apathetic or by permitting themselves to be guided by consensual norms and (2) that the few—those with the real-

ism to adjust policy to the findings of empirical social science
—will be free to make "expedient, utilitarian, practical"
policy judgments. If this theory does not introduce inequality into the political realm, it does serve to rationalize it.
Such a theory places the masses on one side and an elite with
empirical knowledge of the conditions of social cohesion—a
knowledge which it had best not communicate lest it contribute to the rise of skepticism and the consequent disintegration of the liberal society—on the other. Reason governs
the top, sentiment the bottom.

Inasmuch as this defense of elite rule is offered as a
defense of "true constitutionalism," it mocks the liberal pro-
fession of its advocates—their conviction that everyone must
be free to compete on equal terms for the opportunity to
determine the content of the public consensus. After all, these
thinkers believe that the sole argument for institutions
facilitating social cohesion must be derived from practical
necessity, from the evidence that without such institutions
men are deprived of their freedom. It is this belief, and only
this one, that they can reasonably expect the public to share.

It would seem, then, that contemporary thinkers who
seek publicly to formulate relevant theory (1) must use
public procedures to argue for ways of ordering freedom and
(2) cannot argue for the kind of order which confines rationality or virtue to a self-selected group of guardians,
whether they are inspired by religion or by empiricism.
When they violate these imperatives they may be contributing to our nonpolitical life, but their work can have no legitimate bearing on our lives as citizens.

A failure to see the hortatory and merely personal qualities of their work, a tendency to treat all modern thought
indiscriminately as political philosophy, is to give us a false
sense of confidence: it mistakenly leads us to suppose that
political philosophy today is marvelously abundant, that
poets, novelists, psychologists, social scientists, and preachers
all contribute to its specific riches. The fact is that any

genuine contribution to political philosophy must do more than plead for order; its very plea must incorporate the realization that in public there can be no fulfillment, salvation, stability, or completion, that all surrenders are conditional and no treaty of peace the last one.

Foundations for Politics

The argument for a social unity undisturbed by mass participation and supported by consensus on ultimates is an understandable reaction to both liberal theory and liberal practice. After all, there is nothing tranquil about the state liberal theory attempts to justify. Indeed, the liberal state is in principle so constituted that it is always on the very verge of disintegrating. Its constituent elements must forever threaten to secede, to cut their ties and found their own true church. It tends forever to degenerate either into a state of anarchy (thus inviting its totalitarian reunification) or into a state of paralysis (thus inviting programs for totalitarian activism). The specter which haunts it is civil war. Ideally it tolerates but that bare minimum of cohesion, unity, and consensus that enables hostilities to be suspended.[1]

But precisely because the liberal society generates incalculable strains, those committed to its perpetuation must guard against all promise of relief. They must watch that the agenda for public action promotes no more consensus—and no less—than necessary to preserve freedom. The generally meaningful question for public discourse, for political phi-

1. The ideological bias of these programmatic reflections should not be concealed. No doubt an economy of scarcity would deny them expression. In most areas of the contemporary world the problem of sheer physical survival, of creating the material *pre*conditions for a qualitatively rich life, is uppermost. For the elites of underdeveloped countries the question is how to develop large-scale industry and, at the same time, maintain consensus (or support apathy). When this is the issue of the day, there is not likely to be much speculation about what one ought to do with one's life. Such speculation tends to wait until economic "growth" and industrial "development" have led to the plateau where it becomes possible to think of doing something authentically human.

losophy, is therefore how to create the institutions that will steel individuals as they engage in public action and as they seek, simultaneously, to give meaning to their private lives. Its problem is how to compel public agencies to become instruments for private variety.

Although the dimensions of this problem may be illuminated, there can be no abstract solution to it, for there is no science of public policy in the free society. What is initially required, in Hannah Arendt's precise phrase, is that we "think what we are doing," engaging in the kind of exercises in self-awareness she herself has offered.

Like other existentialist thinkers, Hannah Arendt has sought to elucidate the emptiness of our public life, our specific alienation from public undertakings. Seeking to come to terms with the democratic and industrial revolutions in the leading essays collected in *Between Past and Future* (1961), she has maintained that we must act as if we had to found our existence anew, that, to order our life and find a place in our world, we must resolve to rely on our unsupported selves. For us neither a commonly accepted metaphysics nor the memory of a shared past can give the stamp of authenticity to our day-to-day behavior. As she concluded in *Origins of Totalitarianism* (1951):

> Whether we like it or not, we have long ceased to live in a world in which the faith in the Judaeo-Christian myth of creation is secure enough to constitute a basis and source of authority for actual laws, and we certainly no longer believe, as the great men of the French Revolution did, in a universal cosmos of which man was a part and whose natural laws he had to imitate and conform to. . . .
>
> Our new difficulty is that we start from a fundamental distrust of everything merely *given,* a distrust of all laws and prescriptions, moral or social, that are deduced from a given, comprehensive, universal whole.

Our political foundations having been destroyed, each of the revolutions of the modern age (excepting, she says, the American) must be understood as a gigantic attempt to rebuild them, "to renew the broken thread of tradition, and to restore . . . what for so many centuries had endowed the affairs of men with some measure of dignity and greatness." We must realize that we now find ourselves in a political realm "with neither authority nor the concomitant awareness that the source of authority transcends power"; ours is a realm "without the religious trust in a sacred beginning," a realm, what is more, "without the protection of traditional and therefore self-evident standards of behavior." The origins of this condition, according to Arendt, are to be found in the dissolution of an impressive Roman amalgam—authority, religion, and tradition. The Roman loyalty to this trinity had made it possible for Western man to see meaning in his existence after the breakdown of an even earlier form of human existence, the primordial synthesis of classical antiquity.

For Arendt this fundamental synthesis of classical antiquity possesses the highest integrity. Today we have access to it only in the midst of revolution, when we get intimations of its true character. But whereas today we are able to discover our authentic selves and define our public virtue only momentarily during the exhilarating moments of revolutionary action, our lives were continuously meaningful in times of classical antiquity: choices were genuine; deeds were glorious; freedom was action; events were memorable; speech was public; life—the highest form of human life—was lived in the Greek polis. Action and contemplation, work and leisure, were in an ideal state of harmony.

It had been the genius of Roman politics, Arendt says, to maintain the balance by introducing authority, religion, and tradition. This trinity was subverted by Luther, Hobbes, and the secular humanists. Ultimately a modern faith in History replaced the metaphysics that had previously kept our existence from seeming futile. The historical process itself was summoned to dignify our deeds and trials. But having been delivered to an undifferentiated process of his-

tory, we have been deprived of distinctions. We have lost
our balance.

While Hegel inaugurated the reversal of the traditional
hierarchy of values, demoting contemplation and giving preeminence to action, it was Marx, according to Arendt, who
most specifically expressed the break in the tradition of
political thought by recommending that man cease philoso-
phizing and commence acting. Convinced that philosophical
truth was known, that it fully existed in the common world
of man and no longer had to be discovered by philosophers
prepared to leave the cave, Marx could confidently counsel
action. And as he substituted action for philosophy, he substituted labor for contemplation, postulating labor, and not
reason, to be the distinguishing mark of man. He thereby
threw man back on his own resources. And yet he expected
man to use them so as to create a regime of leisure. It is
Arendt's view that the bedeviling, repressive character of
Marxism stems from Marx's accepting man as a laboring
animal now and as a free being only in the future.

Arendt, unlike Marx, seeks to address herself to the
immediate present, to our condition here and now. And this
condition, she observes, is one which presents us, for the
first time since classical antiquity, with a truly extraordinary
option. Because absolutely nothing is left of our past (save in
America where, as she has put it, the revolution to restore
Roman foundations was a success) and because absolutely
nothing blocks our future, we may now confront "the elementary problems of human living-together." Between an
infinite past and an infinite future we stand tensely poised
in the midst of a great void, possessing nothing save our
world and our lives. Evoking the great catastrophes of the
age (catastrophes she lifted out of history and idealized in
her inquiry into totalitarianism), she is able to alert us to a
singular, awesome opportunity: the opportunity to found
our existence anew. Because the sources of authority have
eroded, because the ultimate goals of political communities

have been questioned, it has become necessary for us, as she has said,

> . . . not only to find and devise new laws, but to find and devise their very measure, the yardstick of good and evil, the principle of their source. For man, in the sense of the nature of man, is no longer the measure, despite what the new humanists would have us believe. Politically, this means that before drawing up the constitution of a new body politic, we shall have to create—not merely discover—a new foundation for human community as such.
>
> In historical terms, this would mean not the end of history, but its first consciously planned beginning, together with the bitter realization that nothing has been promised us, no Messianic Age, no classless society, no paradise after death.

The public freedom we have gained is meaningless, however, unless we support it so that it will dignify our personal existence. Our private life lacks point, Arendt has reflected, unless we know that when we find ourselves in solitude we are not alone. We must act on the realization that unless our private existence carries within it the promise of its public vindication, we will be driven to despair.

In her later volume, *On Revolution* (1963), Arendt has proceeded to call attention to the great promise of public life in terms that idealize it, notwithstanding her historical approach. Vindicating unmediated public action, she romanticized the heroic revolutionary bands whose members, all self-selected, fought simultaneously for freedom and for themselves. These individuals stood defiantly at the center of the holocaust, epitomizing what is distinctively political in nature. They aspired to more than private happiness and thus saved their true selves. They had, as Arendt says, "a taste for public freedom and cannot be 'happy' without it." They found it possible to act without masks, to appear "in word and deed without equivocation and without self-reflection. . . ." Releasing energies which normal political settings are designed to keep in check, heroically committed to a public cause, they did justice to man's noblest aspirations. They are the "lost treasure" of revolutions.

For Arendt the practical problem is to make generally available the opportunities for self-actualization provided by revolutionary situations. But when she finally turns to practical matters, she reveals that she is less concerned with remaining relevant to our public issues than with inspiring us to feel uneasy in the modern world. Her policy recommendations are not without reactionary overtones: she would have us re-establish Jefferson's forgotten ward system of government; she would have us revoke "general suffrage as we understand it," and rehabilitate the miniature communities within which an open, natural aristocracy would rediscover its authentic being and conduct the public business.

While Arendt, in seeking to make the exigencies of our contemporary life explicit, takes the position that we are now utterly free to construct our political future, she nonetheless reveals her underlying sympathy for the institutions sustained by classical political philosophy. It is true that she presumes merely to describe the corrosive work of Luther, Hobbes, and the secular humanists; but at the same time her elusive prose suggests that they subverted an ancient edifice of durable worth. Her sympathy for a point of view which empirical philosophies have forced us to abandon takes the form of inviting us to act as if the abandoned values were somehow still legitimate. Without extending a clearly formulated invitation, she appears to tell us that a revival of a meaningful public order would be a more promising possibility if such a revival were somehow oriented by the classical tradition, and not by the more modest empirical approach that finds its representatives in thinkers such as Machiavelli, Hobbes, Locke, Hume, Mill, and Dewey. She is moved, in short, by a sense of loss, by what Hegel had called our unhappy consciousness.

If, however, we are no longer able to share the sense of loss characteristic of Continental existentialist thought, but remain determined to formulate our public policies without supernatural authority, without dependence on elites who claim to have the key to human nature, to divine law, to established tradition, or to the process of history, our policies must be defined by two interlinked objectives: (1) the clarification of procedures for sensible public discussion and (2) the promotion of political institutions likely to facilitate such discussion. The first objective demands a commitment to a method of rational discourse, a method that compels its participants to consider the consequences and contexts of alternative policy recommendations. And the second demands a commitment to a public order that preserves enough peace (but no more) to allow individuals to pursue their own various goods. If the powers of heaven have been shaken, we must jointly make our way by designing the kind of institutions and encouraging the kind of leadership which will protect the individual, and which, by fostering the habits of civility, will clear the ground for private communities outside the bounds of the public order.

One relevant current attempt to move along these lines—and there are others—is Joseph Tussman's *Obligation and the Body Politic* (1960). It is the burden of Tussman's thesis that the traditional interpretation of liberal-democratic theory leads to the erosion of a meaningful political realm. Fair play defined as rational pursuit of self-interest, Tussman has argued, is "our great procedural golden calf, whose worship will destroy us"; we are likely either to become impatient and reckless in the face of self-seeking men who operate behind a façade of procedural fairness or else to accept deadlock and drift as we seek to satisfy all self-seeking parties. By sanctifying the market for votes, at least as it is organized today, we in fact abandon the public arena.

Tussman therefore turns back to Plato's *Republic* to ask,

not to answer, "Is there a guardian type? How can he be found or recruited? How can he be educated for his function? How can we delay his corruption?" And Tussman contends that we must recruit men who satisfy Plato's requirements for leadership: men who can curb their interests, men who have been trained, specifically under the auspices of the humanities, to assume the role of public agent. Moreover, the polity they govern must give each of its members his due public office, that is, make him truly a citizen, enable him to participate in public affairs. This imperative, Tussman concedes, is not easy to implement. "It demands," he says, "the reshaping of the electorate into a genuinely deliberate tribunal capable of dealing responsibly with fundamental issues. It would require vastly more and better education than we have yet been able to achieve, and would require a revolution in our habits and institutions of communication."

If we take our bearings by Tussman's speculations, we will have to act so as to preserve the integrity of the political order. We will have to give vitality to the sovereign public tribunal: the electorate. We will have to take the practical steps that bolster the sense of civic identity, providing the concrete occasions and facilities that allow us to meet and debate as citizens, not merely as representatives of special interests. Thus it becomes our task to reinforce Hannah Arendt's urgent plea in behalf of man's only natural right, his right to citizenship.

To give meaning to our role as citizens we must perennially inquire about the quality of public life, recognizing that unless our polity is so constituted as to make all policies inconclusive, all victories incomplete, and all action symbolic, our private work cannot be redeemed in our generation or in this world.

And if not now, when? If not in this world, where?

Recommended Reading

Arendt, Hannah, *The Human Condition* (Chicago, 1958).

Arendt, Hannah, *On Revolution* (New York, 1963).

Bell, Daniel, "Work and Its Discontents," in *The End of Ideology* (New York, 1962), Chap. 11.

Brown, Norman O., *Life against Death: The Psychoanalytical Meaning of History* (Middletown, Conn., 1959).

Buchanan, James M. and Gordon Tullock, *The Calculus of Consent: Logical Foundations of Constitutional Democracy* (Ann Arbor, Mich., 1962).

Dahl, Robert A., *A Preface to Democratic Theory* (Chicago, 1956).

Downs, Anthony, *An Economic Theory of Democracy* (New York, 1957).

Erikson, Erik, *Childhood and Society* (New York, 1950).

Goodman, Percival and Paul Goodman, *Communitas: Means of Livelihood and Ways of Life* (New York, 1960).

de Grazia, Sebastian, *Of Time, Work, and Leisure* (New York, 1962).

Hayek, F. A., *The Constitution of Liberty* (Chicago, 1960).

Hoggart, Richard, *The Uses of Literacy: Changing Patterns in English Mass Culture* (Boston, 1961).

Huxley, Aldous, *Island* (New York, 1962).

Kateb, George, *Utopia and Its Enemies* (New York, 1963).

Lasswell, Harold D., "The Garrison State," *American Journal of Sociology*, Vol. 46 (January, 1941), pp. 455–68, and "The Garrison Hypothesis Today," in Samuel P. Huntington, ed., *Changing Patterns of Military Politics* (Glencoe, Ill., 1962), pp. 51–70.

Mailer, Norman, *The White Negro* (San Francisco, 1957).

Marcuse, Herbert, *Eros and Civilization* (Boston, 1955).

Macdonald, Dwight, *Masscult and Midcult* (New York, 1961).

Murray, John Courtney, *We Hold These Truths: Catholic Reflections on the American Proposition* (New York, 1960).

Stein, Maurice R., Arthur J. Vidich, and David M. White, eds., *Identity and Anxiety: Survival of the Person in Mass Society* (Glencoe, Ill., 1960).

Tussman, Joseph, *Obligation and the Body Politic* (New York, 1960).

Williams, Raymond, *Culture and Society, 1780–1950* (New York, 1960).

Wollheim, Richard, *Socialism and Culture* (London, 1961).

Young, M. D., *The Rise of the Meritocracy, 1870–2033: The New Elite of Our Social Revolution* (Baltimore, 1961).

SECONDARY WORKS

Shklar, Judith N., *After Utopia: The Decline of Political Faith* (Princeton, 1957).

Stein, Maurice R., *The Eclipse of Community: An Interpretation of American Studies* (Princeton, 1960).

Wolin, Sheldon S., *Politics and Vision: Continuity and Innovation in Western Political Thought* (New York, 1960), Chap. 10.

Index